INTIMATE
RELATIONSHIPS

SOME OTHER VOLUMES IN THE
SAGE FOCUS EDITIONS

INTIMATE RELATIONSHIPS

Development, Dynamics, and Deterioration

Edited by

Daniel Perlman
Steve Duck

SAGE PUBLICATIONS
The Publishers of Professional Social Science
Newbury Park   Beverly Hills   London   New Delhi

For information address:

SAGE Publications, Inc.
2111 West Hillcrest Drive
Newbury Park, California 91320

SAGE Publications Inc.   SAGE Publications Ltd.
275 South Beverly Drive   28 Banner Street
Beverly Hills   London EC1Y 8QE
California 90212   England

SAGE PUBLICATIONS India Pvt. Ltd.
M-32 Market
Greater Kailash I
New Delhi 110 048 India

Printed in the United States of America

Library of Congress Cataloging-in-Publication Data

Main entry under title:

Intimate relationships.

   (Sage focus editions ; v. 80)
   Includes index.
   1. Married people—Psychology. 2. Communication
in marriage. 3. Intimacy (Psychology) 4. Interpersonal
relations. I. Perlman, Daniel. II. Duck, Steve.
HQ728.I64 1987   646.7′8   85-26248
ISBN 0-8039-2609-X
ISBN 0-8039-2610-3 (pbk.)

Contents

Preface

It is simple yet true: Humans are gregarious. In infancy, protection and care are essential for survival. At some point in their lives, over 90% of Americans marry. Not long ago, 107 presumably normal adults carried pagers around the city of Chicago for a week (Larson, Csikszentmihalyi, & Graef, 1982). Once during each two hours of their waking day, they were beeped, and 70% of the time they were in the presence of other people. Via extrapolation, this implies that between the ages of 21 and 65 the average American spends 196,797 waking hours with other people.

Relationships can provide a sense of belonging, feelings of warmth, and help in coping with difficulties. Unfortunately, our dealings with others can also lead to conflicts, disappointment, and jealousy. Whether they be good, bad, or a mixture of both, relationships are a central part of the human experience.

The analysis of personal relationships (PRs) has a long history, dating back as far as Aristotle. In the 20th century, academics in several different disciplines have conducted a substantial number of empirical investigations. All too often, however, these social scientists have worked in isolation and in ignorance of the contributions being made in other disciplines. But in the 1980s, a renaissance has occurred in PR work. There has been greater recognition of the need for interdisciplinary communication among diverse parties with a common substantive interest. Robert Hinde, Harold Kelley, and others have gone so far as to call for a new science of relationships. Not only has research flourished, but subtle shifts have occurred in the kind of research being done.

Given this period of exciting, dynamic growth, we felt that the timing was opportune for one or more volumes charting the advance of the field of personal relationships. This is the second volume the editors have done together (see Duck & Perlman, 1985). The first volume covered a broad range of the PR domain, identifying several recurrent themes that cut across specific areas of research and highlighting new directions of research and practice.

7

The present volume is thematically focused on the development of intimate relations. Chapter 1 is a bibliographic essay providing a conceptually oriented overview of the field. As noted in that chapter, the notion of intimacy has been used in a variety of ways. In the present volume, we focus on relationships, as opposed to individual motives or short-term interactions. Most of the chapters in the book focus on relationships in which people have achieved, or are striving to achieve, intimacy. Some chapters, however, examine close relationships which have failed, or are failing, to provide intimacy. Thus the paradoxical phenomenon of intimate strangers is illuminated.

Although the present book is more thematically integrated than Duck and Perlman (1985), the style and goals of both volumes are similar. In issuing invitations to authors, we encouraged them to present a comprehensive overview of their work rather than focusing on smaller details. While we sought a strong empirical underpinning, we wanted chapters written so that they could be fully understood by statistically naive readers. We exhorted each author to communicate clearly, in a well-organized fashion.

In introducing the earlier volume, we identified trends and needs in the analysis of personal relationships. A few themes from those remarks are worth reiterating, since all are manifest in the present volume. First, the study of personal relationships, while heavily influenced by American psychology, is an international, multidisciplinary enterprise. Among others, sociologists, family scientists, and communication experts are all making important contributions. (The present volume includes contributors from four disciplines and five countries.) Second, there is a shift away from the question of who likes whom to the developmental analysis of long-term relationships. The emphasis on attraction has given way to a more balanced view acknowledging both positive forces and conflict processes (see Chapters 7 and 8). Instead of focusing primarily—as social psychologists did—on causes and consequences, the new PR researchers pay greater attention to stages and processes (see Chapters 4, 9, and 10). Similarly, a variety of new topics have emerged on the PR map such as jealousy, postmarital family reorganization, and female-initiated relationships (see Chapters 3, 5, 9, and 10). With this development has come a movement from laboratory experiments toward the in vivo study of relationships. Another shift has been toward more applied, practical issues. Empirically oriented academics have become more interested in the implications and utilization of their knowledge. Therapists have been using empirical findings as one basis for formulating intervention, and they have also begun doing sophisticated outcome research to demonstrate the effectiveness of their treatments (Chapters 1, 6, 7, and 10 manifest the intersection of researcher and practitioner concerns).

The volume is organized along a time line into three main substantive sections. The first is primarily concerned with the establishment of relationships. In the first chapter within this section, the eminent social psychologist Mark Snyder and his colleague, Jeffry Simpson, ask: Do low self-monitors establish more persisting, intimate relationships than high self-monitors? In the second chapter, Kathryn Kelley and Beverly Rolker-Dolinsky do a nice job of integrating the diverse literature on female-initiated and -dominated relationships. They ask such questions as: How common are female-initiated relationships? Do women gain or lose in other people's evaluations by initiating? How well do female-initiated relationships fare over time? The final chapter in this section ties into the theme of how relationships develop over time. In particular, Surra and Huston provide a fresh, broad analysis of the transition to marriage. They delineate three stages of the transition (precommitment, postcommitment, and the event itself), and then provide new data on how newlyweds graph and explain their courtships.

The second section of the book looks at the dynamics of ongoing relationships. Highlighting the importance that alternative attractions can have on intimate couples, Buunk and Bringle analyze jealousy. They discuss at length how people assess threats to their relationships and how they cope with jealousy-evoking events via impression management strategies. In the second chapter within this section, Patricia Noller of Australia summarizes and updates the findings of her outstanding program of work on how communication patterns differ in distressed versus nondistressed marriages. Given the importance of self disclosure, emotional communication, and gratifying interactions to intimacy, clearly the findings of Gottman, Noller, and others are of prime relevance to the concerns of this volume. The final chapter in this section rests on a creative synthesis of clinical experience and attribution research. Baucom analyzes and spells out the clinical implications of when and why people make attributions. As he notes, maintaining intimacy is one of the main functions of these attributions.

Baucom's chapter leads into the final major section of the book: relationships gone awry. In Chapter 8, Rusbult illuminates four responses (exit, voice, loyalty, and neglect) that people have to dissatisfaction in their relationships. Rodgers then provides a theoretical analysis of family reorganization following divorce. Considering this topic from a developmental perspective, he integrates concepts from four theoretical domains (the binuclear family, social networks, family stress, and family problem solving). Such broad, albeit abstract, theoretical integrations have proved highly valuable in family sociology. Inasmuch as Connie Ahrons is one of the main theorists on whom he draws, Rodgers's contribution leads nicely into the next chapter by Ahrons and her associate, Lynn Wallisch. Ahrons is well known among family scholars for her ground-breaking theoretical and empirical work on family reorganization following divorce. In their chapter for this volume, Ahrons and Wallisch begin by noting that divorce has traditionally been viewed by laypersons and researchers alike as a pathological life event, a threat to basic societal values. By contrast, Ahrons and Wallisch view reorganization as a normal transition in contemporary Western cultures. As such, they recognize that so-called "binuclear" postdivorce families can have benefits for all parties. The bulk of this chapter reports for the first time an analysis of the relationships between ex-spouses over the three years following their divorce. Ahrons and Wallisch concentrate on the determinants and course over time of the quality of these relationships.

In the final chapter of the volume, Linda Acitelli and Steve Duck reflect on controversial issues raised throughout the book. In particular, they focus on three questions: "Does intimacy reside in individuals or in relationships?" "Is intimacy a state or a process?" and "Do insiders' and outsiders' views of intimate couples differ?" They conclude with a prescriptive statement of where the study of intimacy should go next.

Acknowledgments

As anyone who has studied either relationships or the publishing process is well aware, the two are intertwined in a systemic fashion. Our editorial activites have been helped along by the support, advice, and encouragement of several individuals. Our decision to embark on an editorial partnership grew out of two exchange visits between Canada and England. We are very grateful to the British Council for providing the travel funds that made these trips possible. The people at Sage offered advice on the broad directions this volume should take; and a highly distinguished panel of scholars gave us several fruitful leads for recruiting chapter authors doing novel, excellent work.

If preparing this volume has underscored any basic insight, any single theme worth proclaiming in flashing lights, it is the importance of the intimate others in life. Our wives, Elizabeth and Sandra, have respected our tendencies to work 50-55-hour weeks, supported our pursuits, and been most hospitable during our trans-Atlantic visits. Our heartfelt, public thanks are just a small fraction of the ways in which we reciprocate for the great enrichment they add to our lives.

Finally, we have enjoyed working with the contributors and gained from their insights. At the same time, however, we believe that social science knowledge is best when it can be given away. If this volume is to succeed, it must leave its readers wiser. Whether it be for one's personal life, for a course, for a professional practice, or for doing the next generation of research, the chapters should leave the reader better informed about dyadic relations. We hope that all of you will develop an intimate relationship with the contributors' ideas and join with us in helping to disseminate, apply, and/or empirically advance their wisdom.

—D. P. and S. D.

REFERENCES

Duck, S., & Perlman, D. (Eds.). (1985). *Understanding personal relationships: An interdisciplinary approach*. London: Sage.

Larson, R., Csikszentmihalyi, M., & Graef, R. (1982). Time alone in daily experience: Loneliness or renewal? In L. A. Peplau & D. Perlman (Eds.), *Loneliness: A sourcebook of current theory, research, and therapy*. New York: Wiley-Interscience.

1

The Development of
Intimate Relationships

DANIEL PERLMAN
BEVERLEY FEHR

During the past decade, social scientists have significantly added to our understanding of personal relationships (PRs). This volume is designed to feature some of the recent advances in our knowledge. Collectively, the chapters focus on the intersection of two concerns: intimacy and the development of relationships. This introductory chapter reviews the existing literature on the development of intimate relationships.

We concentrate our attention here on past conceptual approaches. In doing so, we cite research for illustrative purposes, but we do not attempt a comprehensive review of empirical evidence. In getting started, we first ask: What is intimacy? Why is it important? Toward the end of the chapter, we briefly discuss ways of promoting intimate bonds. For the most part, intimacy and relationship development have long been treated separately. Thus, sometimes our remarks will apply to both areas, but in other sections of the chapter we reflect exclusively on one topic or the other.

The formal study of intimacy dates back to the writing of Georg Simmel (1950), originally published at the beginning of the century. Starting in the 1930s, such neo-Freudians as Sullivan and Fromm emphasized our need for "chums" and "unity." At about the same time, the negative effects of maternal deprivation among institutionalized children were noted by Spitz. The dramatic impact of these reports was underscored by Harlow's laboratory findings on the detrimental consequences of monkeys being reared by "wire mothers." Not surprisingly, Bowlby and others (see Morris, 1982) later stressed the crucial importance of early maternal attachment. In the 1950s, Buber (1958) analyzed "I-thou" relationships. Whether or

13

not they used the term, all of these investigators drew attention to the importance of intimacy.

Despite the longevity of these roots, many aspects of the PR terrain have been better mapped than the development of intimate relationships. Berscheid (1977, p. 203) laments that "relationship development has been relatively ignored." Undoubtedly, this was due in part to a lack of theoretical interest in developmental issues. The dearth of research also partly reflects the methodological difficulties of doing such research. To study relationship development requires the use of longitudinal designs. One can cite a litany of problems associated with such studies: They can be expensive, they take a long time to complete, keeping track of participants is difficult, subject loss and nonrandom assignment pose threats to the internal validity of results, and change scores are problematic. However, even in the face of these methodological challenges, recent interest in relationship development is helping to fill a previous deficiency in our knowledge.

Dahms (1972) provides a bibliography of the literature on intimacy published prior to his own work. He identifies just over 100 items, spanning such diverse areas as literature, sociology, education, and psychology. While this bibliography may not be exhaustive, and while it is skewed toward Dahms's own humanistic-existential perspective, he identifies only 18 books and articles on the psychological aspects of intimacy.

The *Psychological Abstracts* did not use intimacy as a category until 1973. From 1973 to 1983, 416 items (or an average of 38 per year) were reported in this index. The peak number of entries in a given year (N = 78) was reached in 1979. The number then leveled off to about 40 per year for the period 1980-1983.

A few noteworthy books on intimacy have appeared in the 1980s. In 1982, Fisher and Stricker published a volume on intimacy oriented toward clinical psychologists. In addition, two popular books by social scientists have been well received by the general public. Rubenstein and Shaver (1982) based their *In Search of Intimacy* on a survey of newspaper readers' experiences of loneliness. McGill (1985) focused his report on male intimacy, including the problems men have in achieving intimacy. In 1984 Val Derlega edited a more academically oriented book on communication and intimacy in close relationships. Equally important for the area, Sharon Brehm (1985) has written a textbook on *Intimate Relationships*.

In preparing this chapter, we had to be selective about which treatments of intimacy to include. We have concentrated on social scientific, especially psychological, analyses. Naturally, even within psychology, intimacy can be addressed from a variety of perspectives. Fisher and Stricker's (1982) book provides a clinical viewpoint. It has chapters reflecting humanistic, existential, Gestalt, social learning, and rational-emotive approaches. We have largely ignored these contributions as conceptual analyses of intimacy. In most instances, such statements contain cursory or specifically focused analyses of intimacy coupled with clinical implications based on the author's general viewpoint (some of the treatment suggestions are mentioned briefly in our discussion of promoting intimacy). To date, these analyses have contributed little to the more empirically oriented, social psychological work on intimacy. It is this latter empirical focus that is manifest throughout the present chapter.

What Is Intimacy?

Definition

The word intimacy derives from *intimus,* the Latin term for "inner" or "inmost." In several other Romance and European languages, the root word for intimacy refers to this "most internal" quality. For example, in German the root word for intimacy connotes an awareness of the internal sphere, the most inward reality of the other person. Oden (1974, p. 3) notes: "Influenced by this nuance of innermost, our English word intimate points to a ... knowledge of the core of something, an understanding of the inmost parts, that which is indicative of one's deepest nature and marked by close physical, mental and social association."

Since intimacy is a part of our everyday vocabularies, one would expect it to conjure up various meanings for laypeople. Waring and associates (1980) asked 50 adults living in a university community, "What does intimacy mean to you?" Four themes emerged in their answers. First, sharing private thoughts, dreams, and beliefs was mentioned by a large proportion of the respondents as an important determinant of intimacy. Second, sexuality was considered an important component. Here, the emphasis was on affection and commitment more than on specific sexual activities. Third, respondents noted that anger, resentment, and criticism are not part of intimacy as they result in interpersonal distance. Finally, having a stable personal sense of identity—knowing one's needs and having adequate self-esteem—was mentioned as being essential to establishing intimacy.

Several more formal definitions of intimacy have been offered by social scientists. Ten such definitions are given in Table 1.1. Some common threads which are compatible with lay conceptions of intimacy run through several of these definitions. Three obvious themes are the closeness and interdependence of partners, the extent of self-disclosure, and the warmth or affection experienced. (Later in the chapter we describe in more detail the differences between casual and close relationships.)

Naturally, differences among the definitions can also be found, and it is possible that the nature of intimacy varies across cultures and time (see Gadlin, 1977). Some authors conceptualize intimacy in terms of interdependence and behavior (e.g., Lewis); others conceptualize it in terms of cognitive, evaluative processes (e.g., Chelune et al.). Still others (Erikson, McAdams) conceptualize intimacy as an individual capacity or motive rather than a relationship property.

Derlega and Margulis (1982) note three distinct phases in the development of concepts: (1) establishing interest, (2) conceptual clarification showing similarities and differences with related concepts, and (3) building formal theories. Although all three activities may happen at roughly the same time, work on intimacy appears to be primarily at the second stage. Its status as a unique concept within the science of relationships has not yet been fully established. One often sees references to marriage (or its alternatives) as being synonymous with intimacy. In our view, such relationships have the potential for being intimate, but we prefer to define intimacy in terms of the qualities achieved in the relationship. Turning to other examples of conceptual blurring, Hinde (1979, p. 114) equates intimacy with self-disclosure, while Morris (1971, p. 9) asserts that "intimacy occurs whenever two individuals come into bodily contact." Rubin (1973) treats intimacy as a component of love. We believe that further clarification of how intimacy differs from related concepts will benefit the area's continued evolution.

As concepts are developed and elaborated, a common step is to identify various subtypes. Several dimensions have been used in differentiating types of intimacy (Clinebell & Clinebell, 1970; Dahms, 1972; Davis, 1973; Schaefer & Olson, 1981; Wong, 1981). These include the domains (e.g., sexual, recreational) in which intimacy occurs; the type of relationship involved (e.g., friends, lovers); and time (e.g., intimacy in interactions and short-term relationships versus intimacy in long-term relationships).

TABLE 1.1
Definitions of Intimacy

(1) Intimacy means the degree of closeness two people achieve (Hendrick & Hendrick, 1983, p. 18).

(2) Intimate (n): An intimate friend or confidant. (adj.) Marked by a very close association, contact, or familiarity; marked by a warm friendship developing through long association; suggesting informal warmth or privacy. (*Webster's New Collegiate Dictionary*, 1976).

(3) Intimate relationships: Relationships between loving persons whose lives are deeply intertwined (Walster, Walster, & Berscheid, 1978, p. 146).

(4) Psychologists have evolved their own list of intimacy's defining features: openness, honesty, mutual self-disclosure; caring, warmth, protecting, helping; being devoted to each other, mutually attentive, mutually committed; surrendering control, dropping defenses; becoming emotionally attached, feeling distressed when separation occurs (Rubenstein & Shaver, 1982, p. 21).

(5) The defining characteristics of an intimate relationship are one or more of the following: behavioral interdependence, need fulfillment, and emotional attachment (Brehm, 1985, pp. 4-5, paraphrased).

(6) Emotional intimacy is defined in behavioral terms as mutual self-disclosure and other kinds of verbal sharing, as declarations of liking and loving the other, and as demonstrations of affections (Lewis, 1978, p. 108).

(7) We have defined intimacy as a subjective appraisal that emerges out of a rational process between two individuals in which each comes to know the "inner-most" aspects of the other, and each is known in a like manner (Chelune, Robison & Kommor, 1984, p. 35).

(8) Intimacy: A *process* in which we attempt to get close to another; to explore similarities (and differences) in the ways we think, feel, and behave (Hatfield, 1984, p. 208).

(9) The intimacy motive is a recurrent preference or readiness for *warm, close and communicative exchange with others*—an interpersonal interaction perceived as an end in itself rather than a means to another end (McAdams, 1985, p. 87).

(10) Intimacy ... The capacity to commit [one]self to concrete affiliations and partnerships and to develop the ethical strength to abide by such commitments, even though they may call for significant sacrifices and compromises (Erikson, 1963, p. 263).

On the opposite side of the coin, Orlofsky (in press) has tried to differentiate among people who fail to achieve true intimacy. Using the depth of subjects' ties and whether they were involved in a romantic relationship, Orlofsky identified four types: preintimates, psuedo-intimates, individuals capable of only stereotyped relationships, and isolates. The latter are withdrawn and lack ties with their peers. Pseudo-intimates and individuals capable of only stereotyped relationships have social contacts, but these are superficial, conventional bonds, with a low degree of personal communication and closeness. These two groups differ in that pseudo-intimates have entered into more or less enduring heterosexual relations. Preintimates are capable of closeness but, perhaps because of ambivalence about commitment, have not entered into enduring romantic relations.

Measurement

One factor that has given impetus to an area of research is a widely available, easy-to-administer measuring device. Two strategies have been used for quantifying intimacy. First, the breadth and depth of self-disclosure is often employed. Second, several questionnaire measures, often growing out of clinical work with couples, have been developed. One is Schaefer and Olson's (1981) PAIR Inventory (Personal Assessment of Intimacy in Relationships). It was designed to help marital counselors assess five domains of intimacy in couples' relationships and to reveal discrepancies between desired and achieved levels of intimacy. Other measures include Guerney's (1977) 52-item Likert scale for assessing interpersonal trust and intimacy, as well as Waring's Marital Intimacy Questionnaire (Waring, 1984; Waring & Reddon, 1983).

Tesch (1985) has developed a 60-item questionnaire for assessing intimacy in specific relationships, be they same or cross-sexed, friendships or romantic liaisons. She selected dimensions of intimacy based on the writings of neo-Freudians (Sullivan, Erikson) and humanists (Rogers). Her scale has a very high Cronbach alpha and respectable test-retest reliability over a three-week period. Using factor analysis, Tesch identified three main components contributing to overall scale scores: romantic love, supportiveness, and communication ease.

Miller and Lefcourt (1982) have developed a 17-item measure of the maximum level of intimacy currently experienced in a respondent's closest relationship. The items were derived from students' descriptions of the defining characteristics of relationships they considered to be intimate. (The instructions can be modified to measure intimacy in any designated relationship). This scale has a high Cronbach alpha (alpha = .86 or higher) and a high test-retest reliability (r = .84 to .96 over a one- to two-month period). The authors provide initial evidence of the scale's convergent, discriminant, and construct validity. For example, indicative of "known group" validity, mean intimacy scores were significantly higher for married than unmarried respondents. The Miller-Lefcourt measure correlated strongly with Guerney's measure and inversely with the UCLA Loneliness Scale. We feel that this scale has utility for a variety of research purposes when investigators need a short device to assess intimacy in relationships.

On the Importance of Intimacy

Health and Well-Being

The PR literature is replete with evidence testifying to the importance of relationships in our lives. Klinger (1977) asked 138 college students what made their lives meaningful; 89% mentioned personal relationships. For many students, this was the only source of meaning they mentioned. Sociologists recognize social bonds as the mortar of society. It is through such ties that people are taught the norms of society; without these norms, society would crumble. Elsewhere we have reviewed a considerable body of research showing that married individuals enjoy better health and well-being than the nonmarried (Fehr & Perlman, 1985). In part, this is due to the buffering effect (or protection) of social support in times of crises.

While these lines of evidence indicate the value of relationships in general, they do not necessarily confirm the importance of intimate relations per se. Various threads of evidence do, however, support the specific importance of intimate bonds. Lowenthal and Haven (1968) have demonstrated the unique importance of intimate relations in protecting older adults from the losses accompanying widowhood and retirement. Reis (1984) examined ten studies of the effects of different kinds of relationships on psychological health and mortality. He concludes from these studies that "well-being is most likely to stem from contact with affectively close or intimate partners" (p. 34).

Satisfaction with one's marriage and family life are strongly correlated with people's overall sense of subjective well-being (see Diener, 1984). Freedman (1978) found that among people who were very happily in love, more than 90% were very happy in general. More than any other single element, the unhappy people in his sample mentioned love as the one ingredient that would make them happy.

Scholars have also considered the impact that different kinds of relationships have on loneliness. In his classic analysis, Weiss (1973) distinguishes between social loneliness stemming from a lack of friendship ties and emotional loneliness stemming from a lack of intimate relationships. He claims that emotional loneliness is the more severe of the two forms. Jones (1982) had students keep diaries of their interactions for a two-day period. Loneliness was not related to the total number of interactions that students had. However, lonely students reported more interactions with strangers and mere acquaintances, and fewer interactions with family and friends. This led Jones

(1982, p. 243) to suggest that "lonely students have or exercise fewer opportunities to spend time with others who are intimate." Similarly, Cutrona (1982) provides evidence demonstrating that loneliness is more strongly linked to satisfaction with relationships than to the frequency or number of one's social contacts. Close, satisfying relationships thus appear to be the key in protecting oneself from loneliness experiences.

Additional support for the importance of intimacy comes from evidence on the negative consequences of a lack of intimate bonds. Horowitz (1979) found that intimacy problems formed the largest cluster of clients' complaints when seeking therapy for interpersonal problems. Goldberg (1976) argues that the absence of a close male relationship is strongly related to the significantly higher rate of suicide among men. Brown and Harris (1978) studied women who had experienced severe life events. Those who lacked a confidant were ten times more likely to become depressed than those who had been similarly stressed but who had an intimate relationship.

The Historically Increasing Importance of Intimacy

Intimate relationships appear to have become more important over time. Veroff, Douvan, and Kulka (1981) interviewed Americans about various aspects of their lives in 1957 and 1976. They state: "We have many different pieces of data to support the general conclusion that interpersonal intimacy has become a vehicle for personal fulfillment much more in 1976 than it was in 1957" (p. 537). These authors document an increased sensitivity to interpersonal relations—a desire for friendship, for warm relationships at work and in the family, and for personal impact in everyday encounters. Veroff et al. noticed a profound change in the extent to which people turned to intimate relations to deal with personal problems:

> While people in the earlier generation were more likely to see no solutions to problems they faced, to have a sense of resignation about their miseries, members of the new generation, both young and old, see some possible guidance and help in talking intimately with other people. With the decline of normal structured institutionalized ways of dealing with problems... more people make use of intimate relationships as an arena for working out problems. [Veroff et al., 1981, p. 525]

While the desire for intimacy appears to be on the increase in American society, our capacity to fill those desires may be declining.

Many observers have lamented the increase in urbanism, the high divorce rate, and the number of children reared in single-parent homes. Surveys show that at least one quarter of all Americans are bothered by feelings of loneliness. Unfortunately, other research shows that divorce and loneliness are intergenerationally transmitted (see Lobdell & Perlman, 1986). Thus the deficiencies in intimacy that we are experiencing today may be perpetuated in future generations.

Is Intimacy More Important to Women?

A common theme voiced by social scientists is that women are socioemotional experts while men are more task-oriented. As one feminist quipped, "Women express; men repress." In terms of qualitative aspects of friendship, clear gender differences have emerged. Older women are more apt to have confidants than are older men (Lowenthal & Haven, 1968). In midlife, Booth (1972) found that women have affectively richer relationships than men. In a study of college students, Caldwell and Peplau (1982) found that women place greater emphasis on emotional sharing and talking in their relationships, while men emphasized shared activity. Despite some nuances, it is generally agreed that women are higher in self-disclosure than men (see Brehm, 1985, pp. 216-218).

In a study of the life-span development of intimacy, Hodgson and Fischer (1979) interviewed college students. Participants were placed in one of five intimacy levels based on their interview responses. The authors reported that women had a greater capacity than men for experiencing the two highest levels of intimacy (p. 47). Furthermore, androgynous males achieved higher levels of intimacy than did traditional males.

Lewis (1978) suggests four barriers that prevent contemporary American males from becoming intimate with one another. These are male competition, homophobia, aversion to emotional vulnerability and openness, and a lack of role models. On top of this, reactions to disclosing appear to be a function of the discloser's gender. Derlega and Chaikin (1976) conducted a 2x2-type experiment in which a male or a female did or did not disclose a personal problem. Judges evaluated a male stimulus person as better adjusted when he remained silent. However, they evaluated a female stimulus person as better adjusted when she disclosed. All in all, males appear to be at risk for deficiencies in intimacy.

Is Intimacy Always Beneficial?

We have been stressing the advantages of intimacy, but readers may be wondering: Aren't there disadvantages, too? Undoubtedly, there are. For example, high prior levels of intimacy may make coping with the ending of a relationship all the more painful. Intimacy between two people may also cause others to feel jealous. Therapists such as Albert Ellis (1982) have discussed the unhealthy kinds of intimacy they encounter in their clients.

Hatfield (1984) has articulated six reasons that people shy away from intimate relationships. These include: (1) fear of having one's faults and shortcomings exposed, (2) fear of abandonment, (3) fear of angry attacks—that information disclosed will later be used as ammunition, (4) fear of loss of control, (5) fear of one's own destructive impulses if one were to "unleash" one's feelings, and (6) fear of losing one's individuality or of being engulfed.

The fear of abandonment and/or engulfment has been linked to the alarming incidence of family violence. Dutton (1984) speculates that domestic violence occurs in relationship situations where uncontrollable changes in socioemotional distance occur. For example, battering males may perceive any signs of increased independence from the relationship (such as a wife's new job) as abandonment. Conversely, an increase in demands for affection may be seen as engulfment. Dutton (1984, p. 290) comments:

> While issues of socioemotional distance occur for most couples, wife assaulters may be particularly inept at communicating their own needs in response to intimacy changes or may have exaggerated needs to control intimacy and maintain an 'optimal' zone. Consquently, they may experience arousal which they interpret as anger. If their verbal skills are poor, their prepotent response to anger may be violence.

While family violence is an extreme case of intimate relations gone awry, there is evidence which suggests that even in nontroubled relationships we tend to ignore the ones we love. Birchler, Weiss, and Vincent (1975) observed the verbal and nonverbal behavior of marital partners casually conversing with each other or with a stranger. They found that both distressed and nondistressed married couples were more negative and less positive than were stranger dyads. In fact, they report that nondistressed couples emitted 80% more negative behavior and 30% less positive reinforcement to spouses than to strangers! In the same vein, Rubin (1983) has described marriage as the union of intimate strangers.

This discussion raises the question of whether there are both positive and negative types of intimacy. Our hunch is that the feelings directly associated with intimacy are predominantly positive. We would prefer to consider hollow marriages as unions in which intimacy has not been achieved. We are therefore intrigued by Birchler et al.'s (1975) results. They merit replication and extension in more naturalistic contexts so that we have a better picture of the relative rates of reinforcement in casual versus intimate dyads. At present, we are reluctant to accept them as telling the full story.

Sometimes theoretical insights, especially the limiting conditions of phenomena, can help explain anomalies such as this. Certainly, theories generally have value. They guide research, help explain results, and offer insights into the best forms of treatment. Given these benefits, it is clearly worthwhile to consider conceptual approaches to intimacy. We consider four models: life-span developmental approaches, motivational approaches, equity theory, and equilibrium viewpoints.

Four Approaches to Intimacy

Life-Span Developmental Models

Theorists such as Sullivan (1953) and Erikson (1959, 1963) offer a life-span developmental perspective on the capacity to engage in intimate relationships. In Sullivan's view, the need for interpersonal intimacy first arises in the human life cycle during the short but crucial stage of preadolescence. He posits that the appearance of a same-sex "chum" flags a critical transition in the person's understanding of interpersonal relationships. The individual evidences an unprecedented preoccupation with the well-being of another person. According to Sullivan (1953, p. 246): "So far as I have ever been able to discover, nothing remotely like this appears before the age of, say, eight-and-a-half, and sometimes it appears decidedly later." This developmental transition is also characterized by the painful realization that a lack of intimacy can be a very negative, lonely experience.

Erikson (1963) maintains that successful negotiation of the crisis of identity versus role confusion is a prerequisite for the experience of intimacy. He argues that it is "only after a reasonable sense of identity has been established that real *intimacy* with the other sex (or, for that matter with any other person or even with oneself) is possible" (Erikson, 1959, p. 95). Having established a sense of personal identity, the young adult is anxious to fuse his or her identity with that of others.

Orlofsky (in press) has reviewed research pertaining to the postulated identity-intimacy sequence. Studies typically report an association between these variables, although the correlation is often stronger among men than among women. In one often cited test of Erikson's theory, Marcia (1976) assessed the intimacy status of a group of college males and then interviewed them again six years later. Consistent with Erikson's theory, current identity status was positively correlated with current intimacy status. More important, he found that for those whose identity status remained stable, previous identity was related to current identity status. Marcia (1976, p. 153) concluded: "To the extent that identity status remains constant, it seems to be at least a concomitant and perhaps a precursor to intimacy, as would be predicted by Erikson's theory."

A Motivational Approach to Intimacy

McAdams (1982, p. 134) conceptualizes intimacy as an enduring motive; it reflects the "individual's *preference* or *readiness* for experiences of closeness, warmth, and communication." He measures intimacy motivation by analyzing the quality of interpersonal relationships manifested by characters in imaginative stories written by a subject. Each story must include at least one of two themes before a more detailed thematic analysis takes place. The first prime test is the theme of the relationship producing positive affect (e.g., "The people feel an emotional closeness"). The second prime test is the presence of dialogue—the characters must engage in verbal or nonverbal communication that is reciprocal and noninstrumental (e.g., "They talked about whatever crossed their minds"). The stories are then further categorized on eight dimensions. These include psychological growth and coping, commitment or concern, union, harmony, escape to intimacy, and so forth. Collectively, these dimensions yield a final intimacy motivation score.

McAdams (1980) found that sorority and fraternity members high in intimacy motivation were rated by their peers as significantly more warm, loving, sincere, and less dominant, outspoken, and self-centered than members scoring low in intimacy motivation. McAdams and Powers (1981) report that in a psychodrama situation, students scoring high in intimacy motivation behaved differently than those scoring low. They were warmer and more egalitarian with other group members, positioned themselves closer to others, encouraged others to get involved, and engendered more positive affect in others compared with subjects low in intimacy motivation. McAdams and Constantian (1983) sampled behavior and experience naturalistically. They found that subjects high in intimacy motivation spent more time thinking about people and relationships, engaged in more conversation and letter writing, and expressed more positive affect in interpersonal situations.

Equilibrium Models

Equilibrium models provide another approach to intimacy. Argyle and Dean's (1965) article was the starting point of this tradition, while Patterson's (1976, 1984) ever-evolving formulations have been crucial to expanding and revising this line of analysis. The basic idea of equilibrium models is that we have optimal levels of intimacy that we prefer. Being comfortable involves maintaining a balance between our desires to achieve and to avoid intimacy in our interactions.

Argyle and Dean argue that intimacy is a joint function of topic intimacy and nonverbal behaviors (e.g., eye contact, smiling, and physical proximity). They hypothesized that if one component was changed, one or more of the others would shift in the reverse direction, so that equilibrium would be continually maintained. To test their model, they had subjects approach a confederate whose eyes were open or shut. As predicted, the subjects approached closer to a person whose eyes were shut. Argyle and Dean also examined the opposite side of the equilibrium process, predicting that as a confederate moved closer to the subject, the subject would reduce eye contact. Again, this prediction was supported.

Two implicit features of Argyle and Dean's model are worth noting. First, they view intimacy from a dialectical perspective; they see people as constantly striving to have the right amount of intimacy. This perspective underscores the fact that at times we want to reduce our contact with others. We feel that this is an important point. Many other theorists (e.g., Erikson) seem to imply that striving toward intimacy is good, and frame their analyses in terms of finding the correlates of such closeness. Second, Argyle and Dean imply the substitutability and equifinality of nonverbal behavior. In other words, once the intimacy balance has been disturbed, any of several different ways can be used to restore equilibrium. However, all behavior will be directed toward the same goal. Incidentally, Altman's (1975) analysis of privacy, which has tangential relevance to intimacy, has these same key characteristics.

Argyle and Dean imply that the typical response to intimacy is one or another form of interpersonal distancing. Patterson (1976) extended equilibrium theory to handle results showing that an increase in Person A's intimacy sometimes stimulates an intimate response from Person B. To provide a more comprehensive model, Patterson drew on Schachter's theory of emotional labeling. According to Patterson, we use environmental cues to label our affective reactions to another person's increased intimacy behavior. If our reaction is negative, we engage in compensatory behavior to reduce intimacy. If our response is positive, we reciprocate with intimate behavior of our own.

Patterson also distinguishes between intimacy in interactions and the level of intimacy in the overall relationship. He indicates that the higher the overall level of closeness in a relationship, the more likely two people are to engage in (and reciprocate) intimate behavior. A considerable body of research on such nonverbal behaviors as eye contact and physical proximity is consistent with this conclusion.

Equity Theory

Several popular books have been written on the theme of "looking out for number one" (i.e., oneself). Individuals are frequently depicted as trying to maximize their own outcomes. The problem with this approach is that such individualistic pursuit of material benefits may cause suffering or shortages for others. Therefore, social philosophers have frequently suggested that society must play a regulating function, suggesting rules for the distribution of resources. The operation of equity principles can be seen as one response to the resource allocation dilemma.

Equity theorists (see Walster, Walster, & Berscheid, 1978) believe that people seek a fair outcome, considering both their own costs and the outcomes that others receive. Thus an equitable relationship is one in which an individual perceives his or her input (I)/outcome (O) ratio to be comparable to that of his or her partner. Letting the subscripts refer to person A and B, respectively, equity exists when

$$\frac{(O_A - I_A)}{(|I_A|)} = \frac{O_B - I_B}{(|I_B|)}$$

Here, I_A and I_B designate the absolute value—irrespective of sign—of A and B's inputs.

When relationships are inequitable, we become distressed and try to restore equity. This can be done in various ways. Partners can alter their inputs or try to change their outcomes. They can also use psychological mechanisms to convince themselves that equity really exists, or they can leave the relationship.

Hatfield and her associates have been especially concerned with the application of equity theory to the analysis of intimate relationships (see Hatfield & Traupmann, 1981; Hatfield, Traupmann, Sprecher, Utne, & Hay, 1985). Hatfield et al. (1985) have offered five propositions dealing with intimate relationships. In essence, they claim: (1) equitable (versus inequitable) dating relationships are more likely to progress to higher levels of intimacy, (2) partners will be more content and less distressed in equitable relationships, (3) when inequity exists, intimate partners will try to restore equity, (4) following transitions or crises, couples will either work to reestablish equity or move toward breaking up, and (5) equitable relationships are especially likely to be stable and to persist.

A study by Walster, Walster, & Traupmann (1978) typifies equity research. Members of dating couples were asked to assess their own and their partner's inputs, outputs, and outcomes by responding to questions like, "Considering what you put into your dating relationship, compared to what you get out of it ... and what your partner puts in compared to what s/he gets out of it, how well does your dating relationships stack up?" Based on their responses, the participants were categorized as either overbenefited, underbenefited, or equitably treated. It was predicted that equitable relationships would be more stable over time and characterized by greater sexual involvement relative to inequitable ones. These predictions were supported. One noteworthy feature of these data is that participants who feel slightly overbenefited enjoy satisfying relations. As expected, however, substantially overbenefited individuals were not satisfied with their courtship. Instead, they suffered from feelings of guilt.

Some critics have challenged the application of equity theory to intimate relations. They imply that intimate bonds are special—above the crass considerations of social exchange. Mills and Clark's (1982) work ties into these criticisms. They distinguish between communal and exchange relationships. Communal relations are described as a form of selfless concern in which equity considerations are presumably tossed aside. In communal relationships, concern about the other person's welfare predominates. Benefits are given because they will be pleasing to the other person or because they are needed. Clark and Mills conducted several experiments to test predictions derived from their analysis of the communal versus exchange distinction. For example, in communal relationships they found that if one's partner reciprocated a favor, attraction was decreased (rather than enhanced).

A methodological factor (cum conceptual analysis implied in the writing of equity theorists) may help unravel some of the ambiguity concerning the operation of equity in intimate relationships. At least three different ways of studying equity have been used: an assessment of the resources (money, physical attractiveness, and so on) that people bring to relationships, global assessments by respondents concerning the equity in the outcomes of their relationships, and finally, exchanges in specific situations. It is in studies using the first two procedures that we believe equity principles are generally apparent. In studies of specific situations, we would expect equity to be less apparent for intimate partners than for casual acquaintances, since the latter exchange only a limited range of resources. In such cases, tit-for-tat immediate reciprocity is the order of the day. By contrast, intimate and communal relationships are for the long term, and immediate reciprocity may thus be less important or, according to Clark and Mills, even offensive. In intimate dyads, the members may not keep track of how or when specific benefits get repaid. (Indeed, for parents the mere prospect of future repayment in old age may be enough.) Nonetheless, we suspect that experiencing an overall sense of equity is essential to the members of most intimate relationships.

A Comparative Analysis of Four Approaches to Intimacy

In thinking about these approaches to intimacy, we have identified seven dimensions on which they can be compared. In Table 1.2 we describe the four approaches along these dimensions. Naturally, constructing this table involved making judgments and simplifying details. In large measure, the table is a summary; much of the information has already been presented or is self-explanatory. The table merely organizes information so that the similarities and differences become more apparent.

As the table shows, the four approaches are quite different. Each approach has its own way of conceptualizing intimacy. To some extent, each approach is addressing a different set of phenomena. Although not explicitly indicated in the table, Erikson's and Hatfield's approaches are applications of more general theories to the topic of intimacy. Indeed, Hatfield's postulates are as much an effort to articulate how equity operates in a special class of relationships as they are an effort to illuminate intimacy itself. The other two approaches were developed primarily to account for intimacy per se.

TABLE 1.2
Four Approaches to Intimacy

	Intimacy Motive (McAdams)	Intimacy versus Isolation (Erikson)	Equilibrium Theory (Patterson)	Equity (Hatfield)
View derived from:	McClelland's work on motivation (Buber)	Psychodynamic theories	Research on nonverbal behavior and verbal intimacy	Social psychological research and theory
Central concept:	Need for intimacy	Identity and intimacy	Classes of nonverbal behavior, arousal, labeling and equilibrium	Fairness of input-outcome ratios
Commonly used assessment technique	Projective test	Interview	Assessment of nonverbal behaviors	Questionnaire
Intimacy: individual process or relationship property	Individual process with interpersonal implications	Individual process	Property of the interaction	Relationship property (equity calculations made by individual)
Causes: historical (including earlier life events) versus contemporary	Historical	Epigenetic principle emphasizing importance of resolution of earlier crises	Contemporary	Contemporary
Duration	Traitlike, enduring	Life stage whose resolution has lasting effects	Constantly changing	Lasts as long as outcome ratios in relationships are perceived as fair
Consistency across relationships	Preferences across relationships	Ultimately with one heterosexual partner	Interaction-specific	Relationship-specific

Another classification scheme has important ramifications. Two of these approaches (McAdams & Erikson) stem from a personality perspective, while the other two stem from a social psychological background. Working within the personality tradition, McAdams and Erikson see intimacy as an individual process of a more enduring, transsituational nature. Working within the social psychological tradition, Patterson and Hatfield see intimacy as a property of relationships. For Patterson, levels of intimacy are constantly fluctuating and being adjusted. The two camps also differ in that personality-based approaches place more emphasis on early childhood influences, whereas the social psychological theorists stress the current determinants of intimacy.

Many criteria (e.g., parsimony, logical consistency, testability, stimulation of research, empirical support, the breadth of phenomena addressed, ease of comprehension, and practical utility) exist for evaluating theories. In this case, all four viewpoints can be readily understood. With the exception of Hatfield, however, none of the theorists have focused on ways of enhancing intimacy.

Research is clearly one of the most important criteria for evaluating theories. All four approaches rate favorably in this domain. Each is testable, each has stimulated research, and each has enjoyed at least partial support. Within this generally positive context, some nuances and minor criticisms are in order.

While McAdams has done noteworthy, programmatic research, his formulations have yet to stimulate much work by others. The social psychological approaches are hard to refute because of the numerous ways of restoring equilibrium and reducing inequities. If the theoretical predictions don't work out, it may be because other mechanisms were used. Thus the researcher is faced with either preventing or measuring alternative ways of restoring the equilibrium.

Equity theory has been criticized because of the limits under which the equity phenomenon operates (see Perlman & Fehr, 1986). For example, when the outcomes are small and time constraints large, people are less likely to apportion resources equitably. Even more important, evidence shows that men lean more toward the equity norm than do women. Women are more apt to divide outcomes equally, regardless of how much each individual has contributed to obtaining such rewards.

The breadth and type of phenomena addressed are also a critical concern in evaluating approaches to intimacy. Given our interest in relationships, we are most favorable to theories that more completely illuminate their nature. (We are less concerned with the breadth of phenomena in general that these approaches can explain.) Patterson is concerned with interaction but not with relationships. Erikson is primarily concerned with individual adjustment. McAdams begins with an individual process, and yet he carefully examines how the intimacy motive influences interpersonal relations. Thus both he and Hatfield receive our most favorable evaluations on this consideration.

Using an absolute standard, one can undoubtedly identify faults in all four approaches to intimacy. Yet given the area's youthful stage of development, we would not be too critical. The existing formulations have helped to illuminate the phenomenon and guide empirical work. Certainly we have more knowledge about intimacy than we did 80 years ago when Simmel first offered his analysis.

The Development of Close Relationships

Casual versus Close Relationships

What happens to close relationships as they develop over time? With the exception of equity theory, the four previously discussed approaches to intimacy have not been especially concerned with this issue. Certainly it is reasonable to believe that close or intimate relations differ from casual social ties.

Several authors (Burgess & Huston, 1979; Chelune et al., 1984; Levinger & Snoek, 1972; Walster et al., 1978) have described the ways in which intimate relations are unique. A partial, composite listing of their ideas suggests that the following changes take place as relationships become close:

(1) Interaction increases in terms of the frequency, duration, and number of settings in which it occurs.
(2) Individuals gain knowledge of the innermost being of their partner, the breadth and depth of knowledge exchanged expands, and partners develop personal communication codes.
(3) Individuals become more skilled at mapping and anticipating their partner's views and behaviors.
(4) Partners increase their investment in the relationship.
(5) The interdependence and the sense of "we-ness" experienced by partners increases.
(6) Partners come to feel that their separate interests are inextricably tied to the well-being and outcome of their relationship.
(7) The extent of positive affect (liking or loving) and the sense of caring, commitment, and trust increase.

(8) Attachment develops so that partners try to restore proximity if they are separated.

(9) Partners see the relationship as irreplaceable, or at least special.

Levinger's ABCDE Model

Several models of the stages in the development of intimate relationships have been articulated. Four such models are shown in Table 1.3. There are also theories of friendship formation (see Perlman & Fehr, 1986) and theories focusing on how dyads break up (e.g., Duck, 1982). The most comprehensive theory has been advanced by Levinger and his associates. In 1972, Levinger and Snoek offered an initial formulation which accounted for relationship development from "zero contact" to "mutuality." It concentrated on the initiation of interpersonal ties. More recently, Levinger (1980, 1983) has extended his views to incorporate the deterioration of relationships. In his new ABCDE model, A stands for Acquaintance; B for Buildup; C for Continuation; D for Deterioration; and E for Ending. This new model focuses more specifically on close relationships and places greater emphasis on studying not only the stages per se but also the transitions between stages.

Briefly, at the acquaintance stage people's first impressions or initial images of one another largely determine whether or not there will be any future interaction. To the extent that early interaction is mutually enjoyable, the partners find themselves in the transition from acquaintanceship to buildup. At the next stage, the partners are in the process of becoming increasingly interdependent on one another. Each finds it easy to further the other's goals, and they anticipate that future interactions will also turn out to be mutually rewarding.

Levinger (1983) conceptualizes the transition from buildup to continuation as the development of a commitment to the relationship. In contrast to the novelty, ambiguity, and arousal experienced in the early stages, the continuation stage is accompanied by familiarity, predictability, and the reduction of cognitive and emotional tension. The partner's interconnections are smoothly meshed, and they focus little attention on alternatives to the relationship. The transition from continuation to deterioration "may be marked by an increase in interference or a reduction in the strength, diversity and/or frequency of the pair's interconnections, especially those that entail mutual pleasure" (Levinger, 1983, p. 345). In addition, Levinger comments that downturn is usually accompanied by one or both partners feeling that their outcomes have been unsatisfying. During deterioration, the

TABLE 1.3
Stage Models of Relationship Development

Stage in the Relationship	Kerckhoff & Davis's Filter Theory of Mate Selection	Lewis's Processes in Premarital Dyadic Formation	Murstein's Stimulus-Value-Role (SVR) Theory of Mate Selection	Levinger's ABCDE Model
Early	Similarity in values	Similarities Rapport Mutual self-disclosure Empathic understanding of the other person Interpersonal role-fit (e.g., need complementarity)	Attraction based on external stimulus attributes (e.g., physical attractiveness) Value similarity Successful performance of roles in the relationship (e.g., wife, husband)	Aquaintance—attraction based on impressions Buildup—attraction based on sampling outcomes and expectancies Continuation predictability and commitment develop
	Need complementarity			
Late		Dyadic crystallization (e.g., commitment, identity as a couple)		Deterioration—relations with reduced mutual pleasure often held together by barriers Endings

SOURCE: Adapted from Brehm (1985, p. 145).

relationship is held together primarily by the barriers that surround it. Levinger believes that internal pair processes, personal characteristics of the partners, and internal forces can all lead to the deterioration of relationships. In the transition from deterioration to ending, the partners are engaged in the process of carefully weighing the remaining costs and benefits of the relationship while contemplating alternative solutions. In Levinger's view, the two major tasks involved in the ending stage are to reorganize the intrachain sequences that previously were closely tied to those of one's partner and to begin constructing new relationships to replace the old.

Typical research in this area (see Levinger, 1980) involves presenting subjects with lists of behavior varying in degree of intimacy and asking them to judge how appropriate each behavior is for different relationship types varying in closeness. Not surprisingly, as relationships become closer, the probability that a pair will engage in intimate activities increases. Behavior involving physical contact and self-disclosure is most affected by an increase in closeness, while less intimate behaviors, like going for a walk or running an errand, are least affected by the degree of intimacy.

Evaluating Developmental Models

Two criticisms of developmental theories are worth noting. These theories assume that relationships change over time, perhaps in invariant regular ways, and that the determinants of intimacy are different in different stages. Developmental theorists (see Table 1.3) generally agree that external stimulus attributes (such as physical attractiveness) are important in the early stages of relationships. They also refer frequently to the formation of a dyadic identity ("we-ness", crystallization) in the more advanced stages of relationship development. In between, however, there is no agreement on the stages, the crucial antecedents of attraction, or the exact order in which predictor variables are important. This is the first problem. However, rebuttals on behalf of a developmental position can be offered. For instance, even if only one version is correct, while the others are proved wrong, it would still be a testimonial to the importance of a developmental perspective.

Second, Hinde (1979) claims that the division of any continuous process into stages is bound to be arbitrary, implying the occurrence of sudden changes which do not actually occur in relationships. Levinger (1983, p. 335) seems sensitive to this problem. He notes that transitions do not necessarily occur at a single point in time and acknowledges that processes begun in one stage can carry over into later stages.

Despite such challenges, we feel that developmental theories have had a major impact on PR research in the last decade. The work of Levinger and others has broadened the range of relationship phenomena that researchers have explored, and developmental theorists have posed new types of questions. Thus they have begun to fill the void noted in the 1970s by Berscheid. All in all, their impact has been beneficial.

Promoting Intimacy

In selecting which approaches to intimacy we would review, we noted the gap between practitioners and empirical investigators. While there are a few individuals (e.g., Hatfield) who do both, for the most part the authors writing on these two facets of intimacy are separate groups. We lament this schism. We believe that the broader, more representative view of the problem afforded by empirical investigations has the potential to guide and improve the application of therapeutic techniques for promoting intimacy.

In this last section of the chapter, we identify various ways of promoting intimacy, including lay strategies, psychotherapy, and intimacy workshops. Our discussion will admittedly be cursory. Our primary goal is to draw the reader's attention to a few of the issues involved and to indicate the range of techniques available. For a more comprehensive treatment, the reader will need to consult primary sources.

Lay Strategies

In discussing intervention strategies, we must of course realize that relatively few laypersons turn to professionals for help in achieving intimacy. Most, undoubtedly, try to create intimacy on their own, often without giving much thought to how they might best accomplish their goal. As far as we know, there is no research mapping out the strategies they use. Perhaps this lack of attention stems from the fact that intimacy is positive; it is not a problem. Problems cause pain, and explicit coping efforts ensue. When people's lives are generally satisfactory, missing such life-enhancing experiences as intimacy may go largely unnoticed by scientists and laypersons alike.

Those seeking to make a financial profit, champion specific viewpoints, and coordinate self-help groups are more attuned to our intimacy needs. Gordon (1976) astutely notes the "loneliness businesses" that dot the American landscape. These include introduction services, singles bars, personal ads, organizations such as Parents without Partners, encounter groups, cruises, religious retreats, ski clubs, and the like. Some of these have very worthwhile primary goals, but all capitalize, directly or indirectly, on our hopes and desires to form intimate bonds. The short- and long-term success rate of such activities is a matter of speculation.

Psychotherapy and Programs with Potential for Increasing Intimacy

In their clinical practices, psychotherapists must deal with a variety of intimacy-related problems. These can be divided into three categories: pathological forms of intimacy, underlying problems that prevent clients from achieving intimacy, and transference issues in the therapeutic relationship itself. Psychodynamic theorists such as Ellis have written on how to deal with these problems (see Fisher & Stricker, 1982). Shadish (1984) has also written on intimacy in clinical groups.

Besides general psychotherapy, mental health professionals have a number of more specific programs that may help promote intimacy. These include social skill training, sex therapy, marital enrichment, and even "bibliotherapy" (i.e., books on such topics as overcoming shyness or being assertive). These can be offered as a form of prevention, self-enhancement, or treatment. In distinction to general psychotherapy, these more specialized approaches are designed to help a broad cross-section of society, not just individuals with neurotic difficulties. On the reverse side of this coin, there are also programs for helping people (especially widows) cope with the loss of a loved partner (see Rook, 1984, pp. 1396-1397).

Two specific approaches are especially germane to our concerns. First, using principles of cognitive behavior therapy, Young (1982) has developed a program to help individuals cope with loneliness. The final stages of this therapy focus on enhancing intimacy. Second, Lewis (1978) runs groups for men. He promotes male intimacy via exercises concentrating on self-disclosure and extending physical affection.

Couple-Based Approaches to Enhancing Intimacy

In the past few years, three couple-based approaches specifically designed to enhance intimacy have been published. In 1982, Margolin articulated social learning strategies for enhancing intimacy. She emphasizes discriminating specific behaviors that impact positively or negatively on marriage, increasing positive exchanges, enhancing communication skills (including problem solving), specifying relationship changes, and altering recurrent, dysfunctional thought processes. We should note, perfunctorily, that Margolin fails to discriminate clearly the concept of intimacy. We find little or no difference between her recommendations for enhancing intimacy and her usual approach to enhancing marital satisfaction. Nonetheless, we find behavioral marital therapy as developed by Patterson, Margolin and others a promising general approach to treating distressed couples. This approach may also increase intimacy per se. Indeed, a treatment outcome study by Johnson and Greenberg (1985) provides modest support for this notion.

Hatfield (1984), in a fairly brief explication, encourages people to accept themselves and their partners for what they are. She also encourages people to express themselves and to deal with their partner's reaction, even if that reaction includes anger or hurt.

L'Abate and Sloan (1984) offer a workshop format for facilitating intimacy in married couples. They feature three modules: selfhood and differentiation, emotional communication, and rational negotiations. This model is praiseworthy in that it builds on knowledge of intimacy, the component parts are more fully described in related publications, and its effectiveness has been tested (Sloan, 1984). Although the evaluation lacked either a waiting list or a placebo treatment control group, the results of the outcome study are encouraging; couples exposed to the program increased in intimacy. Sloan's data suggest that a crucial component of the program's effectiveness was training in the prenegotiation sharing of anger and hurt. This finding is consistent with other observations (e.g., Rook, 1984, p. 1393) indicating that dealing with criticism and conflict is a key ingredient to maintaining satisfying relationships. L'Abate and Sloan's work brings us full cycle—from understanding, to knowledge-based intervention, to the enhancement of intimacy.

Conclusion

We believe that intimacy is in the early stages of development as an area of empirically oriented social science work. It is a topic of inherent interest to the general public, and the importance of the phenomenon has been established. While intimacy is seen as special, it has a variety of different referents. In the future, we hope that more precision and consensus will emerge in usage of this term. Existing approaches to intimacy have stimulated empirical research, but the total number of studies done to date is still relatively small. However, development of several scales for measuring intimacy may well serve as a catalyst for future investigations.

There are many directions in which intimacy research could go, either following lines already established or along paths not yet obvious. Our own preference is for conceptually guided, broad examination of intimacy as an individual capacity and especially as a relationship phenomenon. Basic issues and questions are still to be addressed. Some of those we would like to see more fully explored are the demographics of intimacy; signs, symptoms, and behavioral manifestations; strategies people use to achieve intimacy; childhood antecedents; life cycle fluctuations in intimacy and their determinants; the growth and decline of intimacy within specific relationships; and causes and consequences. We suspect that work on intimacy will be further linked with such key psychological factors as cognitions and reinforcement. In addition, we see a natural integration of the literature on bereavement into an analysis of the loss of intimate partners. More connections between research and treatment need to be forged. Questions of the active therapeutic ingredient(s), and of which therapy is needed for different kinds of clients, still need to be addressed. Finally, studies showing the differences between intimate and other kinds of relationships should be undertaken.

We suspect that researchers will be prone to seeing the positive consequences of intimacy and will frequently use personality attributes as predictor variables. We hope that the drawbacks of intimacy and its situational determinants will be made appropriately salient.

We hope that more communication and interaction among intimacy researchers will be established. At the hub of such a network might be a few especially talented, energetic scholars whose work leads and inspires others. Clearly there is a market for greater knowledge about intimacy. Such knowledge can satisfy the curiosity of the general public, inform policymakers, assist therapists, and advance science. The time is nigh. Momentum has been building since the early 1970s; we hope that intimacy will flourish as a focus of social science interest in the decade ahead.

REFERENCES

Altman, I. (1975). *The environment and social behavior*. Monterey, CA: Brooks/Cole.

Argyle, M., & Dean, J. (1965). Eye-contact, distance and affiliation. *Sociometry, 28*, 289-304.

Berscheid, E. (1977). Interpersonal attraction. In B. B. Wolman & L. R. Pomeroy (Eds.), *International encyclopedia of neurology, psychiatry, psychoanalysis, and psychology* (Vol. 2, pp. 201-204). New York: Van Nostrand Reinhold.

Birchler, G. R., Weiss, R. L., & Vincent, J. P. (1975). Multimethod analysis of social reinforcement exchange between maritally distressed and non-distressed spouse and stranger dyads. *Journal of Personality and Social Psychology, 31,* 349-360.

Booth, A. (1972). Sex and social participation. *American Sociological Review, 37,* 183-193.

Brehm, S. S. (1985). *Intimate relationships.* New York: Random House.

Brown. G. W., & Harris, T. (1978). *Social origins of depression: A study of psychiatric disorder in women.* New York: Free Press.

Buber, M. (1958). *I and thou.* New York: Scribner.

Burgess, R. L., & Huston, T. L. (Eds.). (1979). *Social exchange in developing relationships.* New York: Academic Press.

Caldwell, M. A., & Peplau, L. A. (1982). Sex differences in same-sex friendship. *Sex Roles, 8,* 721-732.

Chelune, G. J., Robison, J. T., & Kommor, M. J. (1984). A cognitive interactional model of intimate relationships. In V. J. Derlega (Ed.), *Communicating, intimacy and close relationships* (pp. 11-40). Orlando, FL: Academic Press.

Clinebell, H. J., & Clinebell, C. H. (1970). *The intimate marriage.* New York: Harper & Row.

Cutrona, C. E. (1982). Transition to college: Loneliness and the process of social adjustment. In L. A. Peplau & D. Perlman (Eds.), *Loneliness: A sourcebook of current theory, research and therapy* (pp. 291-309). New York: Wiley-Interscience.

Dahms, A. M. (1972). *Emotional intimacy: Overlooked requirement for survival.* Boulder, CO: Pruett.

Davis, M. S. (1973). *Intimate relations.* New York: Free Press.

Derlega, V. J. (Ed.). (1984). *Communication, intimacy and close relationships.* Orlando, FL: Academic Press.

Derlega, V. J., & Chaiken, A. L. (1976). Norms affecting self-disclosure in men and women. *Journal of Consulting and Clinical Psychology, 44,* 376-380.

Derlega, V. J., & Margulis, S. T. (1982). Why loneliness occurs: The inter-relationship of social-psychological and privacy concepts. In L. A. Peplau & D. Perlman (Eds.), *Loneliness: A sourcebook of current theory, research and therapy* (pp. 152-165). New York: Wiley-Interscience.

Diener, E. (1984). Subjective well-being. *Psychological Bulletin, 95,* 542-575.

Duck, S. (1982). A topography of relationship disengagement and dissolution. In S. Duck (Ed.), *Personal relationships. 4: Dissolving personal relationships* (pp. 1-30). London: Academic Press.

Duck, S., & Perlman, D. (Eds.). (1985). *Understanding personal relationships.* London: Sage.

Dutton, D. G. (1984). Interventions into the problem of wife assault: Therapeutic, policy and research implications. *Canadian Journal of Behavioural Science, 16,* 281-297.

Ellis, A. (1982). Intimacy in rational-emotive therapy. In M. Fisher & G. Stricker (Eds.), *Intimacy* (pp. 203-217). New York: Plenum.

Erikson, E. H. (1959). Identity and the life cycle. *Psychological Issues, 1*(1), Monograph 1.

Erikson, E. H. (1963). *Childhood and society* (rev. ed.). New York: Norton.

Fehr, B., & Perlman, D. (1985). The family as a social network and support system. In L. L'Abate (Ed.), *Handbook of family psychology and therapy* (Vol. 1, pp. 323-356). Homewood, IL: Dow-Jones Irwin.

Fisher, M., & Stricker, G. (Eds.). (1982). *Intimacy.* New York: Plenum.

Freedman, J. (1978). *Happy people: What happiness is, who has it, and why.* New York: Harcourt Brace Jovanovich.

Gadlin, H. (1977). Private lives and public order. In G. Levinger & H. L. Raush (Eds.), *Close relationships* (pp. 33-72). Amherst: University of Massachusetts Press.

Goldberg, H. (1976). *The hazards of being male: Surviving the myth of masculine privilege.* New York: Nash.

Gordon, S. (1976). *Lonely in America.* New York: Simon & Schuster.

Guerney, B. G. (1977). *Relationship enhancement.* San Francisco: Jossey-Bass.

Hatfield, E. (1984). The dangers of intimacy. In V. J. Derlega (Eds.) *Communication, intimacy and close relationships* (pp. 207-220). Orlando, FL: Academic Press.

Hatfield, E., & Traupmann, J. (1981). Intimate relationships: A perspective from equity theory. In S. Duck & R. Gilmour (Eds.), *Personal relationships: Studying personal relationships* (pp. 165-178). London: Academic Press.

Hatfield, E., Traupmann, J., Sprecher, S., Utne, M., & Hay, J. (1985). Equity and intimate relations: Recent research. In W. Ickes (Ed.), *Compatible and incompatible relationships* (pp. 91-117). New York: Springer-Verlag.

Hendrick, C., & Hendrick, S. (1983). *Liking, loving, and relating.* Monterey, CA: Brooks/Cole.

Hinde, R. A. (1979). *Towards understanding relationships.* New York: Academic Press.

Hodgson, J. W., & Fischer, J. L. (1979). Sex differences in identity and intimacy development. *Journal of Youth and Adolescence, 8,* 37-50.

Horowitz, L. (1979). On the cognitive structure of interpersonal problems treated in psychotherapy. *Journal of Consulting and Clinical Psychology, 47,* 5-15.

Johnson, S. M., & Greenberg, L. S. (1985). Differential effects of experiential and problem-solving interventions in resolving marital conflict. *Journal of Consulting and Clinical Psychology, 53,* 175-184.

Jones, W. H. (1982). Loneliness and social behavior. In L. A. Peplau & D. Perlman (Eds.). *Loneliness: A sourcebook of current theory, research and therapy* (pp. 238-252). New York: Wiley-Interscience.

Kerckhoff, A. C., & Davis, K. E. (1962). Value consensus and need complementarity in mate selection. *American Sociological Review, 27,* 295-303.

Klinger, E. (1977). *Meaning and void: Inner experience and the incentives in people's lives.* Minneapolis: University of Minnesota Press.

L'Abate, L., & Sloan, S. (1984). A workshop format to facilitate intimacy in married couples. *Family Relations, 33,* 245-250.

Levinger, G. (1980). Toward the analysis of close relationships. *Journal of Experimental Social Psychology, 16,* 510-544.

Levinger, G. (1983). Development and change. In H. H. Kelley, E. Berscheid, A. Christensen, J. H. Harvey, T. L. Huston, G. Levinger, E. McClintock, L. A. Peplau, & D. R. Peterson (Eds.), *Close relationships* (pp. 315-359). New York: W. H. Freeman.

Levinger, G., & Snoek, D. J. (1972). *Attraction in relationships: A new look at interpersonal attraction.* Morristown, NJ: General Learning Press.

Lewis, R. A, (1972). A developmental framework for the analysis of premarital dyadic formation. *Family Process, 11,* 17-48.

Lewis, R. A. (1978). Emotional intimacy among men. *Journal of Social Issues, 34,* (1), 108-121.

Lobdell, J., & Perlman, D. (1986). The intergenerational transmission of loneliness: A study of college females and their parents. *Journal of Marriage and The Family, 48.*

Lowenthal, M. F., & Haven, C. (1968). Interaction and adaptation: Intimacy as a critical variable. *American Sociological Review, 33,* 20-30.

Marcia, J. E. (1976). Identity six years after: A follow-up study. *Journal of Youth and Adolescence, 5,* 145-160.

Margolin, G. (1982). A social learning approach to intimacy. In M. Fisher & G. Stricker (Eds.), *Intimacy* (pp. 175-201). New York: Plenum.

McAdams, D. P. (1980). A thematic coding scheme for the intimacy motive. *Journal of Research in Personality, 14,* 413-432.

McAdams, D. P. (1982). Intimacy motivation. In A. J. Stewart (Ed.) *Motivation and society* (pp. 133-171). San Francisco: Jossey-Bass.

McAdams, D. P. (1985). Motivation and friendship. In S. Duck & D. Perlman (Eds.), *Understanding personal relationships* (pp. 85-105). London: Sage.

McAdams, D. P., & Constantian, C. A. (1983). Intimacy and affiliative motives in daily living: An experience sampling analysis. *Journal of Personality and Social Psychology, 45,* 851-861.

McAdams, D. P., & Powers, J. (1981). Themes of intimacy in behavior and thought. *Journal of Personality and Social Psychology, 40,* 573-587

McGill, M. M. (1985). *The McGill report on male intimacy.* New York: Holt, Rinehart & Winston.

Miller, R. S., & Lefcourt, H. M. (1982). The assessment of intimacy. *Journal of Personality Assessment, 46,* 514-518.

Mills, J., & Clark, M. S. (1982). Exchange and communal relationships. In L. Wheeler (Ed.), *Review of personality and social psychology* (Vol. 3, pp. 121-144). Beverly Hills, CA: Sage.

Morris, D. (1971). *Intimate behaviour.* London: Jonathan Cape.

Morris, D. (1982). Attachment and intimacy. In M. Fisher & G. Stricker (Eds.) *Intimacy* (pp. 305-323). New York: Plenum.

Murstein, B. I. (1971). A theory of marital choice and its applicability to marriage adjustment. In B. I. Murstein (Ed.), *Theories of attraction and love* (pp. 100-151). New York: Springer.

Oden, T. C. (1974). *Game free: A guide to the meaning of intimacy.* New York: Harper & Row.

Orlofsky, J. L. (in press). Intimacy status: Theory and research. In J. E. Marcia (Ed.), *Identity in adolescence.* Hillsdale, NJ: Erlbaum.

Patterson, M. L. (1976). An arousal model of interpersonal intimacy. *Psychological Review, 83,* 235-245.

Patterson, M. L. (1984). Intimacy, social control, and nonverbal involvement: A functional approach. In V. J. Derlega (Ed.), *Communication, intimacy and close relationships* (pp. 105-132). Orlando, FL: Academic Press.

Perlman, D., & Fehr, B. (1986). Theories of friendship: The analysis of interpersonal attraction. In V. J. Derlega & B. A. Winstead (Eds.), *Friendship and social interaction* (pp. 9-40). New York: Springer-Verlag.

Reiss, H. T. (1984). Social interaction and well-being. In S. Duck (Ed.),

Personal relationships 5: Repairing personal relationships (pp. 21-45). London: Academic Press.

Rook, K. S. (1984). Promoting social bonding: Strategies for helping the lonely and socially isolated. *American Psychologist, 39,* 1389-1407.

Rubenstein, C. M., & Shaver, P. (1982). *In search of intimacy.* New York: Delacorte Press.

Rubin, L. B. (1983). *Intimate strangers: Men and women together.* New York: Harper & Row.

Rubin, Z. (1973). *Liking and loving.* New York: Holt, Rinehart & Winston.

Schaefer, M. T., & Olson, D. H. (1981). Assessing intimacy: The PAIR Inventory. *Journal of Marital and Family Therapy, 7,* 47-60.

Shadish, W. R. (1984). Intimate behavior and the assessment of benefits in clinical groups. *Small Group Behavior, 15,* 204-221.

Simmel, G. (1950). *The sociology of Georg Simmel* (K. Wolf, Ed.). New York: Free Press.

Sloan, S. Z. (1984). Assessing the differential effectiveness of two enrichment formats in facilitating marital intimacy and adjustment. *Dissertation Abstracts International, 44,* 2569B. (University Microfilms No. DA8327354)

Sullivan, H. S. (1953). *The interpersonal theory of psychiatry.* New York: W.W. Norton.

Tesch, S. A. (1985). The psychosocial intimacy questionnaire: Validational studies and an investigation of sex roles. *Journal of Social and Personal Relationships, 2,* 471-488.

Veroff, J., Douvan, E. & Kulka, R. A. (1981). *The inner American.* New York: Basic Books.

Waring, E. M. (1984). The measurement of marital intimacy. *Journal of Marital and Family Therapy, 10,* 185-192.

Waring, E. M., & Reddon, J. R. (1983). The measurement of intimacy in marriage: The Waring intimacy questionnaire. *Journal of Clinical Psychology, 39,* 53-57.

Waring, E. M., Tillman, M. P., Frelick, L., Russell, L., & Weisz, G. (1980). Concepts of intimacy in the general population. *Journal of Nervous and Mental Disease, 168,* 471-474.

Weiss, R. S. (1973). *Loneliness: The experience of emotional and social isolation.* Cambridge: MIT Press.

Wong, H. (1981). Typologies of intimacy. *Psychology of Women Quarterly, 5,* 435-443.

Walster, E., Walster, G. W., & Berscheid, E. (1978). *Equity: Theory and research.* Boston, MA: Allyn & Bacon.

Walster, E., Walster, G. W., & Traupman, J. (1978). Equity and premarital sex. *Journal of Personality, 36,* 82-92.

Young, J. E. (1982). Loneliness, depression and cognitive therapy: Theory and application. In L. A. Peplau & D. Perlman (Eds.), *Loneliness: A Sourcebook of current theory, research and therapy* (pp. 379-405). New York: Wiley-Interscience.

PART I

The Development of Relationships

The three chapters in this section all touch on the question of how relationships develop. Snyder and Simpson suggest that there are two orientations toward relationships. Put simply, the first involves having a few close friends "who are good for all occasions." The second orientation involves maintaining compartmentalized social worlds in which friends are selected for specific activities and situations. Snyder and Simpson explore what implications these orientations have on the initiation, growth, and willingness to depart from romantic relationships. The second and third chapters, respectively, deal with female-initiated relationships and the evolution of courtships.

These chapters underscore and illuminate three issues in the study of relationships. First, there is the question of the extent to which relationships are a function of personalities versus larger social forces and roles. On the one hand, Snyder and Simpson link their two interpersonal orientations to individual differences in self-monitoring. Similarly, Kelley and Rolker-Dolinsky emphasize the importance of chronic self-destructiveness and androgyny. On the other hand, social norms and roles pattern the way in which we typically interact. The second and third chapters in this section explore these pressures, as well as what happens to relationships when they transcend convention.

Second, in focusing on two styles of relating—female-initiated relationships and marriage—these chapters implicitly suggest the importance of different kinds of relationships. Third, all three chapters, especially Huston and Surra's, demonstrate that development per se provides a class of variables that are crucial to understanding relationships. Who starts the relationship, how fast it progresses, and whether or not it backslides are all key factors influencing the short- and long-term outcomes of of our social ties. Questions such as these deserve fuller attention in the personal relationship literature than they have received.

In reading this section of the book, the reader may want to keep these issues in mind. They all add richness and nuance in charting how relationships grow and evolve over time.

2

Orientations Toward Romantic Relationships

MARK SNYDER
JEFFRY A. SIMPSON

It goes almost without saying that romantic relationships can and often do have enormous impact on the lives of most people. When one considers the amount of time that people typically spend in romantic relationships, the range and diversity of the activities commonly shared with romantic partners, the roles that romantic partners play, and the functions that romantic partners serve, there can be no denying the significant involvement of romantic relationships in people's lives (see, e.g., Bachman & Johnston, 1979). Indeed, a substantial majority of people believe that such relationships contribute greatly to the meaningfulness in their lives. In response to the question, "What is it that makes your life meaningful?" only close friends were mentioned more frequently than romantic partners (Klinger, 1977).

Over the past few years, we have been engaged in a program of research that has sought to address a series of fundamental questions. Could there exist, in principle, two distinct orientations that individuals can and do adopt toward romantic relationships? For instance, could there exist one category of individuals who systematically adopt an orientation toward and preference for establishing and maintaining relatively close and exclusive romantic relationships? And could there exist another category of individuals who habitually adopt an orientation toward and preference for establishing and maintaining less close and relatively non-exclusive romantic relationships? And if so, would it be possible to identify individuals who adopt these

AUTHORS' NOTE: This research and the preparation of this chapter were supported by National Science Foundation Grant BSN 82-07632 to Mark Snyder, by an Eva O. Miller Fellowship to Jeffry A. Simpson, and by a grant from the University of Minnesota Computer Center.

45

contrasting orientations through the use of an existing psychological construct, one whose construct validity evidence suggests that differences in orientation toward interpersonal relationships ought to be a member of the set of features that define the construct?

An Investigative Strategy

Our approach to answering these questions represents one of the general strategies for the study of personality and social behavior outlined by Snyder and Ickes (1985, 884-885).

> The phenomena and processes of concern to social psychologists can be understood by focusing investigative efforts on those individuals who characteristically manifest those phenomena and processes ... Accordingly, by identifying those individuals who typically manifest the phenomenon or process of concern, one gains access to the ideal candidates for investigating the social psychology of that phenomenon or process in action. That is, the identification of those individuals who characteristically manifest the phenomenon or process of concern is undertaken, not as an end in and of itself, but rather as a means toward achieving the end of understanding an important social psychological phenomenon or process.

Given that most individuals in our society value (or at least claim that they value) close relationships with others, this strategy suggests that, with an appropriate assessment procedure, we ought to be able to determine whether there exists one category of individuals who especially value close, exclusive romantic relationships and a second category of individuals who place less emphasis on this type of relationship but who especially value a greater number and wider variety of relationships, each of which is characterized by less closeness. Indeed, if two such orientations do exist, and if it were possible to empirically identify individuals who adopt these contrasting orientations, then such individuals could become the focus of investigations designed to examine various features of both close, exclusive and of less close, non-exclusive romantic relationships.

Based on recent research, we believe that we have identified a vehicle—the psychological construct of self-monitoring (Snyder, 1979)—for reliably and validly differentiating between those individuals who generally adopt an orientation toward establishing and maintaining less close and rather non-exclusive romantic relationships (high self-monitoring individuals) and those who typically adopt an orientation toward establishing and maintaining relatively close and exclusive romantic relationships (low self-monitoring individuals). High self-monitoring individuals, identified by their relatively high scores on the Self-Monitoring Scale (Gangestad & Snyder, 1985; Snyder, 1974), typically strive to appear to be the type of person called for by each situation in which they find themselves. Thus they tend to claim, in their endorsement of Self-Monitoring Scale items: "In different situations and with different people, I often act like very different persons. I'm not always the person I appear to be. I would probably make a good actor." These individuals are particularly sensitive and responsive to social and interpersonal cues to situational appropriateness. Accordingly, their social behavior displays pronounced situation-to-situation specificity.

By contrast, low self-monitoring individuals, identified by their relatively low scores on the Self-Monitoring Scale, generally attempt to display their own personal dispositions and attitudes in each situation in which they find themselves. Thus they tend to claim, in their endorsement of Self-Monitoring Scale items: "I would not change my opinions (or the way I do things) in order to please someone or win their favor. I can only argue for ideas which I already believe. I have trouble changing my behavior to suit different people and different situations." These individuals are less responsive to situational and interpersonal specifications of behavioral appropriateness. Rather, they seem to guide their behavior on the basis of information available from relevant inner sources, as reflected in the characteristically substantial congruence between their social behavior and relevant underlying attitudes and dispositions.

For information about the cognitive, behavioral, and interpersonal consequences of self-monitoring, see, for example, Becherer and Richard (1978), Caldwell and O'Reilly (1982), Danheiser and Graziano (1982), Krauss, Geller, and Olson (1976), Kulik and Taylor (1981), Lippa (1976, 1978), Lutsky, Woodworth and Clayton (1980), McCann and Hancock (1983), Rarick, Soldow, and Geizer (1976), Shaffer, Smith, and Tomarelli (1982), Snyder, Berscheid, and Glick (1985), Snyder and Cantor (1980), Snyder and Gangestad (1982), Snyder, Gangestad, and Simpson (1983), Snyder and Kendzierski (1982), Snyder and Monson (1975), Snyder and Swann (1976), Snyder and Tanke (1976), Tunnell (1980), and Zanna, Olson, and Fazio (1980). For reviews of the evidence of the situationally guided behavioral orientation of high self-monitoring individuals and the dispositionally guided behavioral orientation of low self-monitoring individuals, see Snyder (1979) and Shaw and Costanzo (1982).

Psychological Orientations

Why do we suggest that the psychological construct of self-monitoring underlies differences in orientation toward romantic relationships? Recent investigations of personality and friendship have provided considerable evidence that individuals low and high in self-monitoring adopt different orientations toward friendship. In particular, high self-monitoring individuals seem to prefer highly differentiated and compartmentalized social worlds in which they tend to possess different and varied friends for different and varied occasions (Snyder et al., 1983). By contrast, low self-monitoring individuals appear to prefer relatively homogeneous and undifferentiated social worlds in which they tend to have rather exclusive friends who are good for all occasions. Indeed, it appears that, at least for friendships, the social worlds of low self-monitoring individuals are characterized by greater affective closeness and attachment than are those of high self-monitoring individuals (see Snyder & Smith, 1986). Of course, what may be true for relationships between friends may not necessarily be true of relationships between romantic partners. Nevertheless, the differing orientations of individuals high and low in self-monitoring toward their friendships did suggest to us the possibility that these individuals also might differ in their orientation toward closeness and attachment in their romantic relationships.

To investigate the considerations involved when individuals choose partners for leisure-time activities, we presented individuals known to be high or low in self-monitoring with choices that involved engaging in particular social activities with specific partners (Snyder & Simpson, 1984). In all cases, the prospective partners were members of the opposite sex, some of whom were and others of whom were not current dating partners. These choices were of the form, for example, of "going bowling with Jill" (a friend of the opposite sex particularly skilled at bowling) or "going skiing with Ann" (a current dating partner not particularly skilled at skiing). Faced with such choices, high self-monitoring individuals chose to engage in an activity with a friend of the other sex who, although not the current dating partner, was well suited to the activity in question. Low self-monitoring individuals chose to engage in an activity with the current dating partner, despite the fact that he or she was not particularly well suited to the activity in question. That is, high self-monitoring individuals, in accord with their situationally guided behavioral orientation, displayed considerable willingness to substitute a friend of the opposite sex for their current dating partner as the preferred activity partner, while low self-monitoring individuals, in line with their dispositionally guided behavioral orientation, displayed a pronounced unwillingness to substitute a friend for their current dating partner as the preferred activity partner.

Could these differing approaches to choosing activity partners practiced by individuals high and low in self-monitoring actually reveal something about their orientations toward interpersonal relationships more fundamental than their preferences in partners for leisure-time activities? Indeed, might these systematically differing preferences actually be indicative of more generalized differences in their orientation toward establishing and maintaining close and exclusive (as opposed to less close and non-exclusive) romantic relationships? In particular, could the apparent willingness of high self-monitoring individuals to substitute a friend of the opposite sex for the current dating partner as a preferred activity partner be indicative of a more global orientation toward, and preference for, establishing and maintaining less close and rather non-exclusive dating relationships? And could the pronounced unwillingness of low self-monitoring individuals to substitute a friend for the current dating partner be associated with a global orientation toward, and preference for, establishing and maintaining close and relatively exclusive dating relationships?

Moreover, if such differences in orientation toward dating relationships do exist, how might they be revealed in the dating lives, histories, and behavior of individuals high and low in self-monitoring? We suggest that they ought to be reflected in the strategies that these individuals adopt toward "investing" themselves in their dating relationships. Specifically, we propose that they ought to be revealed, first, in the extent to which these individuals tend to adopt a "committed," as opposed to an "uncommitted," orientation toward their dating relationships and, second, in the extent to which these individuals tend to adopt a "restricted," as opposed to an "unrestricted," orientation toward engaging in casual sexual relations with different partners.

Thus, in accord with an orientation characterized by establishing and maintaining relatively close and exclusive dating relationships, low (relative to high) self-monitoring individuals might adopt a committed orientation toward dating relationships and a restricted orientation toward engaging in casual sexual relationships. Moreover, in accord with an orientation characterized by establishing and maintaining less close and relatively non-exclusive dating relationships, high (relative to low) self-monitoring individuals might adopt an uncommitted orientation toward dating relationships and an unrestricted orientation toward engaging in casual sexual relationships.

More specifically, we suggest that these contrasting orientations ought to be revealed in systematic differences between low and high self-monitoring individuals in their stated intentions to change or retain their current dating partners, in the structural features of their past dating behavior, and in the growth of affect in their dating relationships. We also anticipate that these contrasting orientations ought to be revealed in systematic differences between high and low self-monitoring individuals in their patterns of overt sexual behavior and their attitudes toward engaging in casual sex with different partners.

In fact, a series of four separate investigations, each designed to examine the various features that characterize the orientations toward romantic relationships adopted by individuals low and high in self-monitoring, provide considerable support for all of these hypotheses (Snyder & Simpson, 1984; Snyder, Simpson, & Gangestad, 1986). Consider first some empirical evidence which suggests that individuals low and high in self-monitoring adopt differing orientations toward commitment in dating relationships.

Committed and Uncommitted Orientations

Clearly, when it comes to engaging in social activities, low and high self-monitoring individuals differ in their apparent degree of preference for doing these activities with their current dating partners. What is less clear, based only on the outcome of this investigation, is whether they differ in their degree of commitment when actual dating relationships are considered. Does the fact that high self-monitoring individuals prefer to engage in many social activities with specialized partners other than their current dating partners imply a lack of commitment to their current dating relationship and a willingness to consider other members of their social world as replacements for their current dating partners? And does the preference of low self-monitoring individuals for engaging in social activities with their current dating partners, even if their partners are not particularly well suited for those activities, reflect a strong commitment to the dating relationship itself and an unwillingness to consider changing dating partners?

Willingness to Change Dating Partners

To determine whether individuals high and low in self-monitoring differ in their orientation toward commitment to dating relationships, we first presented individuals known to be high or low in self-monitoring with choices that involved the prospect of dating different members of their own social worlds. After having participants identify their current or "most steady" dating partner and four friends of the opposite sex, we presented them with sets of questions, each of which pitted the current dating partner against each of the four friends. In response to the first question set, which asked, "If you could change dating partners, which individual, if any, would you substitute for (name of the current dating partner)?" high self-monitoring individuals typically chose to substitute a friend for the current dating partner, while low self-monitoring individuals overwhelmingly chose to retain the current dating partner. That is, faced with the prospect of changing dating partners, high self-monitoring individuals were relatively willing and low self-monitoring individuals were relatively unwilling to leave their current dating relationships for other potential partners.

In response to the second question set, which asked, "If you could ideally form a close, intimate dating relationship with either (name of the current dating partner) or (name of a friend of the opposite sex), who would you choose?" high self-monitoring individuals, more frequently than low self-monitoring individuals, chose a friend, while low self-monitoring individuals, more frequently than high self-monitoring individuals, chose the current dating partner. That is, given the choice, high self-monitoring individuals expressed a relatively strong desire to form a close, intimate dating relationship with someone other than their current dating partner, while low self-monitoring individuals expressed a comparatively strong desire to form such a relationship with their current dating partner. Viewed together, then, these results suggest that, at least at the level of stated intentions, individuals low and high in self-monitoring differ in their degree of commitment to their current dating relationships and in their preferences for forming close, intimate dating relationships with new partners.

Structural Features of Dating Lives

If, as we suggest, individuals high and low in self-monitoring differ in their orientation toward commitment in dating relationships, then there ought to be differences in the structural features of their dating activities as well. Specifically, if high self-monitoring individuals adopt an uncommitted orientation toward dating relationships, then their dating lives should be characterized by relatively large networks of different dating partners and by dating relationships of relatively short duration. Conversely, if low self-monitoring individuals adopt a committed orientation toward dating relationships, then their dating lives ought to be characterized by relatively small networks of different dating partners and by dating relationships of a relatively long duration.

To investigate these differing structural features of dating histories, we examined the dating lives of individuals involved in multiple, non-exclusive dating relationships ("multiple daters")—defined operationally as those who had dated two or more different individuals within the past year and who were not currently involved in an exclusive dating relationship—and of individuals involved in steady, exclusive dating relationships ("single daters")—defined operationally as those currently involved in an exclusive dating relationship.

Among those classified as multiple daters, high self-monitoring individuals reported that they had dated nearly twice as many different partners in the preceding 12 months (an average of approximately six different partners) as did low self-monitoring individuals (an average of between three and four different partners). For those classified as single daters, low self-monitoring individuals reported having dated their steady exclusive partners for nearly twice as long (an average of approximately 20 months) as did high self-monitoring individuals (an average of approximately 11 months).

Taken together, these findings reveal substantial differences in the structural features of the dating lives and dating behavior of individuals high and low in self-monitoring. For those individuals involved in multiple relationships, the high self-monitoring individuals had dated a greater number of different partners, a finding that would seem to be yet another reflection of an uncommitted orientation to dating relationships. For those individuals involved in single relationships, the low self-monitoring individuals were involved in relationships of relatively long duration, an occurrence that may be yet another manifestation of a committed orientation to dating relationships.

Growth of Intimacy in Dating Relationships

Because dating activities are often the first step in the development of increasingly close and intimate relationships, we turned next to a consideration of the feelings of intimacy associated with dating relationships of wide-ranging duration (from a few weeks to several years). In particular, we sought an answer to the following question: How are self-monitoring propensities reflected in the growth of intimacy in dating relationships?

To answer this question, we had high and low self-monitoring individuals who were involved in dating relationships indicate how long they had been dating their current dating partner and how intimate they considered their relationship to be. We then performed a linear multiple regression analysis, with length of dating relationship as the independent variable and reported intimacy with the dating partner as the dependent variable. This analysis revealed that, as the length of the dating relationship increased, intimacy increased at a faster and more pronounced rate for low than for high self-monitoring individuals. That is, in accord with the other evidence suggestive of differences in orientation toward commitment to dating relationships, length of relationship appeared to be a substantially better predictor of intimacy in the dating relationships of low than of high self-monitoring individuals.

Viewed together, these investigations permit the following characterizations of the dating lives of individuals high and low in self-monitoring: High self-monitoring individuals, as revealed at the levels of intentions, actions, and affect, tend to adopt an uncommitted orientation toward dating relationships. They express considerable willingness to terminate a current dating relationship in favor of an alternative one. Indeed, their dating histories reveal that even if they are involved in an exclusive relationship, they have dated steady, exclusive partners for relatively short periods of time. If they are not involved in an exclusive relationship, they have dated a relatively large number of persons within the preceding 12 months. Moreover, their uncommitted orientation is also revealed through the relatively slow growth of intimacy in their dating relationships.

By contrast, low self-monitoring individuals, as revealed at the levels of intentions, behaviors, and affect, tend to adopt a committed orientation toward dating relationships. Indeed, they profess to harbor no plans or desires to change dating partners. Their dating histories reveal that if they are involved in an exclusive relationship, they have dated steady, exclusive partners for relatively long periods of time. If they are not involved in an exclusive relationship, they have nevertheless dated a relatively small number of partners within the preceding year. Moreover, their committed orientation is revealed through the steady, substantial growth of intimacy in their dating relationships over time.

Restricted and Unrestricted Orientations

If self-monitoring reliably discriminates between those individuals who seek close and exclusive romantic relationships and those who strive for less close and non-exclusive romantic relationships, then it should also be strongly associated with differing orientations toward sexual relations. Specifically, the relatively uncommitted orientation of high self-monitoring individuals ought to be accompanied by an underlying unrestricted orientation toward sexual relations such that these individuals feel that their sexual relations with others need not be restricted to relations between themselves and partners with whom they are psychologically and emotionally close. Similarly, the relatively committed orientation of low self-monitoring individuals ought to be associated with a restricted orientation toward sexual relations in which these individuals feel that their sexual relations with others need to be restricted to relations between themselves and partners with whom they are psychologically and emotionally close.

To determine whether these individuals actually differ in their respective orientations toward sexual relations, both at the level of behavior and at the level of attitudes, we surveyed individuals low and high in self-monitoring about their sexual attitudes, values, and behavior (Snyder et al., 1986). This extensive survey dealt with previous and anticipated overt and covert sexual behavior assessed by items that measured, among other things, frequency of sex in the past month, oral-genital sexual experience, number of lifetime sexual partners, number of sexual partners in the past year, number of sexual partners foreseen in the next five years, number of "one-night stands," frequency of sexual thoughts, frequency of fantasizing about having sex with different partners, and so on. In addition, the survey included indices of attitudes toward engaging in sex with someone to whom one is not committed and attitudes toward being comfortable and at ease engaging in casual sex with different partners. Finally, it solicited judgments of one's own sexual experience and physical attractiveness, both relative to one's age peers. A principal components factor analysis, performed on the correlation matrix of the responses of those individuals who had engaged in sex on at least one previous occasion, yielded two factors.

The first factor reflected variability in individuals' orientation with respect to unrestricted sex. Variables loading highly on this factor included attitudes toward being comfortable and at ease engaging in casual sex with different partners, number of sexual partners foreseen in the next five years, number of sexual partners in the past year, attitudes toward engaging in sex with someone to whom one is not committed, number of "one-night stands," and frequency of fantasizing about having sex with different partners. Accordingly, this factor was labeled the Unrestricted Sexual Orientation Factor.

The second factor that emerged, which was of course orthogonal to the first factor, appeared to reflect variability in individuals' amount of current and past sexual experience. Variables that loaded highly on this factor included frequency of sex in the past month, number of lifetime sexual partners, and personal judgments of amount of sexual experience. Consequently, this factor was labeled the Sexual Experience Factor.

If high self-monitoring individuals adopt a relatively unrestricted orientation toward sex, and if low self-monitoring individuals adopt a relatively restricted orientation toward sex, then participants' self-monitoring propensities should load highly on (i.e., should be highly correlated with) the Unrestricted Sexual Orientation Factor. Indeed, the correlation between self-monitoring and this factor was in fact substantial ($r = .45$). Apparently, self-monitoring is strongly related to one's propensity toward unrestricted, casual sex. At the same time, self-monitoring clearly was unrelated to the Sexual Experience Factor ($r = .03$). Apparently, self-monitoring is not closely linked to sexual experience.

An examination of the variables with the highest loadings on the Unrestricted Sexual Orientation Factor further reveals that at the behavioral level, high self-monitoring individuals (relative to low self-monitoring individuals) reported that they had engaged in sex with a significantly larger number of different partners within the preceding year, that they foresaw themselves having sex with a significantly larger number of different persons within the next five years, and that they were significantly more likely to have engaged in sex with someone on one and only one occasion. At an attitudinal level, low self-monitoring individuals (relative to high self-monitoring individuals) indicated that they would be significantly more reluctant to have sex with someone to whom they were not exclusively committed and that they would be significantly more uncomfortable with and less likely to enjoy engaging in casual sex with different partners.

Taken together, these results provide additional support for our conjectures concerning the contrasting orientations toward dating relationships maintained by individuals high and low in self-monitoring. High self-monitoring individuals, it seems, tend to establish an unrestricted orientation toward sexual relations such that they may engage in sex with others to whom they are neither psychologically nor emotionally close. Low self-monitoring individuals, by contrast, appear to establish a restricted orientation toward sexual relations such that they will engage in sex only with partners to whom they are psychologically and emotionally close.

Close and Exclusive Versus Less Close and Non-Exclusive Orientations

Taking into account all of the findings from this series of investigations, including those dealing with committed and uncommitted orientations toward dating relationships and those dealing with restricted and unrestricted orientations toward engaging in casual sexual relationships, we see in these findings the portrayal of two distinct, global orientations toward romantic relationships—one characteristic of high self-monitoring individuals, and one characteristic of low self-monitoring individuals. Based on their tendency to adopt an uncommitted orientation toward dating relationships and an unrestricted orientation toward sexual relations, high self-monitoring individuals, it appears, tend to adopt an orientation toward and preference for establishing and maintaining less close and rather non-exclusive romantic relationships. In contrast, as evidenced by their tendency to adopt a committed orientation toward dating relationships and a restricted orientation toward sexual relations, low self-monitoring individuals tend to adopt an orientation toward and preference for establishing and maintaining close and relatively exclusive romantic relationships.[1]

What accounts for these contrasting orientations to romantic relationships? What might lead high self-monitoring individuals to establish and maintain less close and relatively non-exclusive romantic relationships and, at the same time, lead low self-monitoring individuals to establish and maintain close and rather exclusive ones? We suspect that systematic differences between high and low self-monitoring individuals in the manner in which they select relationship partners, in the number of alternative partners perceived to be (or actually) available to them, and in their inclination or ability to avoid strong thoughts and feelings about alternative partners may contribute to these contrasting orientations.

Initiating Romantic Relationships

Recent research has revealed pronounced differences between low and high self-monitoring individuals in the type of information they attend to and the kinds of considerations they invoke when contemplating whether or not to initiate a romantic relationship. Specifically, Snyder et al. (1985) provided individuals with a choice of dating either a physically attractive partner who possessed relatively undesirable personality characteristics or a physically unattractive partner who possessed desirable personality characteristics. Faced with this choice, high self-monitoring individuals typically sacrificed desirable interior attributes of personality for exterior attributes of appearance and selected the physically attractive partner. By contrast, low self-monitoring individuals typically sacrificed exterior attributes of appearance for interior ones and chose the partner with the pleasant, desirable personality.

These different sets of considerations might have different implications for the future course of romantic relationships. By choosing romantic partners on the basis of personality considerations (as well as, most likely, their global liking for, general similarity to, and overall compatibility with them; see Snyder et al., 1983), low self-monitoring individuals may be particularly likely to enter relationships that, from the very beginning, stand a greater chance of surviving over time. Indeed, relationships contracted on the basis of exterior physical attributes may be more vulnerable to threat by tempting alternatives than those contracted on the basis of interior personality characteristics. After all, it is substantially easier to assess whether a potential replacement for one's current partner has more pleasing exterior appearance (since one can do so at a glance) than it is to determine whether that potential replacement has appealing interior attributes (since learning about personality attributes often requires extended periods of interaction). Therefore, because of the differing bases on which they are initiated, the romantic relationships of high self-monitoring individuals may be more vulnerable to the threat of alternatives, and hence may be shorter-lived, than those of low self-monitoring individuals.

Availability of Alternative Partners

In addition, the differing orientations to romantic relationships adopted by high and low self-monitoring individuals may be, in part, linked to systematic differences in the number of alternative partners perceived to be available (or actually available) to them. Indeed, three sources of evidence suggest that high self-monitoring individuals have (or at least perceive that they have) a larger number of alternative partners potentially available to them than do low self-monitoring individuals. First of all, as we have already seen, among those individuals involved in multiple, non-exclusive dating relationships, high (relative to low) self-monitoring individuals report having dated nearly twice as many different partners in the preceding year. Second, among those individuals with sexual experience, high (relative to low) self-monitoring individuals report having engaged in sex with nearly twice as many different partners within the preceding year. Third, high (relative to low) self-monitoring individuals indicate that they foresee themselves having sex with nearly twice as many different partners within the next five years.

Taken together, these three pieces of evidence seem to suggest that high self-monitoring individuals may indeed have a larger network of alternative partners than low self-monitoring individuals. Clearly, if an individual has, or perceives himself or herself to have, a limited number of alternative partners other than the current one, he or she might be expected to show strong commitment and attachment to the current relationship. This certainly appears to be the case for low self-monitoring individuals. Thus, perhaps their orientation toward and preference for establishing and maintaining close and exclusive romantic relationships is in part linked to the relatively small number of alternative partners that they perceive to have (or actually have) available to them. By contrast, if an individual has, or perceives himself or herself to have, a large number of alternative partners other than the current one, he or she might be expected to exhibit less commitment and attachment to the current relationship. This clearly appears to be the case for high self-monitoring individuals. Therefore, perhaps their orientation toward and preference for establishing and maintaining less close and non-exclusive romantic relationships is in part related to the rather large number of alternative partners that they perceive to have (or actually have) available to them.

Thoughts and Feelings about Alternative Partners

The contrasting orientations to romantic relationships maintained by low and high self-monitoring individuals may also be tied to systematic differences between these individuals in their inclination toward or ability to avoid, control, or resist tempting thoughts about and strong positive feelings toward attractive alternative partners. Although little is known about cognitive and affective self-control processes as they pertain to romantic relationships (Kelley, 1980, 1983), it has been suggested that such self-control processes may play a critical role in the stability and longevity of romantic relationships (Rosenblatt, 1977).

Recent evidence suggests that low and high self-monitoring individuals may differ in such cognitive and affective self-control processes. For example, when asked to indicate how frequently they fantasize about having sex with someone other than their "most steady" dating partner, low self-monitoring individuals report that they fantasize much less often about such an activity than do high self-monitoring individuals (Snyder et al., 1986). When asked to indicate how often they fantasize about having sex with someone other than their "most steady" dating partner while engaging in sex with that partner, low self-monitoring individuals indicate that they fantasize less frequently about such an activity than do high self-monitoring individuals (Snyder et al., 1986).

To the extent that high self-monitoring individuals are less willing or less able to avoid, resist, or control tempting thoughts or feelings, they may be particularly likely to be drawn away from current relationships toward new ones. Similarly, to the extent that low self-monitoring individuals are more likely to be able to control tempting thoughts and feelings, they may be less likely to stray from their current relationships.

Implications for Long-Term Relationships

What implications might our investigations of romantic relationships have for understanding long-term relationships, including marriages and marriage-like partnerships? Needless to say, there are many differences between romantic relationships of the kind we have studied and marital relationships, not the least of which are differences in the degree of investment and public commitment. Nevertheless, these differences do not diminish the importance of studying the romantic relationships of college students. Such relationships often serve as a significant preliminary step leading to more involved, intricate, and permanent relationships (including marriages). After all, over 90% of all adults marry at some point in their lives (see Kelley, Berscheid, Christensen, Harvey, Huston, Levinger, McClintock, Peplau, & Peterson, 1983). Therefore, it may be of considerable practical importance to examine the implications of our investigations for marriage.

We might expect low self-monitoring individuals to display greater commitment and stronger attachment to their marital partners than high self-monitoring individuals. Furthermore, in line with their differing orientations to sexual relationships, we might expect high self-monitoring individuals to be somewhat more likely than low self-monitoring individuals to engage in extramarital sexual relations. As a result of differences in commitment and attachment within marriages, we might also expect that the marriages of low self-monitoring individuals might last longer and be less vulnerable to dissolution than those of high self-monitoring individuals. Moreover, if such differences in commitment and attachment do exist, we would also expect that low self-monitoring individuals might be more disrupted and distressed by the departure or death of a partner than would high self-monitoring individuals. Given the paucity of theoretical and empirical research devoted to problems of relationship dissolution and termination (see Duck, 1982), the implications of our investigations for marriage take on added importance.

Of course, for now these implications must remain conjectures. Nonetheless, to the extent that the differing orientations that characterize dating relationships also characterize marriages and marriage-like relationships, it may be possible for theorists and practitioners alike to bring fresh perspectives to understanding these relationships. By understanding the differing bases on which such relationships are contracted and maintained, as well as the differing events that threaten to dissolve them, it may be possible to construct two psychologies of relationships—one applicable to the close and relatively exclusive orientation characteristic of low self-monitoring individuals, and the other applicable to the less close and rather nonexclusive orientation characteristic of high self-monitoring individuals.

NOTE

1. At this point one might wonder whether the results from our series of investigations might be attributable to social desirability response sets. That is, perhaps individuals high and low in self-monitoring do not differ in their actual, practiced orientations toward romantic relationships. Perhaps high (relative to low) self-monitoring individuals are more concerned with conveying a desirable impression and thus made claims that led us to believe that they adopted an uncommitted orientation toward dating relationships and an unrestricted orientation toward engaging in casual sexual relationships. This concern, however, does not appear to be warranted. The measure of self-monitoring has not been found to correlate substantially with measures of social desirability response sets (e.g., the Marlowe-Crowne Social Desirability Scale—Snyder, 1974; the MMPI L (Lie)—Snyder, 1979; the Self-Deception Questionnaire—Paulhus, 1984; and the Other-Deception Questionnaire—Paulhus, 1984). In fact, Paulhus (1984) factor analyzed several scales designed to tap social desirability response sets. The Self-Monitoring Scale was found to correlate trivially with good representations of both of the factors that emerged.

REFERENCES

Bachman, J. G., & Johnston, L. D. (1979). The freshman, 1979. *Psychology Today, 13,* 79-87.

Becherer, R. C., & Richard, L. M. (1978). Self-monitoring as a moderator of consumer behavior. *Journal of Consumer Research, 5,* 159-162.

Caldwell, D. F., & O'Reilly, C. A. (1982). Responses to failure: The effects of choice and responsibility on impression management. *Academy of Management Journal, 25,* 121-136.

Danheiser, P. R., & Graziano, W. G. (1982). Self-monitoring and cooperation as a self-presentational strategy. *Journal of Personality and Social Psychology, 42,* 497-505.

Duck, S. W. (1982). A topography of relationship disengagement and dissolution. In S. W. Duck (Ed.), *Personal relationships 4: Dissolving personal relationships* (pp. 1-30). London: Academic Press.

Gangestad, S., & Snyder, M. (1985). To carve nature at its joints. On the existence of discrete classes in personality. *Psychological Review, 92,* 317-349.

Kelley, H. H. (1980). The causes of behavior: Their perception and regulation. In L. Festinger (Ed.), *Retrospections of social psychology* (pp. 78-108). New York: Oxford University Press.

Kelley, H. H. (1983). Love and commitment. In H. H. Kelley, E. Berscheid, A. Christensen, J. H. Harvey, T. L. Huston, G. Levinger, E. McClintock, L. A. Peplau, & D. R. Peterson, *Close relationships* (pp. 265-314). San Francisco: Freeman.

Kelley, H. H., Berscheid, E., Christensen, A., Harvey, J. H., Huston, T. L., Levinger, G., McClintock. E., Peplau, L. A., & Peterson, D. R. (1983). *Close relationships.* San Francisco: Freeman.

Klinger, E. (1977). *Meaning and void: Inner experience and the incentives in people's lives.* Minneapolis: University of Minnesota Press.

Krauss, R. M., Geller, V., & Olson, C. (1976, September). *Modalities and cues in perceiving deception.* Paper presented at the annual meeting of the American Psychological Association, Washington, DC.

Kulik, J. A., & Taylor, S. E. (1981). Self-monitoring and the use of consensus information. *Journal of Personality, 49,* 75-84.

Lippa, R. (1976). Expressive control and the leakage of dispositional introversion-extraversion during role-played teaching. *Journal of Personality, 46,* 541-559.

Lippa, R. (1978). Expressive control, expressive consistency, and the correspondence between behavior and personality. *Journal of Personality, 46,* 438-461.

Lutsky, N., Woodworth, W., & Clayton, S. (1980, May). *Actions-attitudes-actions: A multivariate, longitudinal study of attitude-behavior consistency.* Paper presented at the annual meeting of the Midwestern Psychological Association, St. Louis.

McCann, D., & Hancock, R. D. (1983). Self-monitoring in communicative interactions: Social cognitive consequences of goal-directed message modification. *Journal of Experimental Social Psychology, 19,* 109-121.

Paulhus, D. L. (1984). Two component models of socially desirable responding. *Journal of Personality and Social Psychology, 46,* 598-609.

Rarick, D. L., Soldow, G. F., & Geizer, R. S. (1976). Self-monitoring as a mediator of conformity. *Central States Speech Journal, 27,* 267-271.

Rosenblatt, P. C. (1977). Needed research on commitment in marriage. In G. Levinger & H. L. Raush (Eds.), *Close relationships: Perspectives on the meaning of intimacy* (pp. 73-86). Amherst: University of Massachusetts Press.

Shaffer, D. R., Smith, J. E., & Tomarelli, M. (1982) Self-monitoring as a determinant of self-disclosure reciprocity during the acquaintance process. *Journal of Personality and Social Psychology, 43,* 163-175.

Shaw, M. E., & Costanzo, P. R. (1982). *Theories of social psychology* (2nd ed.). New York: McGraw-Hill.

Snyder, M. (1974). The self monitoring of expressive behavior. *Journal of Personality and Social Psychology, 30,* 526-537.

Snyder, M. (1979). Self-monitoring processes. In L. Berkowitz (Ed.), *Advances in Experimental Social Psychology* (Vol. 12, pp. 85-128). New York: Academic Press.

Snyder, M., Berscheid, E., & Glick, P. (1985). Focusing on the exterior and the interior: Two investigations of the initiation of personal relationships. *Journal of Personality and Social Psychology, 48,* 1427-1439.

Snyder, M., & Cantor, N. (1980). Thinking about ourselves and others: Self-monitoring and social knowledge. *Journal of Personality and Social Psychology, 39,* 222-234.

Snyder, M., & Gangestad, S. (1982). Choosing social situations: Two investigations of self-monitoring processes. *Journal of Personality and Social Psychology, 43,* 123-135.

Snyder, M., Gangestad, S., & Simpson, J. A. (1983). Choosing friends as activity partners: The role of self-monitoring. *Journal of Personality and Social Psychology, 45,* 1061-1072.

Snyder, M., & Ickes, W. (1985). Personality and social behavior. In G. Lindzey & E. Aronson (Eds.), *Handbook of social psychology* (3rd. ed.). New York: Random House.

Snyder, M., & Kendzierski, D. (1982). Acting on one's attitudes: Procedures for linking attitude and behavior. *Journal of Experimental Social Psychology, 18,* 165-183.

Snyder, M., & Monson, T. C. (1975). Persons, situations, and the control of social behavior. *Journal of Personality and Social Psychology, 32,* 637-644.

Snyder, M., & Simpson, J. A. (1984). Self-monitoring and dating relationships. *Journal of personality and Social Psychology, 47,* 1281-1291.

Snyder, M., Simpson, J. A., & Gangestad, S. (1984). Personality and sexual relations. *Journal of Personality and Social Psychology.*

Snyder, M., & Smith, D. (1986). Personality and friendship: The friendship worlds of self-monitoring. In V. Derlega & B. Winstead (Eds.), *Friendship and social interaction.* New York: Springer-Verlag.

Snyder, M., & Swann, W. B. (1976). When actions reflect attitudes: The politics of impression management. *Journal of Personality and Social Psychology, 34,* 1034-1042.

Snyder, M., & Tanke, E. D. (1976). Behavior and attitudes: Some people are more consistent than others. *Journal of Personality, 44,* 510-517.

Tunnell, G. (1980). Intraindividual consistency in personality assessment: The effect of self-monitoring. *Journal of Personality, 48,* 220-232.

Zanna, M. P., Olson, J. M., & Fazio, R. H. (1980). Attitude-behavior consistency: An individual difference perspective. *Journal of Personality and Social Psychology, 38,* 432-440.

3

The Psychosexology of Female Initiation and Dominance

KATHRYN KELLEY
BEVERLY ROLKER-DOLINSKY

Relationships, as scholars working in the field are well aware, come in a variety of types (Duck & Gilmour, 1981). One broad category encompasses those in which interactions between the sexes occur. On a functional level, these relationships can be further subdivided into those either having or not having an important sexual component. The dating couple is an example of the former, and the employee-manager pair qualifies as an instance of the latter. We will call these two types of relationships heterosexual and heterosocial, respectively.

This chapter is about female initiation and dominance in cross-sex relations. It will examine four topics: female initiation of heterosexual relationships, female dominance of these dyads, female initiation and dominance of sexual encounters, and female dominance in heterosocial interactions. These are four separate foci; in terms of specific details, each domain has its own unique features. At the same time, these phenomena are closely aligned. As values and mores change in American society, it appears that all of these phenomena are becoming more prevalent. Thus this is an opportune time for integrating what is known about female assertion in cross-sex bonds.

As with any new area of investigation, three questions are obvious: (1) What is the phenomenon itself? More specifically, one might wonder, What are the styles and strategies women use? (2) What are the antecedents of female assertion in relationships? Here, variables such as attitudes, expectations, norms, and situational factors should be important. (3) What are the consequences of female assertion? Here, specific questions might be asked regarding the success of the relationships assessed via partners' behavior and feelings. Are female invitations accepted? If so, how long do female-initiated couples continue dating? Also, one wonders how other people perceive such relationships.

A crucial assumption running throughout the chapter is that personality variables are important. They may be an antecedent factor and may also have a crucial moderating influence on people's reactions to female initiation and dominance. Figure 3.1 attempts to distill these phenomena into an overall theoretical framework. The antecedents, primarily in the form of attitudinal and affective components, may also function as responses to female assertion. Individual differences, including personality traits and sex variations, may also influence the outcomes of this causal chain. This sequence of determinants and effects has an additional quality of showing the major elements hypothesized to influence the phenomenon of responses to female-dominant behaviors.

Female Initiation of Heterosocial Relationships

Of particular interest is the occurrence of initiating behavior by females compared to males. Although a sizable minority of college males have been approached by the opposite sex (Kelley, Pilchowicz, & Byrne, 1981), social scientists have largely ignored this important aspect of relationships. Several perspectives on this process are considered. First, the perception of an initiator and the effects of this appraisal have been studied by a few investigators. Attitudes toward the appropriateness of different initiators can influence both their success and the evaluation of their personalities. The cultural standards of status accruing to the initiator theoretically result in social rewards for this individual.

We additionally emphasize empirical findings on the self-reported responses to female versus male initiation. The affective results of the prospects, problems, and payoffs associated with the sex of the initiator can thus be assessed. Examples of this assessment include questions such as the following: How do individuals engaged in the establishment of a potentially sexual relationship respond to the person who attempts to accomplish this interaction? Under conditions that contradict the cultural standard for this normative behavior, how does female initiation fare in comparison with the more traditional sort of stimulus—namely, the male undertaking this task? Contrasts can be expected between attitudinal responses to others' behavior and personal responses toward an uncommon experience; questions about sexual processes may prove to be no exception to this general rule.

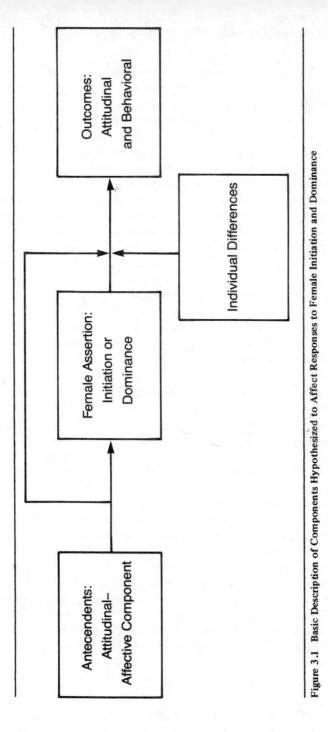

Figure 3.1 Basic Description of Components Hypothesized to Affect Responses to Female Initiation and Dominance

Female Initiation of Heterosexual Relationships

Stereotypes. In an attempt to examine attitudes toward the initiator, Green and Sandos (1983) presented vignettes of heterosexual inter-actions to college undergraduates. They exposed participants to a brief account of a verbal dinner invitation described as extended by a female or male to a person of the opposite sex in a work setting. Another independent variable consisted of the invitation's degree of immediacy. A direct statement placed the invitation before a brief conversation, while indirectness consisted of the conversation preceding the dinner suggestion. Participants evaluated the interactions as being more socially acceptable in the indirect condition, or when a male was the initiator. The female who extended the invitation was seen as relying more on nonverbal cues from her potential date than her male counterpart was assumed to do. The male initiator garnered more positive evaluations, was regarded as socially skilled, and was expected to gain a more readily understood, verbal answer than the females. The results support the notion of male superiority attributed in this social situation by evaluators of both sexes.

Status. Female adoption of male initiation patterns in less approval of the former's behavior. For nonsexual activities, Feinman (1984) has outlined a theory of cross-sex (and age-) role behavior. It regards male deviation as more demaging to his evaluation because female roles receive lower status ranking at the outset. Therefore, females' attempts to perform acts traditionally reserved for males would not necessarily result in more favorable evaluations but would have only a slight negative influence on attitudes toward females. The status differences attributed to the sexes can include assumptions about relationship initiation. However, several unanswered questions remain about the contribution of status differences due to either biological sex or sex roles, including the role of initial heterosexual interactions in combina-tion with nonsexual ones and the relative weights that the two sets of information would receive in stereotypic ratings of actors. For example, since a biological or culturally based sex difference is presumed to be component of most heterosexual interactions, one could investigate how it influences the nonsexual aspects as well.

Male Responses to Female Initiation

Positive Expectations. Theoretically, an affective response toward a topic partially determines the behavioral outcome (Clore & Byrne,

1974). For example, positive attitudes toward females' responsibility in originating a relationship may appear in attributions to oneself. Kelley et al. (1981) interviewed 97 male college undergraduates about their opinions and practices in dating and found that they espoused mainly positive attitudes toward the prospect of a female asking them for a date. In line with the theoretical prediction, the more positive the attitude, the greater the probability that they had actually accepted a female's invitation.

Negative Results. Despite the positive evaluation by males, in Kelley et al.'s study the majority of these female-initiated relationships had ended by the third interaction. Females also neglected to approach some of the males who expressed the greatest interest in this possibility. Older males were less likely either to have received a female's invitation or to have accepted, but the males' ages varied independently of their affect toward the topic. Finally, repeated attempts by a female to gain acceptance did not generally succeed. Kirkendall (1961) describes female initiators as "firecrackers" who might have difficulty in achieving long-term relationships, a characterization not refuted by these data.

Attitude-Behavior Link. Males' stereotyped opinions about such nontraditional female behavior indicated flattery, but the behavioral outcome varied from that attitude. At times, the females' role performance was described as revealing some inadequacy, such as the inappropriate persistence of unwanted attention. As the males saw it, the prospects appeared considerably brighter than the actual experience of female inception. The majority of females would have had less practice with the skills involved here, including skill at handling rejection in the dating situation (Hatfield & Sprecher, 1986). Because this study assessed only males' reactions to opposite-sex initiation, the interpretation of these findings remains tentative; the following study examined both sexes' responses to opposite-sex initiation in order to provide more information about the process, its motivation, and outcomes that can result.

Responses to Opposite-Sex Initiation

In an unpublished study performed by Kelley and Pilchowicz, 28 male and 78 female college students responded to a brief written survey concerning their dating experiences. Questions on the survey focused on the last two relationships begun by members of the opposite sex. Thus females described encounters initiated by males, and males those proffered by females. In agreement with the results reported by Kelley et al. (1981), approximately nine out of every ten respondents reported that they had been asked for a date by a member of the opposite sex. The last two individuals who had done so had repeated the same request of the subject. Statistically, the same frequency of having received an invitation from the opposite sex was reported by both sexes. Participants in this research were not selected on the basis of having had such experiences; rather, they were the typical Introductory Psychology volunteers attending an urban state university. Females enrolled in this course usually outnumber males, giving rise to the relatively small number of males who participated. These data illustrate that both males and females commonly receive requests for dates from the opposite sex. Certain variables can be used to point out the similarities or differences in some of their reactions to this experience.

Similarities Between the Sexes. A number of similarities between the sexes in their responses to opposite-sex initiation can be noted in these data. A series of inquiries about subjects' affective reactions to the general topic of sex variation in requesters revealed these similarities. For example, both sexes expressed pleasure at the prospect of being asked for a date by the opposite sex. The respondents expressed this affect on a seven-point semantic differential scale, rating it as 1.77 to indicate a high degree of expected pleasure from this type of event. Likewise, both sexes expressed approval of a change in current society so that both men and women would feel free to ask one another for dates, with a mean of 1.59 on the seven-point scale. Neither sex expressed much reluctance to refuse an invitation because it might hurt the other person's feelings (mean = 3.55). Finally, the likelihood of reversing the procedure and asking for a later date did not depend on sex. None of these variables covaried with the social desirability component of Bem's Sex Role inventory (Bem, 1974), indicating a low probability that the responses occurred on the basis of the social desirability of stereotypically favorable directions. The foregoing similarities between the sexes make it possible to conclude a generally positive affective response to the concept of opposite-sex initiation, whether by males or females. It remains to be seen whether behavioral assessments agree with the attitudinal portion in this respect.

Sex Roles. A personality variable that could realistically be expected to relate to these measures is that of sex roles, which have often been shown to influence heterosexual relationships. Respondents' sex typing or androgyny was assessed by means of Bem's Sex Role Inventory. Because of the absence of sex-role reversals among this sample, these results omit discussion of feminine males and masculine females. Approximately equal ratios of respondents within sex categories could be classified as sex-typed, as masculine males or feminine females, or as androgynous, self-reporting both masculine and feminine traits.

Rate of Acceptance. Subjects reported their experiences with the last two individuals of the opposite sex who had extended an invitation. Their rate of acceptance depended on their sex and sex role: Androgynous females accepted both persons' requests—rather than only one—with greater frequency than did each of the other categories. Masculinity among females has been associated with greater flexibility in behavior and attitudes. Perhaps this psychological base facilitates a more accepting response than among androgynous males, who apparently exhibited more negativism to some of their female requesters. Androgynous males often report a higher degree of masculinity than similar females, possibly encouraging a greater degree of self-assertiveness among the former. Androgyny had different consequences for relationships among males versus females (e.g., Tesch, 1984), and the present findings support this difference.

Duration of Relationship. Turning to the duration of the subsequent relationship with the requester, some dependence on sex and sex role also occurred here. As Table 3.1 shows, sex-typed males had the briefest female-initiated relationships. Androgyns of both sexes reported longer relationships, perhaps evidence of the greater social skills attributed to them. With the exception of androgynous females, each of the other three groups exhibited shorter durations "the second time around." Perhaps because of a generally effective sexual revolution (Hunt, 1974) or because of changed ideas about romanticism in second and subsequent relationships, most of these respondents provided evidence of the recent cultural changes in Western sexuality.

Affection and Seriousness. The study of friendship and intimacy formation has a long and varied history, with many attempts to describe the factors that facilitate and impede it (e.g., Duck, 1977). Respondents in this study described their relationships on four additional semantic differential scales assessing the degree of affection and seriousness found in both as initiated by a member of the opposite sex. Since they also expressed their affective evaluation of two preceding relationships, this method made it possible to compare their relative outcomes by a mixed design. Sex and sex roles of the respondents could presumably illuminate some of the processes found in their descriptions.

TABLE 3.1
Means for Duration of Relationship
Based on Sex and Sex Role

	Sex and Sex Role of Respondent			
Relationship	Sex-Typed Female	Sex-Typed Male	Androgynous Female	Androgynous Male
First	3.92_d	3.00_b	4.27_{de}	4.65_e
Second	3.05_b	2.57_a	4.65_e	3.47_c

NOTE: The question read: If a relationship developed with the first (or second) person, describe how long it lasted:

	(1)	(2)	(3)	(4)	(5)	(6)	(7)	
Less than 1 week	< 1 week	1 wk.- 1 mo.	> 1-6 mos.	>6 mos. - 1 yr.	> 1 yr. - 2 yrs.	> 2 yrs. -3 yrs.	> 3 yrs. - 5 yrs.	from >3 to 5 yrs.

Means with similar subscripts do not differ by the Duncan procedure (p > .05).

TABLE 3.2
Means for Affection of Relationships
Based on Sex and Sex Role

	Sex and Sex Role of Respondent			
Relationship	Sex-Typed Female	Sex-Typed Male	Androgynous Female	Androgynous Male
First	5.29_{de}	3.45_a	5.21_{de}	4.62_c
Second	4.12_b	3.09_a	4.69_c	5.13_d

NOTE: The question read: How affectionate was this relationship with this first (or second) person? (1 = not at all affectionate; 7 = very affectionate) Means with similar subscripts do not differ by the Duncan procedure (p > .05).

Table 3.2 presents the results of the analyses of variance for this outcome variable of affection attributed to the relationships. Females indicated that less affection occurred in the second relationship compared to the first, perhaps illustrating a self-protective mechanism at work. A broken relationship's negative impact might be reduced by shortening its duration and lessening its impact, thus reducing the tendency toward learned helplessness induced by continuing to suffer in an unhappy pairing. In line with the portrayal of sex-typed males as less sensitive to interpersonal cues than the other groups (e.g., Spence & Helmreich, 1978), these males indicated the least affectionate relationships.

The surprising finding centered on the greater affection experienced by androgynous males in their second relationship. This result contradicted the direction found among females. The so-called liberation of androgynous males may be operating here, in which a second initiation by females of a dating relationship apparently facilitated the males' greater openness to profess affection. Another perspective on these males' data involves the same line of reasoning, pointing out that it was not until the second of the two relationships that the androgynous males' affection equaled that of the females' first report. Males with feminine attributes possibly used the self-protective mechanism of admitting less affection at the outset and subsequently may have experienced less inhibition by the second one. Murstein (1980) claims that males experience romantic affection more strongly than females. The data described here suggest that sex roles intervene in the process of "falling in love."

With respect to the other evaluative dimension, somewhat similar patterns emerged when the respondents evaluated the seriousness of the two relationships. Table 3.3 presents the means for this variable, showing that once again sex-typed males described both relationships as the least serious among the respondent categories. The sex-typed females assessed both encounters as equally and moderately serious. Androgynous females and males attributed different levels of seriousness to the two relationships. The females expressed more seriousness in the first, while males rated the second as comparatively greater in seriousness. The explanation of these findings may follow that offered for the variable of affection. Androgynous males, it should be recalled, were more reluctant than the females to have accepted both initiations. Persistence in embarking on a partially threatening, new relationship may have been defused among these males by either defensively attributing greater affection and seriousness or by expending more effort than usual to encourage a successful outcome.

Chronic Self-destructiveness. From the preceding results, the contribution of sex and sex roles to initiation responses seems important. These two variables produced differences in the relationships initiated by members of the opposite sex. The individual's experiences with this situation thus depended on a biological factor and a personality trait. It seems reasonable to question whether any of the interactive effects might vary with other characteristics and thereby provide additional explanations of these results. One such variable is chronic self-destructiveness (CSD), studied by Kelley et al. (1985). Using multiple samples consisting of hundreds of subjects, these authors have devel-

TABLE 3.3
Means for Seriousness of Relationships
Based on Sex and Sex Role

	Sex and Sex Role of Respondent			
Relationship	Sex-Typed Female	Sex-Typed Male	Androgynous Female	Androgynous Male
First	4.18_{bc}	2.91_a	4.58_c	4.06_b
Second	4.04_b	2.60_a	4.07_b	5.07_d

NOTE: The question read: How affectionate was this relationship with this first (or second) person? (1 = not at all affectionate; 7 = very affectionate) Means with similar subscripts do not differ by the Duncan procedure (p >.05).

oped a reliable scale of CSD that successfully discriminates CSD behavior in various construct validity studies. The construct is defined generally as a tendency to engage in self-defeating behaviors or to avoid self-enhancing ones. Individuals high in CSD drive recklessly, cheat, delay obtaining PAP smears, and exhibit adolescent rebelliousness more often than those at the opposite end of the continuum.

This characteristic's relevance to the present study concerns the correlation between CSD and the duration of relationships. The duration of the first of two relationships correlated significantly with CSD among both males, $r(21) = -.39$, $p < .05$, and females $r(67) = -.24$, $p < .05$. The higher scores on the CSD scale were associated with shorter relationships. This correlation disappeared by the second relationship and did not surface among any other variables. We hypothesized that persons who respond in a chronically self-destructive fashion to items on the scale might have less success in dating, since a consistently self-destructive response would be expected to generalize to interpersonal behavior. Chronically self-destructive acts, which may lead to the breakdown of dating or intimate relationships, would include such things as not attending to the other's needs or feelings and neglecting the relationship, much as a high CSD person ignores his or her own well-being. It is only a short conceptual leap to the conclusion that such individuals would probably report shorter relationships. A person high in CSD might respond counterproductively when faced with a situation perceived as threatening, such as a sex-typed male approached by a female for a date. As mediating variable, CSD may have much to reveal about styles of interaction at crucial points in heterosocial relationships.

Female Dominance of Heterosexual Relationships

A relationship may or may not thrive, once the first encounter has succeeded. This section examines some of the research dealing with the dominance patterns that occur in ongoing heterosexual relationships. Sex roles of feminine passivity continue to affect interactions at the early states of a coupling. Females still occupy the subordinate role in these dating relationships, apparently as part of the ritualization attendant to masculine control (Shehan, 1984).

Dominance Strategies

Evidence for the strategies used to assert perceived power comes from a study by Falbo and Peplau (1980). They studied intimate couples in a university setting and found that the powerful partner tended to use particular tactics to exert control. Attempts at manipulation could be characterized in two categories. Direct strategies used invasive techniques, such as asking, while indirect ones had subtle, unobtrusive implications. Unilateral tactics essentially ignored the response of the other person, by telling, for example, rather than bargaining in an indirect way. The powerholder used direct, unilateral strategies, regardless of sex or sexual orientation. The indirectness of power manipulations by females also appeared in White's (1980) study of their greater tendency deliberately to induce jealousy in their male partners.

The perception of power may not always predict related behaviors in everyday interactions. Minturn (1984) studied the performance of sex-role-related behavior among commune residents. The males among them considered themselves to have higher status than the females but performed a variety of household tasks associated with stereotypical femininity. The work division contrasted with the power and status which the males attributed to themselves. Thus the males seem to have compensated themselves for a loss of perceived dominance in the service of greater equalitarianism in behavior but not in attitude. The attitudes about dominance showed more resistance to change than the related behaviors in this case, illustrating the potential for independence of the two in some situations.

Agreements about Dominance

McDonald (1980) has reviewed the evidence on dominance within marriages and found low marital satisfaction in wife-dominant couples. In this sense, Feinman's hypothesis about negative reactions to female dominance receives some support. The relationship between dominance and other tendencies has appeared in other studies as well. Kotkin (1983) compared married and unmarried couples with respect to the degree of equalitarian attitudes they held concerning their relationships. Of course, this strategy necessarily lacks the element of experimental control through randomization of subjects within groups, so that only comparisons between preexisting divisions can be made. One cannot assume, for example, that the unmarried couples would behave similarly after their entry into marriage. Generally, however, the unmarried cohabitors reported fewer instances of dominance than the other group and expressed more equalitarian attitudes.

An unusual feature of this study concerned the couples' career success, in which males attained higher levels of success in the conventionally nonequalitarian, male-dominant pairs. The need for sympathetic support from an intimate partner of an achieving, dominant person has been cited as a correlate of this type of success (Winter, Stewart, & McClelland, 1977). This may be true when it involves the advantage of assuming the precedence of that person in making decisions about one or both individuals. As an illustration of this notion, Kotkin's data also show that cohabiting women with marriage plans agreed with the assumption of their partner's dominance in career decisions but expected to implement this arrangement only after marriage.

Premarital Attitudes

The possibility thus exists that attitudes toward dominance change with a couple's marital status. Attitudes may or may not have eventually become less equalitarian in Kotkin's study following the formalization of the relationships. More generally, attitudes within couples could provide a basis from which to assess the changes that can be expected to occur at different stages. Other authors have demonstrated that attitudinal agreement is greater among married couples than random pairs (Byrne & Blaylock, 1963) and have assumed that agreement correlates with marital satisfaction (Levinger & Breedlove, 1966). Compatibility of psychological dominance, rather than complementarity, has been found to be correlated with marital adjustment (Meyer & Pepper, 1977).

Kelley performed a study designed to examine some of the factors involved in premarital attitudes and dominance patterns. This study assessed attitudes about role adjustment among premarital couples who visited their religious minister in a large, urban area of the midwestern United States. They responded to 17 items concerning this topic, such as "My family agrees with my choice of a mate," and responded individually in an agree-disagree format. The percentage of agreement was calculated for each of the 60 couples. Variables of interest included age (above and below the medians of the males, 22.5, and females, 21.5) and the number of months remaining before marriage (median = 2.13). Table 3.4 presents the means involved in the between-subjects interaction of the three variables. The pairing of older females with younger males, in conjunction with a closer time to marriage, was associated with the least agreement. The most agreement occurred among the younger female-older male couples at a longer than median time before marriage.

In couples with the more traditional age differences described by Hudson and Henze (1969), attitudinal agreement occurred when the marriage date existed comparatively far in the future. Just before the wedding date, the less traditional age split (older female, younger male) coexisted with less agreement. If age can embody an assumption of dominance (Henley, 1973), then the dominant older male initially found himself in a more advantageous position than the dominant older female.

As the marriage approached, however, this advantage waned and did not exceed that of other combinations. For different groups of the other pairs, disagreement was greater during the same time period and may have set the stage for the development of later problems. Female dominance in this context may have led to greater discord in subsequent interactions. Hatfield and Traupmann's (1981) analysis of equitable relationships may apply to this finding, as a pressure toward inequity. An older female may not have the same physical and financial advantages to bestow on a younger male as in the older male-younger female pairs, for example. At the same time, younger females may eventually perceive disadvantages in an older mate who perhaps may embody a "generation gap." If the equity cannot be established or restored, the relationship may decline in quality.

The Sexual Sphere
Female Sexual Initiation

When females initiate sexual activity, they tend to possess some of the psychological characteristics of dominance. Jesser (1978) found that female college students who approached their male partners asking for sexual activity tended to be more liberal and assertive than

TABLE 3.4

Means for Agreement Percentages for Role Adjustment Topic

| | | Number of Months before Marriage | |
Female Age	Male Age	.25-2	2-7
Younger	Younger	.65$_a$	.74$_a$
Younger	Older	.67$_a$	.91$_c$
Older	Younger	.42$_b$	.77$_a$
Older	Older	.65$_a$	.71$_a$

NOTE: Ages are identified by status above and below the median for each sex. Means with similar subscripts do not differ by the Duncan procedure ($p > .05$).

female noninitiators. Most males who had received a direct request for sex agreed. In contrast, the females in this study thought sexual assertiveness might threaten males. The initiating females tended to enter into involvements with males who also used direct sexual initiatives and whom they assumed would not feel threatened by a female explicitly asking for sex. Therefore, the couple would be expected to agree initially about this mode of initiating sex and would be more likely to use it successfully.

Most offers for sexual interactions occur between acquaintances, friends, or married partners. Males are expected to initiate the majority of sexual encounters (McCormick & Jesser, 1983). When they occur between strangers, they contradict the usual role-play of this behavior. Clark and Hatfield (1984) studied this process by having male or female confederates approach an opposite-sex stranger on a college campus and ask this person for a date, for accompaniment to his or her apartment, or for sexual activity. Few females acceded to the latter two requests. Males agreed to any of the three invitations made by a female, at the rate of 50%-75% in the three conditions. In this study, the preliminary rituals of dating proved unnecessary: Sadie Hawkins can apparently choose from among several routes to success!

Within relationships, sexual activity can provide a significant source of satisfaction. Sexual satisfaction is typically correlated with marital satisfaction, but causative sequences are difficult to study. The sex of the person expected to initiate or control this activity can differ on the basis of social stereotypes, according to which the male may suggest, encourage, or otherwise initiate sex, while the female acts as a regulator to limit it. Peplau, Rubin, and Hill (1977) identified this pattern among couples with either permissive, egalitarian, or more conservative, traditional attitudes. Crain (1978) disputes the typically sociobiological interpretation of these and related findings by emphasizing the socially learned roles of dominance and submission. Strict adherence to the norm of males as the initiator may affect the relationship negatively (Laury, 1983), suggesting that the converse of this situation may improve satisfaction for some.

Marital partners generally report that males initiate sexual interaction more often than females. In a retrospective survey study performed by Brown and Auerback (1981), 50 married couples responded to an extensive series of questions about their sexual habits, satisfaction, and so on. With respect to the frequency of female offers to engage in sex, the couples indicated that she performed this role as a prelude to approximately 25% of their sexual interaction during the first year of marriage. At the time of the survey, the pairs said they experienced female initiation 40% of the time, resulting in an increase of this pattern at a rate of 1% for each year of marriage in this sample. These figures illustrate that with the passage of time and increases in sexual experience, this pattern becomes more frequent, but male initiation still predominates. The style of female assertiveness also varied, becoming more verbal and direct through the years. Type A wives initiate and control sexual interactions more often than Type B wives (Becker & Byrne, 1984).

O'Brien (1981) provides evidence that retrospective self-reports of the pattern of increasing female initiation may be an underestimate. In contrast with the usual agreement that males typically approached females for sex, weekly interviews for six months revealed that wife initiation occurred more commonly than was indicated by retrospective reports. The couples often described the interaction in this manner: She would communicate the cue for sexual readiness, and he then began foreplay.

Activity versus Passivity

During sexual activity, role enactment often continues to consist of male dominance, at least according to the attitudes expressed about this subject. Garcia (1982) found that dominance due to greater sexual experience was evaluated less positively in females than in males. Many consider male sexual dominance the appropriate technique (Fracher, 1980). The concomitant passivity among females would satisfy the need for that outcome (Stein, 1981). In contrast, the behavior connected with delivering pleasure may differ. Davis and Martin (1978) arranged for subjects of both sexes to stimulate the buttocks of a partner with vibrations described as having positive arousal properties. Males and females stimulated their dating partners equally, and more than they did strangers. Passivity in females may be exalted (McCormick, Brannigan, & LaPlante, 1984), but when they had the opportunity to stimulate their partners pleasurably, the women behaved as actively as the male participants.

What Do They Want?

The overused query from Freud about what women want becomes more instructive when questions are asked of both participants in a relationship. Hatfield, Traupmann, Greenberger, and Wexler (1984) surveyed a large number of dating and newlywed couples concerning their desires for improving their interactions. Topics in the survey included a number of dimensions of love, affection, and sexual interaction. With respect to the topics of power and dominance, only males expressed interest in greater assertiveness by their female partners concerning their sexual preferences. They requested instructions about how to make their sexual activities more pleasurable, as well as more frequent requests for sex from females. A portion of the males' requests for more female dominance referred to a need for information. They sought data on the success of their usual activities, as well as guidelines on how to increase "arousingness" using different techniques. The request for more female sexual initiative might reflect any combination of the following factors: a need for information about her interest, avoidance of rejection, and stimulation due to the arousing properties of female dominance itself.

Dominance in Sexual Activity

Position. One route to establishing dominance in Sexual Activity is the position used during heterosexual intercourse. In the United States, the missionary position's popularity indicates a preference for male superiority, but in other societies alternative positions outrank this one. One or more of the face-to-face positions occupy the position of universal preference (Beach, 1978). Despite the greater benefits for sexual arousal, females in Allgeier and Fogel's (1978) study derogated the actors using the female-superior position. This relationship cut across sex roles, so that regardless of their role identification, the effect persisted. A cross-cultural replication of this study would be valuable, especially if it incorporated one of the instruments assessing attitudes toward women's status. These data would facilitate conclusions about status differential as a predictor of responses to female-superior positions. Differences in women's social status may relate to the coital positions approved by various societies.

Perceptions of Sexual Dominance. Several studies have indicated that portrayals of stimulus persons as dominant tend to enhance ratings of their sexual characteristics. For example, Miller and Byrne (1981) describe erotic actors as having degrees of dominance in their relationships. More frequent sexual activity was attributed to the powerful partner of both sexes. Dominance or submissiveness increased ratings of perceived masculinity or femininity, respectively. However, these college student subjects did not report greater sexual arousal in response to the dominance theme. Put differently, these results suggest that one of the components of a positive affective reaction to erotica may be dominance. Kelley (1985) provides evidence that bears on this point. This study exposed undergraduates to a film showing male gang rape of a female. Males with generally positive sexual attitudes reported slightly more positive affective reactions and greater sexual arousal than males with negative attitudes, or in response to control films. The importance of dominance in sexual interaction has been underrated to the extent that one sexologist has suggested different linguistic terms to distinguish male and female coital experiences on the basis of whether giving or receiving is involved (Money, 1982).

Effects of Female Sexual Dominance. The therapeutic effect of exposure to explicit pornography occurred in Wishnoff's (1978) study of sexually anxious, inexperienced female undergraduates. These women viewed an explicit, heterosexual film and subsequently expressed a greater intention to engage in sexual intercourse than those who viewed a nonexplicit sexual film. This benefit for their eventual sexual satisfaction may have been partially dependent on an unpublished aspect of this study. The explicit film's content consisted primarily of coitus with the female in the superior position (R. Wishnoff, personal communication, May 11, 1984). When the subjects were asked which position they preferred to use, these inexperienced women indicated that they would adopt the female-superior position when they engaged in heterosexual intercourse. The female actor functioned as an effective model for these subjects.

Kelley, Miller, Byrne, and Bell (1983) report a series of three studies which attempted to demonstrate a previously hypothesized relationship between anger or aggression and subsequent sexual arousal. While the data did not support this particular hypothesis, they did indicate that the depictions of sexual dominance increased arousal, as well as the tendency to characterize male or female actors as more sexual in their interests and activities. Of course, expressions of anger or aggression can imply dominance, so it is clear that the two contents should be separated to reduce the confounding effects that might otherwise occur. Perceptions of the greater sexual qualities of a dominant erotic actor contrast with females' tendency to ascribe negative characteristics to powerful partners, and with the relatively infrequent use of the female-superior position. These studies investigated perceptions of erotic pictures and as such cannot yield information about how sexual interactions should or should not be conducted.

For a small subset of predominantly male persons, female dominance through sexual aggression is a compelling feature of visits to sadomasochistic prostitutes. Some seek their services so assiduously that they travel long distances to have contact with them (Gebhard, 1969). Another sadomasochistic role-play is the more common one, with males usually enlisting the services of a female prostitute or other consenting adult who will play the subordinate, passive role (Zillmann, 1984). This relatively uncommon form of sexual behavior also reflects the tendencies found in the positivity toward male dominance found in the sexual behaviors of the larger U.S. population.

Female Dominance in Nonsexual Behavior

Heterosocial interactions, in addition to those that involve sexual components, also include nonsexual encounters. Professional contexts for these interactions may place a female in the dominant role of the employer or leader, for example. A number of studies have investigated this aspect of female dominance, often finding that it can result in negative perceptions, attributions, and behavioral outcomes relative to the more traditional male-dominant configuration. A small selection of studies will be summarized here, with the aim of integrating this information with the previous sections.

Perceptions of Female Professionals

It is generally conceded that a prerequisite for the perception of nonsexual dominance is that qualities of masculinity be attributed to the powerholder. Unless the individual occupies a superior position only by assignment to the role, social characteristics become involved in the perception of dominance. Power does not operate in a social vacuum. Thus a whole body of research has illustrated that a person designated as powerful is often described as having male, sex-role-typed qualities such as competence and status. Even one's business lunch menu may imply dominance and success; a popular trade book authored by Pinsel and Dienhart (1984) has identified rare steak and raw oysters as indicative of the consumer's powerful qualities. One who eats chicken and quiche may be dubbed a wimp.

The situational influence of a group setting on this perception can also intervene, as shown in a study by Porter, Geis, and Jennings (Walstedt) (1983). These researchers varied through slide presentations the sex composition of a subordinate group and of the designated leader. In mixed-sex groups, subjects made dominance attributions to the male seated at the head of the table as an indication of group leadership. A female at the same location did not receive ratings reflecting either leadership qualities or a major contribution to the group. Only in all-female groups did she have those characteristics attributed to her. Despite the social desirability of evidence that one operates independently of sex-role stereotypes, these participants discriminated against the female in a potentially powerful position. The effect of the subtle cue of seating position was so robust in this study that androgyns did not differ from the sex-role-typed in their stereotypic responses.

Prejudice Against Dominant Females

When a third party supplies the information about status, the effects on social perceptions of dominance may again occur. Lipton and Hershaft (1984) asked subjects to evaluate an artist and his or her paintings, and identified this person by means of high- or low-status labels. A male artist described in either way received more positive evaluations, while the female was judged more negatively. The description of a female as a person, rather than as a woman or girl, elevated the ratings among both male and female raters. Apparently, the inconvenient machinations that an author sometimes performs to avoid sexist references can have the intended influence against prejudiced perceptions.

The entry of females and other social or ethnic minority groups into traditionally sex-typed fields can be viewed as a threat. Just how this threatened response affects social perceptions was considered by Tawil and Costello (1983). They investigated females' evaluations of applicants to traditional or nontraditional fields for graduate training. The derogation of applicants occurred only among a limited portion of the sample. Older women in traditional occupational roles evaluated most negatively the person seeking entry to a nontraditional field. The females who already occupied nontraditional roles did not differentially evaluate the applicants on the basis of their sex. These data suggest that a female seeking to occupy a masculine role position might face either positive or negative responses from others, as partially determined by the evaluators' social characteristics.

Etaugh and Riley (1983) found that females who applied for a traditional job received the most positive ratings of competence from students of both sexes. When they sought nontraditional occupations of accounting (for females) or nursing (for males), both male and female applicants were derogated. The sex-stereotypic effect of occupational choice lives hardily, and the bias against nontraditional activity in work settings persists.

Even when raters' characteristics are not varied, the behavior of subordinates working for a female superior has shown strongly prejudiced tendencies in at least one study. Sanders and Schmidt (1980) demonstrated this effect among college students working on a task; when informed that their superior was a female rather than a male, their task performance suffered dramatically. In research in business settings, similar effects on performance and evaluation have occurred only infrequently. Terborg and Shingledecker (1983), for example, cite the methodological difficulties of locating sufficiently large samples of males supervised by females. This lack makes it less likely that such studies can be performed in order to answer the questions raised by previous investigators.

Since the perception of female dominance has sexual components, Kelley and Rolker-Dolinsky attempted to examine whether sexual attitudes and dominance stereotypes have any common variance. In a previously unpublished study, they administered the Sexual Opinion Survey (Byrne & Fisher, 1983) and Rosen and Jerdee's (1978) survey of managerially relevant perceived sex differences. The former assesses opinions about a variety of sexual topics using semantic differential rating scales of attitudinal statements. The managerial scale measures the degree of stereotypic assignment of personal characteristics to either males or females. In this study, 119 male and female undergraduates' scores on the two dimensions were correlated, resulting in the finding that positive sexual attitudes facilitated more favorable attributions to males with respect to aptitude, $r(117) = -.24$, $p < .01$, and marginally for interests, $r(117) = -.13$, $p < .10$. This meant that an expression of positive sexual attitudes was related to a tendency to assign to males more than to females the characteristics of approaching problems rationally and understanding financial matters. At least for the variables used in this study, positive sexual attitudes and some unfavorableness toward female dominance were associated. It would be useful to determine whether sexual opinions exert a more powerful influence in the work setting, where the hypothesized threat of a powerful female to the status quo might operate more strongly.

The validity of dominant females' attributed characteristics can, of course, be questioned. Few studies of this issue have been conducted, in comparison to the number of stereotypes about them. Studies of nonprofessional women suggest that they engage in more self-derogation and less self-reward than achieving or superior males (e.g., Crombie, 1983). Searleman, Morris, Becker, and Makosky (1983) found that male academic authors sent reprints more reliably, and that male requesters received them more quickly. But alternative explanations of these results abound, as the researchers themselves have indicated. Kelly (1983) compared the socialization of political and organizational leaders and found that the women had a distinctive background encompassing maternal independence and a similarity to male leaders' experiences. Nevertheless, the lower status of females continues to be taught widely both cross-culturally and across generations (Goldman & Goldman, 1983).

Conclusions

Female dominance continues to evoke ambivalent responses, depending on the aspect under consideration and the psychological or personal characteristics of the beholder. With respect to the initiation of heterosexual relationships, males consider it a titillating idea that upon translation into behavior can have some negative components. Strategies used to exert or maintain dominance among females differ slightly from those of males. Indicants of social status can affect premarital agreement when dominance patterns vary from the traditional norm. The initiation of sexual activity by females involves several aspects of the relationship and is embedded in a number of social psychological phenomena. Female dominance of sexual activity stimulated contrasting sets of responses, depending on whether attitudes, responses to erotica, or self-reported behaviors were being considered.

In the nonsexual, heterosexual area, female-dominant relationships are associated with sex-stereotyping processes. Especially where heterosexual relationships are concerned, attitudes toward female initiation and dominance are considerably more positive than the related behavioral outcomes would suggest. This apparent gap between attitudes and behaviors surrounding this phenomenon can be explained partially as a skill deficit, as suggested in the dating and managerial studies. This single source of disadvantage for females is probably not the whole story, however. Other contributing factors are the conflict between the appealing qualities attributed to female assertiveness and the perceived threat to male dominance. These aspects were supported in the attitudinal and behavioral findings about sexual responses. The studies generally supported the conclusion that affective, attitudinal responses to female initiation and dominance are mediated by a series of intervening variables to contribute to behavioral outcomes, the last of which often possesses negative components as a result. Female initiation and dominance appears to be one of those cases in which fantasy is sometimes better than reality.

It is an open question as to whether future social trends for increased professionalism and economic independence among females will eventually result in a greater correspondence between these attitudes and behaviors. The degree of social change, if any, in this area is certainly worth documenting. At a more scientifically relevant level, studies of female initiation and dominance can continue to investigate the theoretical relationships among affect, arousal, and outcome examined here. Bleier's (1984) treatise, offering a feminist perspective on science and gender, ultimately reveals the goal of the struggle for equality between the sexes as an economic issue. Continued competition for women's piece of the pie may eventuate a return to the more traditional acceptance of male dominance, or it may produce a state of truly equalitarian relationships.

REFERENCES

Allgeier, E. R., & Fogel, A. F. (1978). Coital positions and sex roles: Responses to cross-sex behavior in bed. *Journal of Consulting and Clinical Psychology, 46,* 588-589.

Beach, F. A. (1978). Coital positions in other societies. *Medical Aspects of Human Sexuality, 12,* 135-146.

Becker, M., & Byrne, D. (1984). Type A pattern and daily activities of young married couples. *Journal of Applied Social Psychology, 14,* 82-88.

Bem, S. L. (1974). The measurement of psychological androgyny. *Journal of Consulting and Clinical Psychology, 42,* 155-162.

Bleier, R. (1984). *Science and gender: A critique of biology and its theories on women.* New York: Pergamon Press.

Brown, M., & Auerback, A. (1981). Communication patterns in initiation of marital sex. *Medical Aspects of Human Sexuality, 15*(1), 107-117.

Byrne, D., & Blaylock, B. (1963). Similarity and assumed similarity of attitudes between husbands and wives. *Journal of Abnormal and Social Psychology, 67,* 636-640.

Byrne, D., & Fisher, W. A. (1983). *Adolescents, sex, and contraception.* Hillsdale, NJ: Erlbaum.

Clark, R., & Hatfield, E. (1984). *Gender differences in receptivity to sexual offers.* Unpublished manuscript, University of Hawaii at Manoa.

Clore, G. L., & Byrne, D. (1974). A reinforcement-affect model of attraction. In T. L. Huston (Ed.), *Foundations of interpersonal attraction* (pp. 143-170). New York: Academic Press.

Crain, S. (1978, October). *A model of sexual role enactment and motivational attributions in dyadic interactions.* Paper presented at the Third International Congress of Medical Sexology, Rome.

Crombie, G. (1983). Women's attribution patterns and their relation to achievement: An examination of within-sex differences. *Sex Roles, 9,* 1171-1182.

Davis, D., & Martin, H. J. (1978). When pleasure begets pleasure: Recipient responsiveness as a determinant of physical pleasuring between heterosexual dating couples and strangers. *Journal of Personality and Social Psychology, 36,* 767-777.

Duck, S. W. (1977). *The study of acquaintance.* London: Teakfield (Saxon House).

Duck, S. W., & Gilmour, R. (Eds.). (1981). *Personal relationships 1: Studying personal relationships.* New York: Academic Press.

Etaugh, C., & Riley, S. (1983). Evaluating competence of women and men: Effects of marital and parental status and occupational sex-typing. *Sex Roles, 9,* 943-952.

Falbo, T., & Peplau, L. A. (1980). Power strategies in intimate relationships. *Journal of Personality and Social Psychology, 38,* 618-628.

Feinman, S. (1984). A status theory of the evaluation of sex-role and age-role behavior. *Sex Roles, 10,* 445-456.

Fracher, J. C. (1980). Women's role in coitus: Active or passive. *Medical Aspects of Human Sexuality, 14*(12), 16-17.

Garcia, L. T. (1982). Sex-role orientation and stereotypes about male-female sexuality. *Sex Roles, 8,* 863-876.

Gebhard, P. H. (1969). Fetishism and sadomasochism. *Science and Psychoanalysis, 15,* 71-80.

Goldman, J.D.G., & Goldman, R. J. (1983). Children's perceptions of parents and their roles: A cross-national study in Australia, England, North America, and Sweden. *Sex Roles, 9,* 791-812.

Green, S. K., & Sandos, P. (1983). Perceptions of male and female initiators of relationships. *Sex Roles, 9,* 853-870.

Hatfield, E., & Traupmann, J. (1981). Intimate relationships: A perspective from equity theory. In S. Duck & R. Gilmour (Eds.), *Personal relationships 1: Studying personal relationships* (pp. 165-178). New York: Academic Press.

Hatfield, E., Traupmann, J., Greenberger, D., & Wexler, P. (1984). *Male/female differences in sexual preferences in dating and newlywed couples.* Unpublished manuscript, University of Hawaii at Manoa.

Hatfield, E., & Sprecher, S. (1986). *Mirror, mirror on the wall* (Vol. 2). In D. Byrne & K. Kelley (Eds.), *Human sexual behavior*. Albany: State University of New York Press.

Henley, N. M. (1973). Status and sex: Some touching observations. *Bulletin of the Psychonomic Society, 2,* 91-93.

Hudson, J. W., & Henze, L. F. (1969). Campus values in mate selection: A replication. *Journal of Marriage and the Family, 31,* 772-775.

Hunt, M. (1974). *Sexual behavior in the 1970s.* Chicago: Playboy Press.

Jesser, C. J. (1978). Male responses to direct verbal sexual initiatives of females. *Journal of Sex Research, 14,* 118-128.

Kelley, K. (1985). The effects of sexual and/or aggressive film exposure on helping, hostility, and attitudes toward women and men. *Journal of Research in Personality, 19,* 472-483.

Kelley, K., Byrne, D., Przybyla, D.P.J., Eberly, C., Eberly, B., Greendlinger, V., Wan, C. K., & Gorsky, J. (1984). Chronic self-destructiveness: Measurement and construct validity. *Motivation and Emotion, 9,* 135-151.

Kelley, K., Miller, C. T., Byrne, D., & Bell, P. A. (1983). Facilitating sexual arousal via anger, aggression, or dominance. *Motivation and Emotion, 7,* 191-202.

Kelley, K., Pilchowicz, E., & Byrne, D. (1981). Responses of males to female-initiated dates. *Bulletin of the Psychonomic Society, 17,* 195-196.

Kelly, R. M. (1983). Sex and becoming eminent as a political/organizational leader. *Sex Roles, 9,* 1073-1090.

Kirkendall, L. A. (1961). *Premarital intercourse and interpersonal relationships.* New York: Julian Press.

Kotkin, M. (1983). Sex roles among married and unmarried couples. *Sex Roles, 9,* 975-986.

Laury, G. V. (1983). Which partner should take the sexual initiative? *Medical Aspects of Human Sexuality, 17*(9), 288-293.

Levinger, G., & Breedlove, J. (1966). Interpersonal attraction and agreement: A study of marriage partners. *Journal of Personality and Social Psychology, 3,* 367-372.

Lipton, J. P., & Hershaft, A. M. (1984). "Girl," "Woman," "Guy," "Man": The effects of sexist labeling. *Sex Roles, 10,* 183-194.

McCormick, N. B., Brannigan, G. G., & LaPlante, M. N. (1984). Social desirability in the bedroom: Role of approval motivation in sexual relationships. *Sex Roles, 11,* 303-314.

McCormick, N. B., & Jesser, C. J. (1983). The courtship game: Power in the sexual encounter. In E. R. Allgeier & N. B. McCormick (Eds.), *Changing boundaries: Gender roles and sexual behavior* (pp. 64-86). Palo Alto, CA: Mayfield.

McDonald, G. W. (1980). Family power: The assessment of a decade of theory and research, 1970-1979. *Journal of Marriage and the Family, 42,* 841-854.

Meyer, J. P., & Pepper, S. (1977). Need compatibility and marital adjustment in young married couples. *Journal of Personality and Social Psychology, 35,* 331-342.

Miller, C. T., & Byrne, D. (1981). Effects of dominance cues on attributions of sexual behavior. *Journal of Research in Personality, 15,* 135-146.

Minturn, L. (1984). Sex-role differentiation in contemporary communes. *Sex Roles, 10,* 73-86.

Money, J. (1982). To quim and to swive: Linguistic and coital parity, male and female. *Journal of Sex Research, 18,* 173-176.

Murstein, B. L. (1980). Mate selection in the seventies. *Journal of Marriage and the Family, 42,* 777-792.

O'Brien, C. P. (1981). Commentary. *Medical Aspects of Human Sexuality, 15*(1), 117.

Peplau, L. A., Rubin, Z., & Hill, C. T. (1977). Sexual intimacy in dating relationships. *Journal of Social Issues, 33*(2), 86-109.

Pinsel, E. M., & Dienhart, L. (1984). *Power lunching: How you can profit from more effective business lunch strategy.* Chicago: Turnbull & Willoughby.

Porter, N., Geis, F. L., & Jennings (Walstedt), J. (1983). Are women invisible as leaders? *Sex Roles, 9,* 1035-1049.

Rosen, B., & Jerdee, T. H. (1978). Perceived sex differences in managerially relevant characteristics. *Sex Roles, 4,* 837-843.

Sanders, G. S., & Schmidt, T. (1980). Behavioral discrimination against women. *Personality & Social Psychology Bulletin, 6,* 484-488.

Searleman, A., Morris, C. D., Becker, M., & Makosky, V. P. (1983). Are the fruits of research available to all? The effects of sex and academic rank on reprint-sending behavior. *Sex Roles, 9,* 1091-1100.

Shehan, C. L. (1984). Dating behaviors of women. *Medical Aspects of Human Sexuality, 18,* 90-91.

Spence, J. T., & Helmreich, R. L. (1978). *Masculinity and femininity.* Austin: University of Texas Press.

Stein, T. S. (1981). Passivity during coitus. *Medical Aspects of Human Sexuality, 15* (3),24.

Tawil, L., & Costello, C. (1983). The perceived competence of women in traditional and nontraditional fields as a function of sex-role orientation and age. *Sex Roles, 9,* 1197-1204.

Terborg, J. R., & Shingledecker, P. (1983). Employee reactions to supervision and work evaluation as a function of subordinate and manager sex. *Sex Roles, 9,* 813-824.

Tesch, S. A. (1984). Sex-role orientation and intimacy status in men and women. *Sex Roles, 11,* 451-465.

White, G. L. (1980). Inducing jealousy: A power perspective. *Personality & Social Psychology Bulletin, 6,* 222-227.

Winter, D. G., Stewart, A. J., & McClelland, D. (1977). Husband's motives and wife's career level. *Journal of Personality and Social Psychology, 35,* 159-166.

Wishnoff, R. (1978). Modeling effects of explicit and nonexplicit sexual stimuli on the sexual anxiety and behavior of women. *Archives of Sexual Behavior, 7,* 455-461.

Zillmann, D. (1984). *Connections between sex and aggression.* Hillsdale, NJ: Erlbaum.

4

Mate Selection as a Social Transition

CATHERINE A. SURRA
TED L. HUSTON

The idea that heterosexual relationships in this culture are going *from* somewhere *to* somewhere is inherent in most conceptions of dating. In our research on dating and the transition to marriage, in which we ask people to tell us how and why their level of commitment changed, it is common for them to make statements like, "Well, I was graduating from college in May and we just *had* to decide where our relationship was headed." In some instances, the quality of a relationship is judged by its lack of movement, as in, "I decided to break it off because our relationship just wasn't going anywhere." Participants also have implicit standards for what relationships should be like, given their timing: "We weren't spending as much time together as we should have been for someone who'd been dating that long [six months]."

Social scientists, too, make suppositions that heterosexual relations are developing toward some goal. After hearing one of our research reports, a graduate student noted with amusement our use of the phrase "relationships that end in marriage." The teleological nature of assumptions made about developing relationships is evident in the kinds of dependent measures used by researchers, including, for example, courtship progress and advances or regressions in involvement.

Hinde (1979) suggests that participants imbue their relationships with a sense of continuity between successive interactions over time. Thus a concern with constancy and advancement may be central to the phenomenological experience of being in a dating relationship. Many premarital relationships established by young adults are, in fact,

AUTHORS' NOTE: Preparation of this chapter was supported by grants to the first author from the University of Illinois Agricultural Experiment Station and the Research Council of the College of Family Life, Utah State University, and to the second author from the National Institute of Mental Health (Grant MH-33938).

headed toward matrimony. Although the rates of first marriages and remarriages have been declining, about 90% of young adults will marry at some time in their lives (Glick, 1984). Given the fact that most persons in the United States marry only once, it is not wonder that, in ordinary and scholarly practice, the momentum of dating relations is weighed against progress toward marriage.

Conceptualizing mate selection as a transition from dating to marriage makes explicit some hidden but agreed upon meanings attached to opposite-sex relations in this culture: The mettle of a dating relationship is gauged in part by its future prospects and the rate, timing, and character of its movement toward a commitment to permanence.

Acknowledging the role of time and timing in relationships underscores the importance of understanding the precursors of transitions and the processes by which they are made. Social scientists have traditionally focused on viewing transitions as the movement of an individual through a fixed sequence of stages. Family developmentalists, for example, describe the passage of families through a series of life cycle stages, such as the birth of the first child, the oldest child leaving home, and retirement from work. Similarly, researchers who study dating often use such stages as casual dating, serious dating, and engagement as markers of involvement. The problems with these approaches lie in the tendency to reduce the study of development to a set of stages or, worse, to an event that marks a stage, rather than to examine the processes by which individuals, couples, and families move from one stage to another (Surra & Cate, 1984).

Our goals in this chapter are to define what is meant by the phrase "social transition" and to delineate the components of social transitions. A framework for describing the processes by which social transitions occur is provided, and the transition from dating to marriage is used to illustrate the applicability of the framework. A method for gathering data about courtship processes will also be presented along with results from studies that have used the framework.

A Scheme for Describing Social Transitions

On the Nature of Social Transitions

What is meant by the phrase "social transition"? The term *transition* captures the idea that there is movement over time; however, the word is typically used to denote a particular kind of movement, one that concerns the passage of individuals from one social status to another (Hagestad & Smyer, 1982). When studying transitions, it is important to recognize that they are made either by individuals or groups of individuals. For example, a person who is making the transition to retirement passes from being a wage earner to being unemployed. To some degree, the transitions made by an individual affect others connected to the person who is changing statuses. For example, the act of retiring reverberates through the retiree's immediate and extended families and his or her friendship network. However, with individual transitions, the statuses and roles that intertwine a target individual with the family and with members of the social network who are not co-workers remain essentially unchanged. A retiring married man with children is still a husband to his wife and a father to his children. Although the nature of their (role) relationships is probably altered, the actual positions and roles that define and bind them as a group are not.

In the case of social transitions, by contrast, there are multiple, simultaneous changes in social status for the members of a group. Group members adopt new roles that simultaneously define their interrelationships. An examination of social transitions such as marriage, divorce, and the birth or loss of children suggests that these transitions involve the formal and legal incorporation or decomposition of close relationships. With a wedding, for instance, a dating couple becomes married, and with the birth of a first child, the spouses become parents and the three-person group a family. In the same way that making a transition influences an individual's environment, the passing of group members from one status to another alters the larger systems in which they are embedded.

When examining transitions, the distinction between the individual and the group as the unit of analysis has several implications. First, this perspective emphasizes the fact that personal relations are unique entities with their own defining properties (Kelley, 1986) and points to the need for investigating changes in group-level properties, especially role interrelationships, when studying transitions. Theorists have specified many ways of characterizing the properties of groups. Kelley (1979), for example, has theorized that two-person groups are interdependent with regard to the behavioral outcomes derived from interaction as well as the symbolic outcomes expressed in the dispositions that people display during interaction. Another approach to describing a group is in terms of the role expectations and behaviors that link the members of the group. Although it is desirable to study the effects of both individual and social transitions on various properties of groups, changes in positions and roles are those most directly altered by the making of social transitions. Unfortunately, most researchers have studied individual indicators thought to covary with changes in roles (e.g., degree of crisis, stress, or satisfaction) rather than changes in group properties per se (Surra & Cate, 1984).

Recognizing the social nature of some transitions further accentuates the idea that, although transitions help prepare group members for the new roles to be assumed, it is impossible to literally take on the new roles beforehand. As a result, the period prior to assuming the new status is an imperfect testing ground. This observation is especially important for the transition to marriage, during which time people are supposed to be trying out their suitability as marriage partners. Persons who cohabit before marrying are able to try out a number of aspects of the routines of married life, but each of the routines established during the transition period will be variously affected by the act of assuming the roles of husband and wife on the wedding day. This may be one reason that researchers have failed to find strong predictability between cohabitation and marriage (Newcomb, 1981), and for the common lament heard even from partners who cohabited prior to marrying: "He (she) changed the day we got married; all of a sudden I was supposed to act like a wife (husband)." Regardless of how consciously and actively partners approach courtship as a time of compatibility testing, the act of marrying is, to some extent, a new venture.

When the group is treated as the unit of analysis, the idea that close relationships connect individuals to the larger society and vice versa becomes apparent (Kelley, 1986). Two ramifications of this observation are especially relevant here. The first derives from Kelley's argument that personal relations affect society through their cumulative impact. When many individuals choose to make (or not make) the same transition, their aggregate behavior becomes a demographic trend, which influences the likelihood of other persons' making the same or different transitions in the future.

In the contemporary United States, social transitions that were once more or less programmed have become less orderly and predictable. To begin with, although most adults eventually marry, the proportion of single women between the ages of 25 and 29 increased from 10% in 1970 to 24% in 1983; for single men, the respective figures are 19% and 38% (Saluter, 1983). Moreover, in 1983, the median age at first marriage for women was 22.8 years—the highest that has ever been documented. For men the median age at first marriage has increased each year since 1975 to its present level of about 25 years (Saluter, 1983). Third, between 1975 and 1980 the number of unmarried persons of the opposite sex who were living together more than tripled (Spanier, 1983). The number of out-of-wedlock births is also on the rise (U.S. Bureau of the Census, 1983), and projections indicate that 50% of young adults will end their first marriages in divorce (Glick, 1984). Finally, about 85% of divorced men and 75% of divorced women eventually remarry (Glick, 1984).

In short, individuals and families are now making more social transitions during the course of their lives than they have previously (Norton, 1983). The passages from singlehood to marriage to parenthood occur in alternate sequences for many people, and for others not at all. The cumulative impact of such trends is that sanctions for and against making social transitions, and making them in a certain manner, are reduced. Whether to make a transition at all has become more voluntary and more under the control of participants.

A second implication of conceptualizing close relations as the link between persons and the larger society concerns the fact that transitions involve the passing of individuals from one group to another. As early as 1908, Van Gennep (1908/1960) described three kinds of rites of passage—separation, transition, and incorporation—each of which assists individuals and groups with the processes of detachment from one group and assimilation into another. With regard to social transitions, it is useful to observe that individual group members, as well as the group as a whole, are moving in and out of larger collectivities.

Changes in social network relationships brought about by the transition to marriage illustrate this point. Huston and Levinger (1978) make a distinction between the networks of individual pair members and the joint network of the couple. They proposed that with deepening involvement, the individual network shrinks in size while the joint network grows. Recent research has documented that as dating partners become more involved, they withdraw from their separate networks (Johnson & Leslie, 1982; Milardo, Johnson, & Huston, 1983; Surra, 1985) and form a couple network of associates held in common (Milardo, 1982). Rands (1980) collected similar data showing that networks of divorcing persons decrease in size as they drop members of the marital network and replace some of them with individual friends. Such descriptive information verifies that making social transitions requires changes in the social memberships of both the target group and its individual members. What is needed now is information on when and why these changes come about (Johnson, 1982).

To summarize, social transitions have several common features. They involve the passage of a couple or a larger group in and out of other established social groups. As such, the parties to a transition affect and are affected by the sociocultural context. Despite the features that social transitions share, it is assumed that people now have more freedom of choice about whether and how transitions are made than in the past. Today, how and why people make transitions is highly variable.

The Phases of Social Transitions

In order to conceptualize transitions in a way that reflects these assumptions, it is useful to start with the recognition that social transitions are marked by a series of phases: precommitment, postcommitment, and event. The pre- and postcommitment phases involve a series of processes, some of which are voluntary, that ultimately carry participants toward an event which signifies a change in status (e.g., a wedding, birth, or divorce). Although participants who are making a transition are, to some extent, caught in a web of forces beyond their control, movement toward an event also involves making voluntary decisions along the way. The degree of voluntariness, however, decreases the nearer one gets to the event.

The psychological, interpersonal, and social processes involved in social transitions are different for different persons. Some couples decide to marry only after considerable thoughtful debate about matrimony's good and bad points and their suitability for marriage, while others are more passive, and seem to "fall into" marriage. Another route to marriage, which is assumed to be the common one, centers on the interaction between partners themselves, through which they get to know each other, fall in love, intertwine their life plans and goals, and make formal commitments (Bolton, 1961). For other partners the decision to wed is prompted by such unexpected happenings as the discovery of a pregnancy.

Although the net result of the processes characteristic of the pre- and postcommitment phases is that participants are propelled toward the event, the movement through the transition is not unidirectional. Individuals may alternately move closer to or away from the event during the course of a transition. Even though such fluctuations can happen during either the pre- or postcommitment phase, they are more common during the former because of the processes characteristic of this period. Likewise, individuals typically pass through the precommitment, postcommitment, and event phases in an orderly sequence. In some instances, however, they may alternate between phases. For example, a couple may become formally engaged—a period which is equivalent to the postcommitment phase—then break off the engagement and return to the precommitment phase, which is marked by relative uncertainty about whether the wedding will actually take place. Resolution of the uncertainty and a return to the postcommitment phase—even for a short time—precedes the wedding itself. Similarly, some couples who divorce pass through the entire sequence again, including the event, by remarrying each other.

The generic characteristics of each of the phases in social transitions are discussed more fully in what follows. Although we focus on the transition to marriage, similar arguments apply to other social transitions (see Hagestad and Smyer, 1982, for an analysis of the transition to divorce during middle age).

The Precommitment and Postcommitment Phases

Ryder, Kafka, and Olson (1971) gathered detailed information about social transitions made by couples, especially the transition to marriage, and the results of their analysis fit well with the framework presented here. They found that the preparatory stage of a transition, which is like our precommitment phase, is marked by a "feeling of freedom—[the] activity can be dropped with no great effort of will" (Ryder et al., 1971, pp. 452-453). The potential consequences of their behavior and circumstance are not yet apparent to the participants, so they enter and proceed with the transition unaware of where they are headed. The responses of family and friends typically influence the couple to join together during this phase (Ryder et al., 1971).

Later in the precommitment phase, the momentum of the transition becomes apparent to the participants. The likelihood of the wedding is high, and partners often experience a period of overt or covert resistance and struggle over the structure of the relationship and whether they want the relationship to go forward (Ryder et al., 1971; also see Braiker & Kelley, 1979; Eidelson, 1980). The intensification of conflict and negativity that has been found to accompany the movement from casually to seriously dating no doubt reflects, in part, couples' working through issues pertaining to commitment (Braiker & Kelley, 1979; Kelly, Huston, & Cate, 1985). Because the likelihood that the event will occur is now obvious to third parties, the latter may act to separate the pair or fail to support them if they are opposed to the continuation of the transition (Leslie, Johnson, & Huston, 1986; Ryder et al., 1971).

The postcommitment phase commences when the parties become certain and remain relatively sure that the event will occur. A formal or informal engagement is a usual marker of this phase for the transition to marriage. As the likelihood of the event increases to virtual certainty, the voluntariness of the transition decreases. Ryder et al. (1971, p. 454), found that the sense of freedom of choice is gone at this stage and that persons "feel themselves swept along by an inexorable social process." The partners themselves have made promises to one another, promises are made public, and family members and friends come to accept the unavoidable. Ryder et al. note that the activities of the network during the postcommitment phase are aimed at reaffirming the unity of the pair.

There may be questioning or doubt during the postcommitment phase, but it is accompanied by an awareness that the event will probably take place anyway. Therefore, people attempt to resolve ambivalences by employing such dissonance reduction strategies as focusing on the good features of the new status and minimizing the importance of troublesome concerns (Bolton, 1961; Waller, 1938).

The major undertaking of this phase is not whether to go through the transition but how best to manage it (Ryder et al., 1971). The tasks surrounding preparations for the wedding or other event give opportunities to practice role-related behaviors and, depending on the transition, joint decision making (Rapoport, 1973; Van Gennep, 1960). There are opportunities to imagine the event, its effect on life circumstances, and the self in the new role. Rites of passage are designed to ease the donning of new roles and the changing of group affiliations (Rapoport, 1973; Van Gennep, 1960). Rituals like bridal showers and bachelor parties signify the impending loss of old roles and the assumption of new ones, and often directly aid the transition by providing implements needed to carry out new roles. The psychological, dyadic, and social influences of the postcommitment phase combine to set in motion a process that is difficult for any one party to reverse.

The Transition Event

The act of marrying is usually accompanied by ritual and ceremony which serve to celebrate the event, commit persons to the transition, and assist in the alteration of group memberships (Rapoport, 1973; Van Gennep, 1960). Rosenblatt and his colleagues (Rosenblatt, 1974; Rosenblatt & Unangst, 1974) have examined the marriage rituals that occur in a variety of cultures in search of the commitment mechanisms involved. Families relinquish control over offspring, accept alliances with other families, and join together in a series of financial or work transactions. Many societies, according to Rosenblatt, require the partners to engage in effortful activity or to participate in acts that publicly commit them to one another. These activities consist of "elaborate preparation [for the marriage], sexual intercourse in front of witnesses, ... learning a difficult sequence of words or acts, a long-term labor such as brideservice, trials of strength and suffering, hazing, teasing, or other public embarrassment" (Rosenblatt, 1974, p. 90).

It is common for couples in Western societies to go on a honeymoon immediately after the wedding. The honeymoon has functions similar to the wedding ceremony; it physically separates (indeed isolates) the pair from intrusion by others; gives an opportunity to recuperate from the wedding itself before assuming the duties of married life; and, at least in theory, provides an intensely intimate setting in which spouses can try out acting as husband and wife (Rapoport & Rapoport, 1964).

Objective and Subjective Influences on Commitment

To comprehend more adequately the influences that operate on social transitions, it is useful to distinguish between two types of research on this topic. In the first type, investigators make *objective inferences* about the variables that affect transitions. They decide before gathering data which factors are influential in social transitions and measure how these variables are associated with movement closer to or further from an event. In research of this sort, the researcher takes an outsider's perspective on how and why people make transitions and, guided by theory, makes causal inferences about the factors that affect transitions.

In research of the second type, investigators ask participants themselves to explain the decision processes involved in making a social transition. In this case, the researcher is concerned with examining peoples' *subjective inferences* about how and why an event came about. There are three distinct but interconnected ways of viewing the theoretical significance of participants' causal analyses of transitions. First, the researcher might assume that participants' accounts are accurate reflections of the causal forces that shaped the transition and that the accounts provided by the parties to a transition would essentially agree with a causal analysis done by an outside observer. Second, subjective inferences might be investigated because they are seen as functional reconstructions that serve to explain, justify, or otherwise account for the making of a transition. Finally, an investigator may presuppose that subjective inferences actually affect the character of social transitions, along with other causes the researcher believes to be influential. In this case, the examination of subjective attributions might also be classified as research on objective inferences.

Examples of the two types of research and of the various kinds of research on subjective inferences are available in the literature. With regard to the transition to divorce, for instance, researchers have studied subjective inferences by obtaining participants' accounts of the process of marital deterioration (Harvey, Weber, Galvin, Huszti, & Garnick, 1986; Harvey, Wells, & Alvarez, 1978; Weiss, 1975). Consistent with the second line of research on subjective inferences, Harvey and his colleagues have argued that, irrespective of whether accounts are valid representations of the causal processes operating in divorce, they play an important role in enabling individuals to make sense from and simplify a complex network of causal forces so that their explanation is acceptable to themselves and others.

Johnson's (1982) work on the personal and structural components of commitment and Levinger's (1976, 1979) work on the attractions to relationships and the barriers to divorce illustrate the approach whereby scientists make objective inferences. These authors maintain that such determinants as the reward-cost balance derived from the relationship, an individual's sense of moral obligation to continue the relationship, social pressures, the attractiveness of available alter-natives, and the difficulty of or costs associated with terminating the relationship are influential in marital dissolution. Indeed, research has documented the fact that these variables are linked to the deteriora-tion of marital relationships (for reviews, see Levinger, 1976, 1979; Lewis & Spanier, 1979).

Concerning the transition to marriage, research on commitment by Rusbult (1980, 1983) and Johnson (1978, 1984) illustrates the objec-tive-inference approach. Both have demonstrated that increases in commitment or depth of involvement are associated with variables similar to those just described as operative in marital breakups.

Bolton's (1961) research on the decision to wed is a good example of studying subjective inferences in order to examine causal processes directly (also see Rubin, 1976). From case study interviews of 20 newly married couples, Bolton delineated five types of mate selection pro-cesses, each of which represents different causes of commitment; (1) partners perceive that their personalities mesh; (2) partners establish bonds and commitments through interaction; (3) partners clarify their separate identities through their romance; (4) one or both partners feel a strong desire to wed; and (5) one or both partners manipulate the other into marriage.

As in the third kind of research on subjective inferences, we believe that participants' attributions about changes in commitment are one type of influence on the transition to marriage. Kelley's (1983) analysis of the causes of commitment in romantic relationships provides the foundation for this hypothesis. Kelley theorized that a partner's level of commitment is determined by the causes that act to keep that person in the relationship (pro-causes) and by those that draw the person out of the relationship (con-causes). Specifically, the extent of an individual's commitment is a function of (1) the average level of the difference between these pro- and con-causes, and (2) the variability in this difference. If the balance of causes consistently favors stability, the partner will adhere to the relationship.

Kelley (1983) also reviewed the kinds of processes that affect the pro-con balance. These include some mentioned previously (i.e., the reward-cost balance or satisfaction derived from the relationship, irretrievable investments, social costs of termination, and the attractiveness of available alternatives), as well as agreements or pledges made between partners, processes of dissonance reduction and self-regulation, the formation of intentions to maintain the relationship, the identification of the self with the relationship, and the breadth of the individual's time perspective on the relationship.

The most important part of Kelley's (1983) analysis for our purposes is the distinction he makes between objective and subjective assessments of causes:

> A proximal causal condition necessary for commitment is the person's relatively invariant *perception* that the pros of membership outweigh the cons. For membership to be stable, it is only necessary that the person's subjective assessments of the pros and cons consistently yield a balance in favor of continuation. [p. 294]

Causes that are not a part of a person's subjective assessments are distal influences on commitment. Thus a comprehensive analysis of the growth of commitment considers the impact of influences from both an insider's and outsider's perspective and maintains a clear distinction between the two vantage points.

Because objective inferences about why commitment changes have been systematically studied more than subjective inferences, we have focused on the latter in our research.

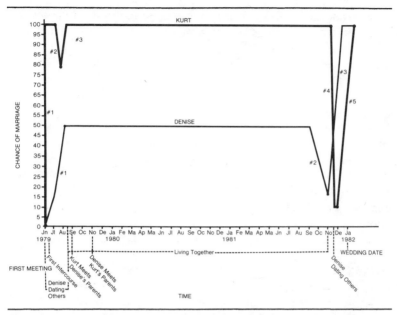

Figure 4.1   Graphs of Changes in the Chances of Marriage for Two Newlyweds

Studying the Subjective Causes of Commitment

Delineation of Approach

How can one capture the key elements of a social transition, including its temporal evolution, the decision process, and fluctuations in the movement toward or away from the event? One method that we have found useful in our work on the transition to marriage is to have the parties involved independently chart its course, noting significant circumstances and happenings that they believe were central to the decision to wed. The procedure creates a graphed representation of the transition to marriage by asking individuals to show changes in the probability that the event would occur (see Figure 4.1). To depict the transition to marriage, we ask newlyweds to graph changes in the "chance of marriage" from the day they met until the wedding day (see Huston, Surra, Fitzgerald, & Cate, 1981).

The chance of marriage is a measure of perceived joint commitment (Surra, 1985). Commitment is usually defined as the likelihood that a person will continue to adhere to a relationship once it has begun. Measures of commitment typically include some assessment by participants of the probability that their relationship will endure (Surra, 1985). In our research newlyweds are told, "Of course, on the day of your wedding, you were 100% sure you would marry." We assume that the act of marrying is indicative of a 100% commitment to marriage and that it signifies the end of the decision-making phases of a transition.

Changes that take place during a transition in things other than commitment might also be plotted on a graph. It is possible, for example, to have newlyweds (or daters) map changes in the amount of love, trust, time spent together, or other indicators. We chose to plot commitment primarily because it is a more global construct than such things as love or intimacy, and because it is sensitive to a broader range of causal forces that affect the choice of a mate (Kelley, 1983). Moreover, because the concept of commitment can be applied to understand acts other than marrying, it is easily adapted to the study of other individual and social transitions. The transition to divorce, for example, might be plotted as the movement from 100% to 0% commitment or, more precisely, to a 100% probability of divorce.

Shown in Figure 4.1 are two graphs of changes in the chance of marriage drawn independently by newlywed spouses who participated in one of our studies. The shapes of the graphs in Figure 4.1 are quite similar, although that of the husband, Kurt, has a downturn in the chance of marriage early on that was not reported by his spouse, Denise. Although Surra (1985) found that the average correlation between the graphs of husbands and wives is higher than the average for randomly paired partners (r = .80 compared with r = .56), it is not always the case that partners' graphs are as similar to each other as those seen in Figure 4.1. A description of the procedure used to obtain the graphs in Figure 4.1 and of the factors responsible for each turning point is presented below.

We began the interview by informing the respondents of our belief that all dating relationships have unique histories. Participants were exhorted to think back and remember accurately the happenings that led up to their decision to marry. They were shown a blank graph, the axes of which were described, and they were told that the grid would be used to represent the courtship as a series of changes in the chance of marriage. In order to jog memory and aid in construction of the graph, they were asked when certain key events occurred. The timing of the events, including the dates of the first meeting and the wedding, was marked along the bottom of the graph. The chance of marriage was then defined this way:

There must have been times when you thought, with different degrees of certainty, that you would indeed marry (*name*). These ideas were based on both your ideas about marrying (*name*) and what you believed (*name*'s) ideas were about marrying you. Taking both of these things into consideration, we will graph how the chance of marrying (*name*) changed over the time in which you knew (*him/her*).

Participants were told that the chance of marriage is not the same thing as how much they were in love with or wanted to marry their partner, but rather an estimate of, all things considered, the likelihood of marrying him or her. The chance of marriage on the wedding day (100%) was marked on the graph with a dot, and then the interviewer asked what this value was for the time the partners met. For both Kurt and Denise, the first value was 0%. For other respondents, however, the first value was often above 0%, sometimes as high as 50%. Participants were then asked to identify the month in which they were first aware that the chance of marriage was different from its initial value. The interviewer marked the new value on the graph with a dot; ascertained the shape of the line, giving several options; and drew the line. This line constitutes the first turning point in the graph. In order to get a description of why the chance of marriage had changed during the turning point, the interviewer pointed to the appropriate period on the graph and said, "Tell me, in as specific terms as possible, what happened from [*date*] to [*date*] that made the chance of marriage go [*up/down*] [_____%]?"

For Kurt, the chance of marriage reached 100% at the very first turning point:

> The first time I met her I was 99% sure I would marry her. I knew right off she had many of the things I was looking for in a wife. For one thing, she was really good looking and a great conversationalist.

For Denise, the first turning point occurred because:

> He was good looking and outgoing. He liked to do lots of outdoor things—swimming—things like that, that we both enjoyed. We started discovering all these things we both liked and were doing them.

Once the explanation for the first turning point was obtained, the interviewer, pointing to the end of the turning point, asked, "When were you next aware that the chance of marriage was different from this point, either up or down?" A series of structured questions similar to those just described were asked until the second turning point was drawn. For Kurt, this was a downturn. It occurred because, "I found out she had been dating someone else." He explained that it shocked him because he had assumed that he was the only one Denise was seeing.

Respondents were asked about each turning point in sequence, using the same series of questions, until the graph was completed to the wedding date. Once the graph was drawn, it was divided into three premarital stages of involvement: casual dating, serious dating, and engaged. In this way, a continuous account of the courtship unfolds. For example, in explaining the third turning point, Kurt described how Denise's handling of her relationship with Jeff affected the chance of marriage:

> She told me about Jeff and explained to me that she was just biding her time to drop him—letting him down slow and easy, you know. Once I found out and she explained, I appreciated her honesty. It only made me love her more.

According to Kurt, the third turning point covered a long period of unwavering commitment. The commitment was formed early on as the result of several things: They began having intercourse on a regular basis, exchanged vows of love, spent virtually all of their time together, began living together, and often talked of marriage. From Kurt's perspective, it was just a matter of time until they would marry.

Although Denise's level of commitment was stable at 50% for 25 months, her version of this period deviates from Kurt's. For her, the decision to live together was in part "convenient ... because we were practically living together anyway." She also reported that during the second of their two years of living together, they bought a trailer together. However, she felt that she maintained a noncommittal stance about marriage throughout the period. She purposely kept an open mind:

> We were both trying to experiment with each other—how we felt about things, responsibilities.... I felt like I was married when we were living together, but we were prepared to spend a long time getting to know each other.... We still knew that at any time either of us could say, 'It's not going to work out for me.'"

In November of 1981, that was precisely what Denise told Kurt before she packed up and moved out, which accounted for the downturn late in his graph. For Denise, the downturn began happening sooner because:

> I did not really like our life in the trailer and I grew to be very unhappy there—with it and the neighborhood. Kurt was working a lot and doing other things, too, and for the first time in our relationship we didn't have all that time together. So I was left alone in an environment that really bothered me. I just had to get out of there. So I moved home.

For the first time since they met, Kurt began to doubt whether they had a future together. His despair grew worse because they were not seeing each other daily, and Denise began dating another man. For a while he thought, "I am completely out of the picture," and wanted to move out of town. Denise, on the other hand, believed that the decision to date others was mutual. Her involvement with another man was responsible for the final upturn in her graph. As she put it:

> I went out with this guy a few times and he was very nice, but he wasn't Kurt. He just didn't appeal to me physically. Besides that, I felt like a married woman going out—like I was being unfaithful.... We really did some heavy talking about that kind of thing. By the end, we decided we wanted to get married right away.

This summary of Kurt and Denise's descriptions of their courtship is representative of those typically obtained by means of the graphing procedure. The complexity of the accounts is apparent in the variety of inferences made about why the chance of marriage changed. There are references to relationships with alternative dating partners, the dynamics of partners' interaction with each other, and personal preferences for the ideal mate. Moreover, the case study shows that, even in situations where the shapes of the graphs of each spouse are similar, their accounts of key events and experiences sometimes differ.

Coding Participants' Inferences about Changes in Commitment

In order to preserve the richness of the data, a four-category coding scheme was devised to classify subjective inferences as to their content (Surra, 1980). The categories and their definitions were developed from a content analysis of inferences reported by 50 newlywed couples who participated in the first study to employ the graphing procedure (Cate, Huston, & Nesselroade, in press). The derivation of categories from the content analysis was influenced by the assumption that individuals attribute causality to different types of causes (e.g., personal versus environmental), and by Huston and Levinger's (1978) suggestion that variables from different levels of analysis are needed to explain relationship development. These authors proposed that variables located within the individual partners, their relationship, and their social and cultural environments are needed to fully explain changes in attraction. The four categories of subjective inferences that resulted from these procedures are intrapersonal/normative; dyadic; social network; and circumstantial.

Intrapersonal/normative inferences are those in which the self, the partner, or the relationship is evaluated against some ideal or normatively derived standard. The standards, which reflect personal beliefs brought to the relationship at its inception, usually stem from cultural or subcultural prescriptions about the appropriate timing or pace of relationships, or about important qualities in a dating partner, a spouse, or the character of a dating or marital relationship. When the ongoing relationship is implicitly or explicitly evaluated against any of these kinds of standards, the inference is classified as intrapersonal/normative.

Examples of intrapersonal/normative inferences include: "I graduated from high school and it was time to find a husband" or "He wasn't as interested in marriage as he should have been for someone who dated only one person for so long." Another kind of intrapersonal/normative inference is one in which individuals assess their readiness for a particular type of premarital involvement or marriage based on some preconceived belief about what dating or marriage is like. For example, "I wasn't ready to get seriously tied down and have to give up my independence." Intrapersonal/normative inferences are especially easy to identify when they include a reference to the socialization agents from whom the beliefs and standards were learned, as in "I knew from my parents' marriage that..." or "I learned from my past disasters with women...."

Dyadic inferences are statements about phenomena rooted in interaction between partners. Any reference to self-disclosure, conflict, agreement on stage of involvement, or participation in joint activities is classed as dyadic. Examples of dyadic inferences are: "She told me she was falling in love with me"; "We decided it was okay to date others"; or "We spent a lot of time together." Also included here are interpersonal attributions (Newman, 1981)—that is, attributions about the partner or about their interaction (e.g., "We were really compatible on what we liked to do" or "She was considerate, fun, and kind"). It is important to emphasize that when attributions about the partner or the relationship are made in conjunction with standards for acceptability (e.g., "He just didn't have what it would take to make a good husband—fun, but not reliable"), the inference is coded as intrapersonal/normative rather than dyadic.

Inferences about interaction with third parties, anticipated interactions with third parties, or attributions about interaction with third parties are classified as *social network* inferences. Any person, such as kin, friends, neighbors, co-workers, or other dating partners, who is a member of the respondent's psychological or social environment (other than the dating partner) is considered a member of the social network. Examples of social network reasons are: "I met his parents"; "I knew my sorority sisters would think he was beneath me, so I didn't tell anyone about him for a long time"; and "He started hanging around with a wild crowd of friends." This category includes interaction involving either or both partners and others. It also includes references to network members independent of the dyad (e.g., "My dad worked with his dad and thought he was a jerk").

The fourth category of inferences is *circumstantial*. It includes statements about events over which the respondent has little or no control. The cause of change in commitment is attributed to institutions or forces external to either partner or their relationships with others. References to luck, fate, the weather, God, and accidents or illness fall into this category (e. g., "I had a car accident and was laid up for a month"), as well as statements about "actions" taken by institutions (e.g., "I got fired") or about events controlled by the calendar (e.g., "It was Christmastime," or "School let out for the summer").

Results of Research on Participants' Inferences

The four-category coding scheme was used in a study of 50 couples who provided graphs of changes in the chance of marriage and explanations for why each turning point occurred. The respondents, who were married for the first time and for 10 months or less, were recruited for participation through the marriage license records in Centre County, Pennsylvania. Interviewers were trained to use open-ended probes until inferences that could be coded into one of the four categories were obtained. All interviews were tape recorded (for further detail on the procedure, see Surra, 1985b).

As illustrated in the quotations from Kurt and Denise, explanations are often long and convoluted, involving two or more inferences, each from a different category. Therefore, the coding rules specify that more than one kind of reason can be coded for each turning point

(Surra, 1980). In addition, the descriptions are usually given as a series of logically interconnected inferences that fit various categories. For example, a respondent might say, "I got a job in a different town [circumstantial inference], and so we were apart all during the week [dyadic inference]." Although the original interviewers were trained to probe until inferences could be coded, they were not trained to probe for a complete chain of reasons. Therefore, it was decided to recode the inferences from the audiotapes so that only the first inference in a chain was coded; if there was more than one separate chain of inferences, more than one distal inference was coded. Two independent coders agreed an average of 82% of the time on the number of distal inferences and an average of 93% of the time on the categorization of each inference into one of the four categories.

Changes in Commitment and Participants' Explanations

In this sample, a total of 1039 different (distal) inferences were reported for a total of 606 turning points. The average number of turning points reported was 6.1, with a standard deviation of 2.9 and a range of 1 to 16. The span of time covered by a turning point averaged 4.0 months; the average amount of change reported for turning points was 24.6% ($sd = 20.0\%$; range = 2% to 100%). The mean number of inferences reported per turning point was 1.7 (range = 1 to 8). Most of the inferences were classified as dyadic (64%), while 7%, 20%, and 10% were intrapersonal/normative, social network, and circumstantial, respectively.

In order to provide additional descriptive information about turning points, the rate of change, or slope, of each turning point was calculated. Each turning point was categorized as (1) a rapid increase (slope greater than 5% per month), (2) a moderate increase (slope equal to or less than 5% but greater than 1% per month), (3) a negligible increase (slope equal to or less than +1% but greater than 0% per month), (4) a negligible decrease (slope equal to or greater than −1% but less than 0% per month), (5) a moderate decrease (slope equal to or greater than −5% but less than −1% per month), or (6) a rapid decrease (slope less than −5% per month).

Table 4.1 shows that the overwhelming majority of turning points were increases rather than decreases in commitment. This finding no doubt reflects our decision to study the courtships of partners who married, but it also introduces the possibility that the pattern of generally positive changes may produce a sense of momentum that helps carry couples through the transition. This momentum may

TABLE 4.1
Distribution of Turning Points by Characteristics

Variable	n	%
Increase in Commitment		
Rapid	259	42.7
Moderate	201	33.2
Negligible	34	5.6
Total	494	81.5
Decrease in Commitment		
Rapid	65	10.7
Moderate	41	6.8
Negligible	6	1.0
Total	112	18.5

contribute to the phenomenon described previously, whereby participants feel swept along toward the wedding. Changes in commitment
were as often as not rapid, and this was true for both increases and
decreases. Many courtships alternate between moving forward rapidly
and then leveling off in commitment; some partners reported no
periods of decline, whereas for others the upward movement was
broken by more frequent setbacks.

To find out whether the kinds of inferences were different for
increases as compared with decreases in commitment, chi-square
analyses were performed. As shown in Table 4.2, respondents reported a greater proportion of dyadic inferences for positive turning
points than negative and more intrapersonal/normative, social network, and circumstantial reasons were given for downturns in commitment χ^2 (3, N = 1039) = 45.3, p $<$ .001.

The results indicate that inferences about the relationship itself
may contribute to progress toward marriage, while beliefs about external influences and assessments of the relationship against prede-
termined standards may be partially responsible for downturns in
commitment. Commitment may decline as partners perceive changes
in their environment or as their standards for acceptability are invoked
by dyadic or nondyadic events. Alternatively, periods of decline in
commitment may motivate individuals to do a more thorough causal
analysis by looking beyond 1986 relationship itself for explanations
(Harvey et al., in press). In the idealized world of dating (or in
remembering it), people may be motivated to make inferences about the
nature of the relationship when commitment is on the upswing and
about intrapersonal and external factors when things are going poorly.

TABLE 4.2

Percentage of Inferences in Coding Category
by Direction of Turning Point

	Direction			
Category of Inference	*Positive*		*Negative*	
Intrapersonal/normative	5.8	(50)	12.3	(21)
Dyadic	68.2	(592)	41.5	(71)
Social Network	17.3	(150)	32.7	(56)
Circumstantial	8.8	(76)	13.5	(23)
Total	100.1	(868)	100.0	(171)

NOTE: Number of inferences is in parentheses.

TABLE 4.3

Percentage of Inferences in Coding Category
by Rate of Change of Turning Point

	Rate of Change				
Category of Inference	*Rapid Increase*	*Moderate Increase*	*Negligible Increase or Decrease*	*Moderate Decrease*	*Rapid Decrease*
Intrapersonal/ normative	6.1 (29)	5.5 (19)	5.3 (3)	9.4 (6)	14.7 (14)
Dyadic	68.7 (327)	66.6 (231)	71.9 (41)	39.1 (25)	41.1 (39)
Social network	18.9 (90)	15.9 (55)	12.3 (7)	29.7 (19)	36.8 (35)
Cricumstantial	6.3 (30)	12.1 (42)	10.5 (6)	21.9 (14)	7.4 (7)
Total	100.0 (476)	100.1 (347)	100.0 (57)	100.1 (64)	100.0 (95)

NOTE: Number of inferences is in parentheses.

Looking at the association between the kinds of inferences reported and the rate of change of turning points reaffirms and adds to the findings discussed so far [χ^2 (12, N = 1039) = 67.5, p < .001]. The data in Table 4.3 again show that dyadic inferences were more likely to be given for increases in commitment, but especially for rapid increases. In addition, 72% of the inferences for neglible increases or decreases were dyadic, suggesting that these kinds of inferences may operate in slow progressions and declines in commitment.

Social network inferences, by contrast, were connected to rapid and moderate decreases in commitment. Moreover, of the inferences mentioned for rapid increases, 19% were social network inferences. These findings indicate that beliefs about the network are more likely to be implicated in dramatic changes in commitment, especially when the change is a negative one. The distribution of intrapersonal/normative inferences on rate of change is somewhat similar to that for social network inferences. Reports of intrapersonal/normative inferences were most often associated with rapid downturns in commitment. It may be that as standards of suitability come into play, commitment declines because these standards act as thresholds against which the partner and the relationship are monitored.

Circumstantial inferences were more likely to be given for moderate changes in the chance of marriage. About 12% of the inferences for moderate increases, and 22% of those for moderate decreases, were circumstantial. Beliefs about life circumstances may have effects similar to social network inferences, but the impact on commitment of the former does not appear to be as strong as the impact of the latter. Participants' attributions about the state of affairs in their lives may affect commitment more indirectly than other kinds of inferences by setting the stage for other beliefs to take hold. For example, beliefs about occupational or educational circumstances may influence perceptions of the appropriate time for marriage or the quality of the interaction that transpires between partners.

Courtship Types and Inferences about Commitment

In other research based on data drawn from the same sample, Surra (in press) inquired as to whether partners in different types of courtship gave different kinds of reasons for why their commitment evolved as it did. According to the results of previous work (Surra, 1985), couples were assigned to four types of courtship based on variation in the shapes of their commitment graphs: (1) an accelerated type, in which graphs moved relatively smoothly and quickly to certainty of marriage (mean length of courtship = 14.2 months); (2) an accelerated-arrested type, in which the graphs progressed most rapidly of all the types to a high chance of marriage and then lost their momentum so that partners spent, on the average, nearly 60% of their courtship engaged (mean length of courtship = 13.6 months); (3) an intermediate type, in which females' graphs were typically more turbulent than their male counterparts, and the graphs generally took a somewhat slow ascent to asymptote (average length = 28.0 months); and (4) a prolonged type, in which courtships had an average length of 64.1 months and partners spent a comparatively large part of their courtship seriously dating but a short portion of it engaged (65% versus 22%, on the average).

Comparing the courtship types on the proportion of inferences made to the four categories revealed that partners in the accelerated type reported a higher proportion of intrapersonal/normative reasons for all turning points, and for upturns in particular, than partners in the other types. Partners in the prolonged type gave proportionately more circumstantial inferences than partners in the accelerated and intermediate types. There was also some indication that partners in the accelerated-arrested type gave more social network reasons, while those in the intermediate type reported more dyadic inferences for downturns in commitment, although these findings only approached significance.

These results were interpreted to mean that variation in participants' inferences about causality may contribute to variation in the way commitment develops. Accelerated relationships may move rapidly to marriage in part because partners are highly predisposed toward marriage in the first place, because they believe that the time is right for marriage, or because they are convinced that they have found a marriageable partner and relationship. In contrast, the development of commitment in prolonged relationships seems to be affected by partners' beliefs about their life circumstances. Given the fact that these partners usually met while they were still in high school, it is not surprising that changes in commitment might be influenced by their perceptions of their occupational, residential, and educational circumstances, and by other events outside of their control. Partners in intermediate courtships may have incongruent beliefs about the meaning of their interaction and their relationship, which affect downturns in commitment; progress in these relationships may result from the subsequent resolution of differences between partners. Finally, there is evidence that the initially rapid development of commitment in accelerated-arrested relationships is hampered by interaction with the social network and by partners' beliefs about this interaction (for further discussion of these patterns, see Surra, in press).

Reflections on Analyzing Explanations for Changes in Commitment: Toward a More Refined Coding Scheme

The results available so far from the classification of subjective inferences about why the probability of marriage changed were promising but underscored the need for more precise coding of inferences. A more refined measurement scheme would make it possible to draw

TABLE 4.4
The 19-Category Coding Scheme: Categories and Definitions

Coding Category	Definition
Intrapersonal/ Normative Inferences	
timing or social clock beliefs	a reference to an internalized belief that a particular stage or type of involvement is appropriate given either P's or O's age, education, occupation, or other life circumstance
standards for a suitable partner	an evaluation of the characteristics of the self or the partner against a preconceived standard for suitability or ideal
standards for a suitable relationship	an evaluation of the characteristics of the relationship against a preconceived standard for suitability or ideal
fear or attraction predispositions	a reference to P's or O's fear of or attraction to escalating the depth of involvement that is based upon preconceived beliefs about the qualities of premarital or marital relationships
Dyadic Inferences	
agreement on stage of involvement	a statement that describes an occasion or episode in which P and O together redefined their stage of involvement
conflict	a reference to any exchange of (or lack of) negative affect, tension, hostility, or fight between P and O on one or more occasions or over a period of time
self-disclosure	a statement about a particular interaction or episode when information with special meaning was (or was not) discussed or with new meaning was (or was not) expressed
behavioral interdependence	a reference to doing or planning to do activities or behaviors together; to change in the kinds of behaviors done together; or to spending or planning to spend time together (or not doing any of the above)
subjective interdependence	a statement in which a characteristic is attributed to O, P in relation to O, or the P-O relationship. The attribution may describe an emotional reaction, motive for behavior, personality characteristic, or quality of the relationship
behavioral-response interdependence	a reference to a transaction or episode in which P voluntarily and independently of O and of members of the social network performed some behavior or took an action that generated a behavioral response or an attribution on the part of O

(continued)

TABLE 4.4 Continued

Coding Category	Definition
Social Network Inferences	
P's behavioral interaction with social others	a reference to behaviors or activities done by one partner with any network member, except for other dating partners
P-O's behavioral interaction with social others	a reference to behaviors or activities done by P-O and any network member, except for other dating partners
others' behavioral interaction independent or P, O, or P-O	a statement about behaviors or activities done by members of the network independent of either partner or the dyad
involvement with alternative dating partner	a reference to a behavior performed with, an attribution about, or an anticipated involvement with an alternative dating partner
positive social comparison	a statement in which a positive attribution is made about O, P-O, or a network member that results from a comparison of the characteristics of O, P-O, or network member against those of a third party
negative social comparison	a statement in which a negative attribution is made about O, P-O, or a network member that results from a comparison of the characteristics of O, P-O, or network member against those of a third party
positive attribution	any statement of a positive attribution about P, O, or P-O interaction with the network or interaction among network members independent of P and O
negative attribution	any reference to a negative attribution about P, O, or P-O interaction with the network or interaction among network members independent of P and O
Circumstantial	any statement of an event, force, or institutional action that is external to either partner or their relationships with others, over which P and O have little control

NOTE: P refers to one partner, O the other, and P-O the dyad.

more definitive conclusions about the linkages between attributions and the growth of commitment. Consequently, a content analysis was performed on inferences gathered in the Surra (in press) study and on those obtained from 30-40 pilot interviews. The procedures used in the pilot interviews involved only slight modifications of those described here. A coding scheme was derived, with 19 subcategories of the original four and rules for coding and probing (Surra, 1984; see Table 4.4).

The expanded coding scheme has been used to gather data on inferences in two studies to date. In the first, retrospective reconstructions of courtship were obtained from 66 newlywed couples; in the second, 60 dating couples provided retrospective as well as concurrent reports using a modification of the graphing procedure. Although interviewers were thoroughly trained in the probing and coding rules, inferences are always recoded from audiotapes to improve accuracy. The data from both studies are now being recoded from audiotapes and analyzed; however, we would like to offer some preliminary observations about procedures and about subjective inferences that became apparent in conducting the interviews.

The codes in the 19-category scheme are mutually exclusive but not exhaustive. There are two kinds of inferences that are rare, but when they are mentioned, they are not coded. These are statements in which the respondent makes an attribution about the self or describes a behavior performed alone which did not involve or affect the partner or members of the network. In addition, there were cases in which the interviewer did not follow proper probing techniques and, therefore, an inference cannot be categorized from the audiotapes. The statement, "We got to know each other better," for example, fits more than one dyadic subcategory in its present form. These kinds of statements are not coded. Percentage agreement between independent coders for 64 randomly selected audiotapes averaged 90% and ranged from 54% to 100%. Percentage agreement is typically somewhat higher when agreement on "uncodables" is included in the calculation.

Although some authors have suggested that categorizing persons' reasons for why they do what they do is arbitrary (Locke & Pennington, 1982), our experience has been that respondents are careful to make fine distinctions among different kinds of inferences as captured by the code. For instance, one woman explained, "You can't pin the change on getting the job [circumstantial reason], but getting the job made it so I could think about marriage right then [timing or social clock inference]." It is common for respondents to ensure that interviewers are clear about reasons, as in this case: "No, it *wasn't* that I had a fight with the fellows at work [P's behavioral interaction with social others], but that I got *suspended* for it [circumstantial] that made the chance of marriage go down." The impression one gets from conducting interviews is that people have definite notions about their reasons for changes in commitment and that they are able to communicate them.

It became clear early on that respondents tend to explain why the probability of marriage changed in terms of causal chains and that these causal chains are sometimes long, complex, and consequential for respondents. One man said, for instance, "A conflict she had with her family was a big influence [P's behavioral interaction with social others] in that it led to our decision to live together [agreement on stage of involvement], which, in turn, led to our finding out we had similar routines and ways of doing things [subjective interdependence]." There is, of course, wide variation among respondents on the complexity and interconnectedness of their inferences. The probing and coding techniques being used at this time are aimed at measuring the degree and pattern of the interconnectedness of inferences. nectedness of inferences.

With regard to the kinds of inferences made by participants, especially as compared to those made by outsiders, some initial observations are apparent from consideration of Table 4.4. Although social scientists make attributions about the effects of culture on relationships, participants in relationships are presumably like "fish in water." Respondents vitually never make statements like, "Well, in this day and age, because of the women's movement and economic conditions, women are more career-minded. I was affected by that and not sure I wanted to marry." Instead, they give intrapersonal/normative reasons such as, "The whole idea of marriage was foreign to me then because I was concentrating on getting my career off the ground. I knew marriage would interfere with my career goals." Cultural influences on subjective inferences are indirect, shaping beliefs about the way things are or ought to be. Moreover, intrapersonal/normative reasons are constantly being modified through an ongoing socialization process. Respondents consistently report on what they learn from watching their parents and friends in relationships and from their own past experiences in relationships.

In terms of their analysis of the environment, respondents seem to be aware of two major sources of external influence—one social and the other circumstantial. Social scientists tend to assume that through interaction, network members exert a very direct and active influence on relationships. Although the behavioral-interaction subcategories of social network inferences demonstrate that participants make similar attributions, the remainder of the network subcategories underscore the more passive, but equally potent, effects that stem from respondents' psychological interconnectedness with members of their networks. As seen in the subcategories of positive and negative social comparison and of positive and negative attributions about the network, subjective inferences are often based on the anticipated or imagined reactions and characteristics of others. The study of subjective inferences emphasizes the internalization of network relationships.

The other kind of subjective inference about the environment—circumstantial—comprises a set of forces that have in common the fact that they are described in impersonal terms and as being beyond one's reach or influence. Although to the outside observer some circumstantial inferences, such as starting school or changing jobs, may appear to be the result of conscious decisions, the language used to talk about them conveys the idea that life deals out some events almost by happenstance. Instead of saying, for example, "He decided to take a job in a factory," respondents are much more likely to say, "He finally got a job in a factory." The content of other circumstantial reasons, such as references to luck, God, or coincidence, is more clearly stated in terms that communicate the participant's detachment from the forces that shape his or her decisions. Even though an outsider might view both circumstantial and network inferences as external, the content of these inferences communicates the interactive and psychological closeness of network members to participants, on the one hand, and their detachment from life circumstances on the other.

Of all the subcategories, those that are dyadic are probably the most similar to social scientists' inferences. In describing dyadic inferences, participants make reference to the same kinds of factors studied by researchers, such as falling in love, partners' believing that they share goals and are compatible, and spending time together. The major difference between the two points of view lies in the fact that participants often take a more discontinuous view of the influence of dyadic factors. It is common for participants to give accounts of isolated interactions and happenings that fit each of the dyadic subcategories. The method used to elicit inferences, in which respondents identified turning points as they became aware of them, may be partially responsible for inferences to singular dyadic events.

Conclusions

The aims of this chapter were to devise a framework for characterizing social transitions and to apply that framework to the transition to marriage using data we have gathered. In conclusion, we comment on the value of studying subjective inferences and offer some thoughts on the connections between subjective inferences and what transpires after the transition is made.

The investigation of participants' attributions has good potential for yielding information about the process by which persons consider and draw conclusions about their relationships and about attributional processes in general. For example, the study of intrapersonal/normative inferences may provide evidence on how prior experiences affect the formation of inferences and how these inferences, in turn, affect later involvements. Thus, for instance, persons who learn from past hurts that fidelity is the most important quality in a good partner may focus inordinate amounts of attention on seeking that quality in a spouse. Similarly, persons' descriptions of why the chance of marriage changed, some of which are intricate accounts of multiple, interconnected reasons, while others are more simplistic, are informative about individual differences in attributional style.

Although we presently have no evidence on the connections between subjective inferences about the transition to marriage and marital outcomes, we can speculate on this point. The accuracy of persons' subjective assessments about such things as the characteristics of their partner and their relationship, about what is important for a successful marriage, and about the reactions of third parties to the relationship is probably related to marital stability and to the ease with which an individual passes through the transition. By "accuracy," we mean the validity and comprehensiveness of subjective, as compared with objective, assessments.

Theoretically, commitment derives from both subjective and objective causes, and individuals differ in the extent to which they are mindful of the objective conditions that affect their level of commitment. Kelley (1983) argues that commitments formed as the result of a thorough, farsighted analysis of the conditions affecting permanence are likely to be more stable than those formed with little consideration, because of impulse or a temporary state of affairs. It is quite common, for example, for our participants to make an assessment that their partnership is highly compatible on activities and interests, but these judgments are probably more correct in some cases than others.

Applying this argument to the problem at hand, it is likely that the kinds of causes considered during the formation of marital commitment, as well as the validity and thoroughness of subjective assessments, are associated with the changeability of commitment after marriage. As discussed previously, research to date indicates that the kinds of objective causes that shape commitment premaritally are similar to those that affect commitment postmaritally. However, as our data show, some partners have reasons for marrying that have little to do with the objective conditions that actually promote stability. In addition, the processes underlying subjective assessments are probably quite different before and after the transition is made. Before marriage, many partners are highly motivated to make assessments of conditions that favor continuation of the relationship. As a result, participants' analyses of causal conditions may be quite different from those of an outsider. Dating partners, for example, are often adept at explaining away problem areas or ignoring difficulties in their relationships; at seeing qualities in the partner and the relationship that others cannot see; and at detecting stabilizing conditions but overlooking destabilizing ones. All of these processes may be central to the idealization that occurs during dating (Bolton, 1961; Waller, 1938).

Of course, there is always the possibility that the objective conditions necessary to promote stability are present without the partners' knowing it (Johnson, 1982; Kelley, 1983). Nevertheless, it is probably difficult to sustain inaccurate subjective assessments over the long run. As the objective evidence accumulates during the course of married life, and as spouses become less motivated to idealize their situation, they may change their initial assessments. Consequently, commitment will fluctuate as the balance is struck between objective and subjective reality.

REFERENCES

Bolton, C. D. (1961). Mate selection as the development of a relationship. *Marriage and Family Living, 23*, 234-340.

Braiker, H., & Kelley, H. H. (1979). Conflict in the development of close relationships. In R. Burgess & T. Huston (Eds.), *Social exchange in developing relationships* (pp. 135-168). New York: Academic Press.

Cate, R. M., Huston, T. L., & Nesselroade, J. R. (in press). Premarital relationships: Toward a typology of pathways to marriage. *Journal of Social and Clinical Psychology*.

Eidelson, R. J. (1980). Interpersonal satisfaction and level of involvement: A curvilinear relationship. *Journal of Personality and Social Psychology, 39*, 460-470.

Glick, P. C. (1984). Marriage, divorce, and living arrangements. *Journal of Family Issues, 5*, 7-26.

Hagestad, G. O., & Smyer, M. S. (1982). Dissolving long-term relationships: Patterns of divorce in middle age. In S. Duck (Ed.), *Personal relationships 4: Dissolving personal relationships* (pp. 155-187). London: Academic Press.

Harvey, J. H., Weber, A. L., Galvin, K. S., Huszti, H. G., & Garnick, N. N. (1986). Attribution in the termination of close relationships: A special focus on the account. In R. Gilmour & S. Duck (Eds.), *The emerging field of personal relationships*. Hillsdale, NJ: Erlbaum.

Harvey, J. H., Wells, G. L., & Alvarez, M. D. (1978). Attribution in the context of conflict and separation in close relationships. In J. H. Harvey, W. Ickes, & R. F. Kidd

(Eds.), *New directions in attribution research* (Vol. 2, pp. 235-260). Hillsdale, NJ: Erlbaum.

Hinde, R. A. (1979). *Towards understanding relationships.* London: Academic Press.

Huston, T. L., & Levinger, G. (1978). Interpersonal attraction and relationships. In M. R. Rosenzweig & L. W. Porter (Eds.), *Annual review of psychology* (Vol. 29, pp. 115-156). Palo Alto, CA: Annual Reviews.

Huston, T. L., Surra, C. A., Fitzgerald, N. M., & Cate, R. M. (1981). From courtship to marriage: Mate selection as an interpersonal process. In S. Duck & R. Gilmour (Eds.), *Personal relationships 2: Developing personal relationships* (pp. 53-88). London: Academic Press.

Johnson, M. P. (1978, October). *Personal and structural commitment: Sources of consistency in the development of relationships.* Paper presented at the National Council on Family Relation, Philadelphia.

Johnson, M. P. (1982). Social and cognitive features of the dissolution of commitment to relationships. In S. Duck (Ed.), *Personal relationships 4: Dissolving personal relationships* (pp. 51-73). London: Academic Press.

Johnson, M. P. (1984, July). *Courtship as the development of commitment to a relationship.* Paper presented at the International Conference on Personal Relationships, Madison, WI.

Johnson, M. P., & Leslie, L. (1982). Couple involvement and network structure: A test of the dyadic withdrawal hypothesis. *Social Psychological Quarterly, 45,* 34-43.

Kelley, H. H. (1979). *Personal relationships: Their structures and processes.* Hillsdale, NJ: Erlbaum.

Kelley, H. H. (1983). Love and commitment. In H. H. Kelley, E. Berscheid, A. Christensen, J. H. Harvey, T. L. Huston, G. Levinger, E. McClintock, L. A. Peplau, & D. R. Peterson (Eds.), *Close relationships* (pp. 265-314). New York: Freeman.

Kelley, H. H. (1986). Personal relationships: Their nature and significance. In R. Gilmour & S. Duck (Eds.), *The emerging field of personal relationships.* Hillsdale, NJ: Erlbaum.

Kelley, C., Huston, T. L., & Cate, R. M. (1985). Premarital relationship correlates of the erosion of satisfaction in marriage. *Journal of Social and Personal Relationships, 2,* 167-178.

Leslie, L. A., Johnson, M. P., & Huston, T. L. (1986). Parental reactions to dating relationships: Do they make a difference? *Journal of Marriage and the Family, 48,* 57-66.

Levinger, G. (1976). A social psychological perspective on marital dissolution. *Journal of Social Issues, 32,* 21-47.

Levinger, G. (1979). A social exchange view on the dissolution of pair relationships. In R. L. Burgess & T. L. Huston (Eds.), *Social exchange in developing relationships* (pp. 169-193). New York: Academic Press.

Lewis, R. A., & Spanier, G. (1979). Theorizing about the quality and stability of marriage. In W. R. Burr, R. Hill, F. I. Nye, & I. L. Reiss (Eds.), *Contemporary theories about the family: Research-based theories* (pp. 268-294). New York: Free Press.

Locke, D., & Pennington, D. (1982). Reasons and other causes: Their role in attribution processes. *Journal of Personality and Social Psychology, 42,* 212-223.

Milardo, R. M. (1982). Friendship networks in developing relationships: Converging and diverging social environments. *Social Psychology Quarterly, 45,* 162-172.

Milardo, R. M., Johnson, M. P., & Huston, T. L. (1983). Developing close relationships: Changing patterns of interaction between pair members and social networks. *Journal of Personality and Social Psychology, 44,* 964-976.

Newcomb, M. D. (1981). Heterosexual cohabitation relationships. In S. Duck & R. Gilmour (Eds.), *Personal relationships I: Studying personal relationships* (pp. 131-164). London: Academic Press.

Newman, H. (1981). Communication within ongoing intimate relationships: An attributional perspective. *Personality & Social Psychology Bulletin, 7,* 59-70.

Norton, A. J. (1983). Family life cycle: 1980. *Journal of Marriage and the Family, 45,* 267-275.

Rands, M. (1980). *Social networks before and after marital separation: A study of recently divorced persons.* Doctoral dissertation, University of Massachusetts. *Dissertation Abstracts International, 41,* 2828B.

Rapoport, R. (1973). The transition from engagement to marriage. In M. E. Lasswell & T. E. Lasswell (Eds.), *Love, marriage, family: A developmental approach* (pp. 250-258). Glenview, IL: Scott, Foresman.

Rapoport, R., & Rapoport, R. T. (1964). New light on the honeymoon. *Human Relations, 17,* 33-56.

Rosenblatt, P. C (1974). Cross-cultural perspective on attraction. In T. L. Huston (Ed.), *Foundations of interpersonal attraction* (pp. 79-95). New York: Academic Press.

Rosenblatt, P. C., & Unangst, D. (1974). Marriage ceremonies: An exploratory cross-cultural study. *Journal of Comparative Family Studies, 5,* 41-56.

Rubin, L. R. (1976). *Worlds of pain: Life in the working class family.* New York: Basic Books.

Rusbult, C. E. (1980). Commitment and satisfaction in romantic associations: A test of the investment model. *Journal of Experimental Social Psychology, 16,* 172-186.

Rusbult, C. E. (1983). A longitudinal test of the investment model: The development (and deterioration) of satisfaction and commitment in heterosexual involvements. *Journal of Personality and Social Psychology, 45,* 101-117.

Ryder, R. G., Kafka, J. S., & Olson, D. H. (1971). Separating and joining influences in courtship and early marriage. *American Journal of Orthopsychiatry, 41,* 450-464.

Saluter, A. F. (1983). Marital status and living arrangements: March, 1983. *Population Characteristics* (P-20, No. 389). Washington, DC: U.S. Bureau of the Census.

Spanier, G. B. (1983). Married and unmarried cohabitation in the United States: 1980. *Journal of Marriage and the Family, 45,* 277-288.

Surra, C. A. (1980) *Turning point coding manual I.* Unpublished manuscript, University of Illinois at Urbana-Champaign, Department of Human Development and Family Ecology.

Surra, C. A. (1984). *Turning point coding manual II.* Unpublished manuscript, University of Illinois at Urbana-Champaign, Department of Human Development and Family Ecology.

Surra, C. A. (1985a). Courtship types: Variations in interdependence between partners and social networks. *Journal of Personality and Social Psychology, 49,* 357-375.

Surra, C. A. (in press). Reasons for changes in commitment: Variations by courtship type. *Journal of Social and Personal Relationships.*

Surra, C. A., & Cate, R. M. (1984, October). *Developmental variation in families: Theoretical and methodological issues.* Paper presented at the National Council on Family Relations Preconference Workshop on Theory Construction and Research Methodology, San Francisco.

U. S. Bureau of the Census (1983). *Statistical abstracts of the United States: 1984* (104th edition). Washington, DC: Author.

Van Gennep, A. (1960). *The rites of passage* (M. B. Vizedom & G. L. Caffee, Trans.). Chicago: University of Chicago Press. (Original work published 1908)

Waller, W. (1938). *The family: A dynamic interpretation*. New York: Gordon.

Weiss, R. S. (1975). *Marital separation*. New York: Basic Books.

PART II

The Dynamics of Relationships

The present section is particularly concerned with intimacy in loving relationships, defined to include long-term, committed sexual partnerships as well as marriage. The section explores the communicative and interpretative bases of intimacy that lie behind the experience of long-term commitment and satisfaction, although the chapters deal mostly with unsatisfactory relationships.

Buunk and Bringle consider the issue of jealousy in long-term relationships and propose a new definition of the phenomenon that takes account of the cognitive work that goes into the emotion as well as the communicative elements, the situational factors, and individual differences. Taking similar themes, Baucom's chapter on marital attributions in distressed relationships also ask some searching questions about the circumstances in which partners make attributions, the structure and form of the attributions, their purposes in distressed relationships, and their role in marital adjustment.

Noller considers the role that nonverbal communication plays in informing partners about their relationship with one another. She addresses the question of whether happy couples are better able to understand one another than are distressed couples. She finds considerable and interesting differences in the accuracy of decoding nonverbal messages by spouses in happy and unhappy marriages, especially insofar as it concerns comparative differences between the two sexes.

As a whole, this section gives us several new insights into intimacy and its dependence not only on the cognitive work of the partners but also on the communicative skills that contribute to their understanding of one another and their intimate activity.

5

Jealousy in Love Relationships

BRAM BUUNK
ROBERT G. BRINGLE

Jealousy has been widely acknowledged as one of the most prevalent and potentially destructive emotions within love relationships. In the world's literature—Shakespeare's Othello, for instance—the encompassing nature and tragic consequences of jealousy are often elaborated upon. In both research and therapy, jealousy has been found to be a serious marital problem. Jealous behavior may have morbid consequences; spousal killing and physical abuse, for example, have in many cases been related to jealousy (Faulk, 1977; Gelles, 1972; Mowat, 1966).

Despite its ubiquity and potentially violent character, jealousy has not been a prime topic of research and theory in social psychology. Furthermore, most previous studies have dealt with either the personality and relationship variables related to this emotion—such as self-esteem and dependency—or with the affective and behavioral responses characteristic of jealousy (for a review, see Bringle & Buunk, 1985). Social psychological theorizing on this topic is still scarce. Nevertheless, there are many important questions to be answered, including: What exactly is jealousy? Why are some types of extramarital relationships innocuous while others evoke rage? Why do some individuals and relationships seem immune from jealousy? What is the role of cognitive factors in mediating jealous reactions?

Using existing research on jealousy and social psychological

AUTHORS' NOTE: This chapter was largely prepared while the second author was a visiting scholar at the Department of Social Psychology of the University of Nijmegen. It was facilitated by a travel grant to the first author from the Netherlands Organization for the Advancement of Pure Research (Z.W.O.) and by a Fulbright Scholarship to this author spent at the University of California, Los Angeles. We thank Hedy Kleyweg Buunk for her editorial assistance.

theories and concepts, this chapter is intended as a first step toward an analysis of the jealous response. We present a definition of jealousy and explain and elaborate the elements of this definition. Additionally, some of the possible cognitive processes involved in jealousy are discussed, and, lastly, an analysis is made of the coping processes involved in jealousy.

The Nature of Jealousy: A Definition and Elaboration

Jealously has been referred to as a Rorschach word, since it evokes a rich variety of images and associations and means different things to different people (Clanton & Smith, 1977). Individuals experience and express their jealousy in different ways (Bryson, 1976). In addition, there are important differences in the stimuli evoking jealousy (Bringle, Renner, Terry, & Davis, 1983). Furthermore, while it is likely that most people think of jealousy as the painful reaction to a partner's interest in someone else, for some individuals jealousy is primarily the feeling of envying someone else for his or her material possessions, achievements, or characteristics. Another way in which the meaning of jealousy varies is the extent to which one uses the word to refer to a particular emotion or to a stable personality characteristic.

It is quite possible that several types of jealousy can be distinguished, differing in emotional and behavioral manifestations, in perceptions and interpretations, in the stimuli evoking these responses, and in stability over time. However, we limit our discussion to those types that fit the following definition: *Jealousy is an aversive emotional reaction evoked by a relationship involving one's current or former partner and a third person. This relationship may be real, imagined, or expected, or may have occurred in the past.* The various elements of this definition and the considerations behind them, as well as some of their consequences, will be elaborated in what follows.

Aversion

Jealous reactions are unpleasant responses that, in general, are neither sought nor desired. Jealousy is not being described here as a specific type of emotional experience; it may be experienced in divergent ways. Feeling betrayed, angry, afraid, resentful, depressed, aggressive, or inferior are only a few of the emotions that may occur as part of the jealous response (e.g., Bryson, 1976; Buunk, 1984;

Clanton & Smith, 1977; Hupka, 1981). There is some evidence that jealousy is relatively distant from certain aversive emotions, including fear, powerlessness, and shame, yet closely linked to others, such as anger, disgust, contempt, and suspicion (Buunk, Bringle, & Arends, 1984).

In addition to aversive responses, the person may concurrently experience relief, joy, or even competence or pride as a result of the partner's behavior (Buunk, 1981). These reactions are experientially separate from the negative feelings. It must therefore be emphasized that a person's reaction cannot simply be described on a continuum varying from "happy" to "upset" but will often include positive and negative emotions simultaneously.

Emotional Reaction

While jealousy in general has a behavioral manifestation (e.g., physical aggression) and a cognitive aspect (e.g., obsessive thoughts), it is the *emotional* component that is viewed here as necessary and sufficent for defining the jealous reaction. We conceive of jealousy as a primary, direct, affective response that often occurs with a minimal amount of cognitive work and despite rational or conscious decisions and interpretations. Reports on the so-called "jealous flash" (Clanton & Smith, 1977) illustrate that affect and cognition are partially independent processes, such that one can have an affective response prior to conscious cognitive activity (Leventhal, 1980; Zajonc, 1980). Most of the significant cognitive "work" follows the initial affective reaction and colors the emotional experience in a specific way. In this sense, cognitive strategies will not prevent jealousy, as such, but can modify its development, course, and consequences.

Current or Former Partner

Jealousy can occur in different types of relationships—between business associates, friends, family members, and lovers. All of these relationships can be close in the sense indicated by Kelley, Berscheid, Christensen, Harvey, Huston, Levinger, McClintock, Peplau, and Peterson (1983): characterized by strong, frequent, and diverse interdependency that lasts over a considerable period of time. The necessity of some degree of interdependency is assumed here in order for the other to evoke jealousy; when two people are not at all interdependent, the behavior of one will not affect the behavior of the other. By using the word "partner," we refer in particular to marital and other committed love relationships, in which the level of interdependency is generally higher than in any other type of bond. Jealousy is therefore more likely to occur and to be more intense than in other relationships. In our definition we do not speak only of current but also former partners. Even though a relationship has ceased to exist, emotional attachment to another can continue for a substantial period of time (see Kitson, 1982), and intense jealousy can arise. Little research has been done on jealousy in relation to former lovers or spouses, but given the continued attachment in the first period after a divorce (see Weiss, 1975), one would expect jealousy to be a rather common phenomenon during this time.

If no prior or actual relationship exists, then the situation is one of rivalry. The latter occurs when two persons are attempting to establish a relationship with a third person when neither has a prior existing relationship. If it is someone else's relationship, then envy exists, in which case the envious person begrudges another person's relationship to some other person or possession. Jealousy is thus a three-person situation in which the partner's relationship with the third person has objectionable implications for the jealous person.

Evoked by a Relationship

The term "relationship" is used here to denote some level of dependency. If the partner is unilaterally dependent on positive outcomes from another relationship (the other person's outcomes are not influenced by the relationship), or if the partner and the other person are both dependent on the relationship in that the outcomes of both are positively affected by the interaction, then, from the point of view of the jealous person, an extradyadic relationship exists for the partner. It must be emphasized that such a relationship does not necessarily evoke jealousy. This will only occur when the partner's behavior in such a case is appraised as threatening.

Real or Imagined

Although most social psychologists have focused on jealousy as being provoked by some actual interaction or relationship between the partner and a third person, jealousy can also arise out of suspicion or mistrust, even when no actual rival is known to exist. Clinicians are well aware that in extreme cases, such an attitude takes the form of delusional or paranoid jealousy (i.e., the person is convinced of the partner's infidelity and is constantly on the lookout for evidence to "prove" their infidelity). This type of pathological jealousy must be distinguished from obsessive jealousy, in which there is no severe distortion of reality but the person is nevertheless plagued with recurrent doubts about the partner's infidelity (see Hoaken, 1976). In either case, the emotional reaction to the mistrust is real and constitutes a jealous response.

Expected

Another relationship may not yet exist, but the partner's dissatisfaction may imply the expectancy for the development of one. Dissatisfaction, however, does not evoke jealousy per se, except when there is the real possibility of the partner becoming involved in an additional relationship. If, for example, as a result of dissatisfaction with the marital relationship the partner begins going to singles bars, or expresses the desire to have an open marriage, or to "swing," then the partner's behavior implies a real potential for extramarital relationships, one that may result in jealousy.

Has Occurred in the Past

Jealousy can arise because of one partner's past love relationships, especially if the partner talks favorably about a former lover or shows pictures of him or her. These former relationships will generally not constitute a threat in the sense that the other person may replace the relationship. They are probably more often threatening to the exclusivity of the relationship in the sense that they give rise to the feeling that the partner has shared certain previous intimacies and experiences with others or continues to have a particular type of relationship from which one is excluded (e.g., the joint parenthood one has with a former spouse or a kind of special friendship that has developed over the years).

Assessment of Threat to the Relationship

The jealous reaction starts with an individual's immediate, largely unconscious assessment of the partner's behavior as threatening. However, once the emotion has arisen, processes that are more deliberate will come into play. Jealous individuals will try to evaluate the degree to which the particular extradyadic behavior of the partner constitutes a threat to the relationship. They will attempt to obtain a more precise and clear idea of what is really going on and to get an estimate of the implications of the partner's behavior.

To be more specific, we suppose that the jealous person will try to assess (1) the immediate losses being incurred as a result of the behavior and (2) the implications the behavior has for the future rewards and losses in the relationship by analyzing the motives for his or her partner's behavior. It is assumed here that the intensity of jealousy is influenced by both assessments, as well as by personality characteristics, such as neuroticism, and relational factors, including dependency and insecurity.

Assessing Threats Due to Contemporaneous Losses

There have been several theoretical analyses of immediate losses experienced when jealous. Clanton and Smith (1977) state that the two basic factors defining a behavior as threatening are the feeling of being excluded and the fear of losing one's partner. Mazur (1977) makes a distinction between five types of jealousy, all of which represent a different kind of threat: (1) *possessive* jealousy, characterized by the perception that one's property rights are being violated; (2) *exclusion* jealousy, being left out of a loved one's important experiences; (3) *competitive* jealousy, competing with the partner as the result of feeling inadequate; (4) *egotistical* jealousy, stemming from the inability to expand one's ego awareness and role flexibility; and (5) *fearful* jealousy, the fear of being lonely or rejected. Based primarily on clinical work with jealousy, Constantine (1976) suggests that jealousy always involves the perception that some valued aspect of the relationship has been lost (e.g., face or status, need gratification, control, predictability, territory, or amount of time spent with the partner).

These analyses principally refer to the immediate losses experienced in a relationship as the result of one partner's extradyadic behavior. However, little work has been done on empirically verifying these delineations and assessing the relative importance and frequency of the different kinds of losses experienced. Buunk's (1980, 1981) research has explicitly attempted to test some of these theoretical ideas. In this work, all respondents had a partner who had been involved in at least one extramarital sexual relationship during the past two years. Respondents were presented with a number of different perceptions and were asked to respond with respect to the most significant extramarital relationship that their partner had had in the past and to their partner's extramarital sexual involvement in general.

Elaborating on some of the findings of this work, we propose the following immediate losses as particularly salient in jealousy:

Inequality. Feelings of inequality will sometimes play a role in the experience of jealous individuals. In Buunk's (1980, 1981) work, some subjects indicated that they felt upset because their partner had had an extramarital affair while they themselves did not have such a relationship or had never had one. In line with our earlier definition, these people were envying their partner's "asset" (i.e., an extramarital affair). They compared their own outcomes with those of the partner, who was obviously perceived as getting relatively more outcomes. As has been emphasized by many theorists, people will often evaluate a partner's behavior against a general notion that there should be a fair or even distribution of outcomes in the relationship.

Some additional evidence for the operation of principles of equality in the area of extramarital behavior comes from another study by Buunk (1982) conducted on three different samples. This study showed high negative correlations between one's own intention to engage in several types of extramarital sexual and erotic behavior and anticipated jealousy if the partner would indulge in the same behavior. Obviously, considerations of reciprocity and equality lead people to adjust their own extramarital intentions to their ability to tolerate similar behavior from their partner, and vice versa; people seem to feel that it is not justified to react jealously to a spouse's specific behavior when they want the freedom to exhibit the same behavior themselves.

Loss of Self-esteem. To a large degree, jealousy is competitive in nature. The person who notices that his or her partner is attracted to a third person is likely to see that person as a rival. He or she will then experience a sense of competition, vying for the exclusive love and attention of the partner. Knowing that the partner is attracted to this person will make the rival a very salient target for social comparison: the jealous person can hardly escape comparing his or her own qualities with those of the rival. Two drives for social comparison that have been distinguished in the literature—the *hedonic* drive and the *adaptive* drive (Brickman & Bulman, 1977)—can both play a role. First, people probably hope to discover that the other is inferior to them, thus enhancing their self-esteem. On the other hand, when the other is seen as superior, the self-esteem is lowered. Second, they want to assess what the other is like in order to be able to cope with the situation.

A study by Buunk et al. (1984) showed that threats to the self-esteem were manifested especially when the rival was seen as superior in sexual abilities. Other qualities, such as social skills or being an interesting personality, were much less important. Among women, there was also competition in professional capacities and physical attractiveness. There are probably several reasons why sexual competition is so prevalent in jealousy. First, most people in our culture have had only a few sexual partners before their marriage (Hunt, 1974), mostly with people who also had a limited experience in this respect. Hence, it is difficult to obtain reliable feedback about one's capacities as a sexual partner and to acquire a sense of confidence that one can meet the the sexual needs of partners with different sexual make-ups. Second, nearly all sexual contact occurs in privacy in dyadic relationships, so a direct comparison of oneself versus others in this area is difficult. These (and other) factors make the sexual realm very sensitive to insecurity and competition.

Loss of self-esteem can also occur for other reasons. In some cases, people can feel upset because their partner feels attracted to an unattractive person (Bryson, 1977). One explanation for this effect is based on balance theory (Heider, 1958). It is particularly aversive to be associated with someone who displays bad taste and is not very discriminating. A second explanation for this effect refers to the attributions being made by the jealous person. Specifically, it is upsetting to realize that the partner is attracted to someone who does not seem to have very favorable qualities. This can lead to the inference that the partner must really be vulnerable, inclined, and predisposed to engaging in extradyadic relationships, since the threshold needed to evoke the behavior seems so low.

Violation of Specialness. Despite the role the processes just described play in the experience of jealousy, the most upsetting factor is probably the violation of specialness. Jealousy will, in general, occur because the partner's behavior threatens one or more of the following closely interrelated aspects of the relationship: (1) the degree of *exclusivity*—certain experiences, feelings, thoughts, and activities are desired to be shared only with the partner and are not open to outsiders; (2) the degree of *togetherness*—one wants a certain amount of time spent together and a certain degree of attention from the partner; (3) the degree of *superiority*—one wishes the experiences in the relationship to be better than elsewhere. Lewin (1948, pp. 99-100) made some remarks on jealousy that have bearing on this theme, especially on the first two issues:

> It is understandable, from the great amount of overlapping regions and from the tendency of love to be all-inclusive, that emotional jealousy may be easily aroused if the relation between two persons is very close. The intimate relation of one partner to a third person not only makes the second partner "lose" the first one, but the second partner will have, in addition, the feeling that something of his [or her] own intimate life is thrown open to a third person. . . . The relation of the partner to the third person is felt as a breach in the barrier between one's intimate life and the public.

Buunk's (1980, 1981) study confirms the importance of these experiences in jealousy. The three perceptions that stood out were the idea of getting less attention than before, the perception that the partner enjoyed certain things more with another person, and the feeling of exclusion from the partner's activities. Within the total Gestalt of these perceptions, there also fits a somewhat less often endorsed statement of not liking the idea that one was no longer the only one for the partner.

Loss of Partner. Many theorists suppose that the fear of losing the partner is a central feature of jealousy (e.g., Bohm, 1960; Clanton & Smith, 1977; Miller & Siegel, 1972; Shibles, 1974). This is probably indeed the case in the earlier phases of a relationship, when one is not yet sure of the other's commitment. In addition, it constitutes a central factor when one feels unilaterally dependent on the relationship and perceives the other as having a higher "comparison level for alternatives" than oneself (White, 1981b). In such a situation, one considers the possibility of loss likely, coupled with the feeling that one has a lot to lose.

Nevertheless, the fear of loss is not always the central factor in jealousy. In the study by Buunk (1980, 1981) where all subjects were aware of their partner's behavior, this fear turned out to be of minor importance. Why did this perception play a relatively unimportant role among these subjects? For one, it could be the consequence of their ideology concerning extramarital relationships, leading them to believe that such relationships could or should be an addition to instead of a replacement for the relationship (see Buunk, 1980; Knapp, 1976). Second, these people may have learned that their partner's extramarital involvement did not mean that their partner was planning to leave the relationship.

Future Losses: Analyzing the Motives for Behavior

In addition to the manner in which jealousy has disrupted the current state of the relationship, the behavior also has implications for future losses in the relationship. Assessments of these losses are speculative for the jealous person; however, their consequences for his or her attitude toward the relationship are quite real. The basic question that has a bearing on this assessment is, Why did the partner engage in the jealousy-evoking behavior? Buunk's (1978) research shows that virtually everyone who is jealous is compelled to identify causes for their partner's behavior. However, only a few studies have attempted to identify and examine the motives of the partner. White (1981a) used both judges' ratings and a factor analysis to identify the following four motives: sexual attraction, nonsexual attraction, dissatisfction with the relationship, and desire for greater commitment. Only commitment failed to produce significant correlations on measures of the subject's jealousy, the partner's jealousy, perceived threat in the relationship, or anger with hypothetical jealousy-evoking incidents. Buunk (1984) found that the intensity of jealousy was positively correlated with variations in the perception that the partner's behavior was due to deficiencies in the marital relationship and to aggressive intentions on the part of the partner.

Although these studies describe lists of motives that may relate to perceptions of losses threatening the future of the relationship, there has been no theoretical integration available. Due to the nature of the underlying question posed by the jealous person, we feel that attribution theory can provide this needed conceptual integration.

Research by Kelley and his associates (Kelley, 1979; Orvis, Kelley, & Butler, 1976; Passer, Kelley, & Michela, 1978) suggests that people will interpret and evaluate a partner's behavior from two perspectives: first, the extent to which it manifests a positive or negative attitude toward them; and second, the stability of the behavior. Concerning the first dimension, it is clear that extradyadic relationships are seldom engaged in for the benefit of the partner. To the contrary, it is painful for one to realize that a partner is seeking other rewarding relationships at the expense of or with disregard for the interdependencies within the current relationship. Although there are possible exceptions to this discussion, such as open marriages or "swinging," the overwhelming majority of cases indicate that the partner's behavior is assumed by the jealous person to show the lack of a positive attitude by the partner for at least some aspect of the current relationship. The attitude may be seen as merely reflecting disinterest, or it may be viewed as much more negative, indicating dissatisfaction, antagonism, or aggression. Subsequent aspects of the attribution process will determine the degree of negativity of the inferred attitude and, thus, to what extent future losses are anticipated.

The second dimension—stability—will help determine what inferences the jealous person constructs from the partner's behavior. In general, we hypothesize that stable attributions will be more threatening than unstable attributions, assuming that, in jealousy, stable attributions will typically be negative. Thus, viewing the partner's behavior as being triggered by an unusual situation or an atypical mood (unstable attributions) will be accompanied by less jealousy than attributing the extradyadic behavior to the partner's selfishness or lack of self-control (stable attributions).

One of the reasons that stable attributions are more threatening than unstable attributions is that they imply chronicity. When past behaviors are assumed to imply future behaviors, it is particularly upsetting to learn that the behavior causing the current loss in outcomes can be expected to occur in the future. This is one reason why learning about a past affair is upsetting to a person, as it means that the behavior and subsequent losses could continue to occur. One might argue that it is easier for someone to adapt to predictable, rather than to unpredictable, events; however, most people are probably unable or unwilling to adapt to regularly incurring losses in a relationship due to a partner's extradyadic behavior.

Stability can also imply a lack of control. The jealous person may feel less able to change the situation or, more specifically, the partner when a stable, rather than unstable, attribution is made. Thus, if the conclusion is that the partner is someone who is easily flattered, this is more of a threat to the future of the relationship than if the behavior were attributed to a transient cause, such as not having given the partner enough love and attention lately. The individual's track record within a relationship with a particular partner will be important in determining the stability of the attributions made. If a partner has consistently engaged in extradyadic behavior during the relationship and in past relationships, then the behavior shows high consistency (and maybe low distinctiveness), and stable attributions are likely. If, however, after a long history of fidelity an initial extradyadic relationship occurs, then the situation is, at this point, highly ambiguous.

The jealous individual does not know whether, given the history of fidelity, the incident is an isolated event (an unstable attribution) or whether it represents a significant change in the partner and, therefore, warrants a new stable attribution.

This situation can lead to feeling a lack of ability to predict future behavior, as well as a lack of perceived control. If the partner had once been involved in an extradyadic relationship but had since demonstrated fidelity over a long period of time, then a stable, positive attribution becomes possible, as the incident can then be attributed to unstable causes. This is possible if the incident can be viewed as an isolated event attributable to atypical circumstances. The situation also suggests some level of control by both the partner and the jealous individual in that they are successfully avoiding similar incidents. The longer the period of renewed fidelity, the greater the sense of control and predictability. The couple may never, however, attain the level of trust that existed prior to the extradyadic relationship.

A third dimension to be proposed here is the level of personalism (Jones & Davis, 1965) or ego involvement implied by attributions. The dimension of personalism is relevant to the attributional task of finding explanations for the partner's behavior because of its implications for the jealous person's self-esteem and self-concept. The most personal attribution would occur if, for example, the jealous individual concluded that the partner's extradyadic behavior took place as a result of the jealous person's deficiencies. This could be a stable attribution, signifying that the person lacks the qualities necessary to satisfy the partner. However, it could also be an unstable attribution, assuming that negligence or lack of effort resulted in the partner's behavior but supposing that this can be altered in the future. Nevertheless, what is of crucial importance is the degree to which one considers oneself responsible for the partner's jealousy-evoking behavior. For example, it has been found that in traditional marriages, women often blame themselves for their husband's infidelities (see Safilios-Rothschild, 1969). In modern marriages people may also feel responsible for problems within the relationship that may have instigated their partner to look for affection or sexual gratification elsewhere. It seems likely that one is relatively reluctant to express too much jealousy when there is self-blame, and one may feel relatively more motivated to improve the relationship. In general, the more dependent one feels on the relationship, the more likely that one will put the responsibility for the event on one's own shoulders (Buunk, 1978; White, 1981b).

A less personal attribution would be that there is nothing wrong with oneself but that the relationship, for whatever reasons, is not working and that this caused the extradyadic behavior. To blame the partner would be even less personal, except that blaming the partner is nearly always blaming oneself because one did choose this partner and maintain a relationship with him or her. To be able to blame the incident on idiosyncratic circumstances would be the least threatening attribution.

Generally speaking, the more ego-involving and personal the attributions become, the more negative the subsequent implications. Negative-reflected appraisals, particularly from significant others who have had frequent contact with the person (e.g., a romantic partner), are especially likely to provide a threat to the self-concept (see Schlenker, 1980, p. 63). The stronger the intimacy has been within the relationship, the more intense this threat will be. Thus, to conclude that your partner engaged in the extradyadic behavior because he or she considers you unattractive or overweight is more negative than to attribute it to a relationship deficiency. The partner's dissatisfaction with you as a person conveys a threat to your self-esteem and jeopardizes the outcomes from the relationship. The severely negative implications of attributions to the self will often be transformed into attributions to the relationship, partner, or circumstances.

Bringle et al. (1984) tested these predictions by presenting the following situation to unmarried subjects: "You suspect your partner might express a desire to spend some more time with the opposite sex because your partner ... " Based on the previous hypotheses, 15 different reasons for this occurrence were provided (five levels of ego involvement: me, us, you, other person, and circumstances and three levels of stability: high, moderate, and low). The findings indicate that highly stable attributions were perceived as more threatening than those moderate and low in stability. Attributions citing the cause for the partner's behavior as "me" or "us" were perceived as more threatening than when the partner's behavior was attributed to the partner or to circumstances.

Relational Factors Affecting the Assessment of Threat

The tendency to react with jealousy in a particular situation, and to be concerned with finding an explanation for the partner's behavior, depends in part on such personality characteristics as low self-esteem, arousability, anxiety, and repression-sensitization (e.g., Bringle & Williams, 1981; Buunk, 1981; Jaremko & Lindsey, 1979; Mathes, Roter, & Joerger, 1982). Despite the obvious importance of such variables, in this section we focus only on some of the temporary and permanent characteristics of the relationship that make the occurrence of jealousy more likely and its experience more intense.

Kinsey, Pomeroy, Martin, & Gebhard (1953) reported that as the length of the marriage increased, the respondents were less threatened by their spouse's extramarital involvements. Buunk (1980) also found jealousy to be negatively correlated with the length of the relationship. While it is possible that these findings merely indicate that people get less jealous as they get older (Constantine & Constantine, 1973), we suggest that these data indicate that jealousy is in part evoked by insecurity as to the degree that the partner is committed to the relationship and feels attracted to his or her spouse (see Berscheid & Fei, 1977). As Duck and Sants (1983, p. 37) eloquently note, "One of the great human dilemmas appears to be the problem of deciding how much real affection a partner has for oneself."

In general, insecurity stemming from this dilemma will diminish as the length of the relationship increases and one learns that the partner is willing to remain in the relationship despite any problems and conflicts that arise. However, in the first stages of the relationship, insecurity will often be quite prevalent, especially when one has started to become emotionally involved in the relationship, to take risks and to show vulnerability and dependency, but when a clear commitment has not yet been made by the other. Research by Braiker and Kelley (1979) indicates that people in these stages not only experience feelings of insecurity about the partner's commitment but also about their own. Buunk's (1980) finding that cohabiting women reacted more jealously than married women can be interpreted to mean that, for the former group, insecurity about the partner's commitment is higher and that getting married contributes to a feeling of security in the relationship. For men, this factor was not at all related to jealousy. This could indicate that marriage does not provide the kind of security for men that it offers women. It could also mean that among men, other factors indicate security or that jealousy for them is not at all related to security about the partner's commitment.

Insecurity is not limited to the first phase of the relationship. Even when the partner has made a clear commitment to get married, or when a couple is actually married, insecurity on an emotional level can still exist, especially regarding the other's intention to put real effort into the relationship or to pursue the kind and degree of exclusivity that one desires. As Duck and Sants (1983) point out, in relationships that have developed further, there may still exist uncertainty about the stability of the other's feelings and about the future of the union. The development of an emotional sense of security and confidence in a relationship probably requires years of exposure to the partner, and in the first years of a relationship, even when one is married, insecurity will be relatively high and people may feel easily threatened when their partner feels attracted to someone else. Furthermore, insecurity can exist in all phases of a relationship to the extent that lack of perceived control over events exists. As noted earlier, it is likely that this factor is related to jealousy.

A second variable relevant to jealousy is emotional dependency. People who are relatively dependent on a relationship will be more inclined to react with jealousy when their partner shows interest in someone else. As conceived here, emotional dependency has two components that are closely related but conceptually different. One component concerns the number of actual or potential alternative sources of satisfaction and fulfillment outside of the relationship. For example, someone who has no outside job or only a few friends (actual sources of satisfaction), or someone who has the feeling that it is unlikely that he or she will find a partner as attractive as the current partner (potential source of satisfaction) is more dependent on the relationship than someone for whom the opposite is true. A second aspect of dependency concerns the emotional involvement in the relationship, reflected by the degree to which a person is emotionally affected by the partner's actions. Emotional involvement partially develops concurrently with the process of commitment to a relationship in which the partners develop a history of positive interaction and shared memories, make "irretrievable investments," show their vulnerability and reveal their dependency to each other, and link the relationship to their personal identities (Kelley, 1983). Personality factors play a role in this process. For example, some neurotic individuals may become anxiously detached and overinvolved, having problems with their own and their partner's autonomy. In contrast, others may become compulsively independent, trying to avoid closeness and intimacy.

Whatever the roots of emotional dependency in a relationship, it will make the occurrence of jealousy more likely—first because one feels that one has a lot to lose, and second because such dependency will make one more sensitive to any of the partner's actions. A high degree of emotional dependency does not necessarily mean, however, that the relationship is characterized by the frequent occurrence of strong emotions. Such relationships can function quite smoothly, provided that the partners coordinate their behavior to a high degree. If one partner interrupts this interdependent pattern of behavior by becoming involved with someone else, a response similar to a divorce will occur, as detailed by Berscheid (1983, p. 145)—namely, the thus far hidden interdependencies are unmasked "to wreak their emotional vengeance upon the individual." The person then becomes aware of his or her emotional involvement in the relationship.

Several studies underline the importance of dependency for understanding the occurrence of jealousy. In particular, it has been suggested that relative dependency vis-a-vis the partner is of crucial importance. White (1981b) has identified perceived inadequacy and the perception of differences in relative involvement as independently influencing vigilance, worrying, and jealousy. The components of relative involvement in the relationship identify contextual elements influencing a particular behavior as threatening. For example, differences in physical attractiveness or perceptions of differences in effort (White, 1981b) are background factors heightening the suspiciousness, vigilance, and appraisals of a particular behavior as threatening. One's dependency in an absolute sense, regardless of the partner's involvement in the relationship, has also been found to be related to jealousy (Buunk, 1981).

Coping with the Jealousy-Evoking Event:
The Role of Impression Management

It is not always clear which activity or sequence of activities elicited by a jealousy-evoking situation should be defined as coping strategies. We want to differentiate between jealousy and coping strategies by maintaining that in general, jealousy should be limited to the emotional responses, while coping strategies refer to cognitive and behavioral responses that are goal-directed attempts to change or influence the self, the partner, the relationship, or the situation. Such strategies are not limited to deliberate, conscious attempts to modify the threat inherent in the situation. Nonverbal reactions, such as sighing or muscular tension, are examples of nonconscious behavioral responses which at times may be instrumental as a coping strategy. Furthermore, coping strategies are not necessarily confined to those activities represented externally and visibly to others. For example, redefinition, cognitive reappraisal, and some defense mechanisms are purely cognitive processes often seen as part of coping strategies.

In the following section, we do not present an extensive review of the literature on coping (see Bringle & Buunk, 1985) but elaborate instead on an analysis of how a couple copes with a jealousy-evoking event. This is primarily done from an impression management perspective borrowing from the work of Schlenker (1980). We deal with some of the psychological dynamics of self-esteem maintenance for both partners. This is followed by a look into the possible interaction of both partners' strategies in a relationship.

Psychological Dynamics of Impression Management

The occurrence of jealousy may, using Schlenker's (1980 terminology, constitute a predicament insofar as it can potentially damage a person's self-concept and the image portrayed to others. The degree to which the jealous person will be concerned with impression management—to maintain or enhance the self-concept or to prevent further erosion of it—will depend on several factors. First, the severity of the event is assumed to increase to the degree that the jealous person and others who have knowledge of the event consider the jealous person responsible for the predicament. As Hupka (1981) points out, it is much more common for the blame or attribution of responsibility to be shouldered by the partner who evoked the jealousy. However, what can occur is that the jealous person assumes some blame for the incident, either through global association (Heider, 1958; Schlenker, 1980; Shaw & Sulzer, 1964) or through the attribution of more direct responsibility (e.g., not investing enough in the relationship).

Second, the severity of the jealousy-evoking event as a predicament depends on the degree to which it has undesirable implications for the jealous person—that is, if the event draws into question the person's image as an adequate mate. Both the attribution of responsibility and the undesirable implications for the self are consistent with the personalism or ego-involvement dimension previously posited in analyzing threat.

In addition to concern for the self-esteem highlighted by Schlenker's theory, the jealous person can also be concerned with maintaining or improving the quality of the relationship (Rodgers & Bryson, 1978) and with reducing and handling the jealous feelings. However, the assumption is made here that all of these attempts will be moderated by concerns of impression management to maintain or enhance the individual's self-esteem or to prevent further erosion of it. White (1981c) suggests that when the threat is perceived as minimal and the resources are moderate to high, the focus will be on the relationship. The emphasis will be balanced between the relationship and the self, however, when the threat is moderate to high and resources are moderate. It is the self that will be of primary concern when the threat is high and the resources low.

According to Schlenker's theory of impression management, the transgressing partner also faces a predictment. As with the jealous person, the severity of the predicament is a function of the ascription of responsibility and the undesirability of the event. The contrast lies in the fact that in most cultures, the attribution of culpability for the partner is much stronger and will be strongest when it is apparent to observers that the partner freely and purposively engaged in the jealousy-evoking behavior.

When faced with the predicament of having provoked jealousy, the trangressing partner is faced with minimizing the "potential negative repercussions and maximiz[ing the] expected reward/cost ratios" (Schlenker, 1980, p. 134). If the partner has decided that the relationship is not salvageable, the coping strategies are rather straightforward. The partner will withdraw from the relationship while making egotistical attributions ascribing blame to the jealous person and minimizing the negativity of what has occurred. These attributions may include inferences consistent with predictions from the Just World Hypothesis (Lerner & Simmons, 1966) derogating the victim (e.g., "He asked for it" or "She deserved it").

However, if the partner is committed to the relationship, the greater his or her dependency on it, the greater the tendency to incorporate the jealous person's values into the selected coping strategies. Schlenker's (1980) analysis suggests that the partner's first task is in assessing (given what the jealous person knows about the situation) the worst conclusion that could be drawn. Subsequent coping strategies must then be directed at preventing a "worst-case interpretation" of the event.

Faced with their respective predicaments, both the jealous person and the transgressing partner can respond in a number of different ways. The first broad category of responses identified by Schlenker (1980, p. 136) is *accounts,* defined as "explanations designed to minimize the apparent severity of the predicament." Three types of accounts can be used: innocence, excuses, or justifications. First, the person may profess innocence (i.e., denying that the event occurred). This strategy would probably work best for the partner when he or she had committed minor jealousy-evoking events such as flirting, as opposed to extradyadic relationships, where the costs for professing false innocence would be too great. For example, the partner could contend that the event did not take place ("I wasn't flirting, I was just talking"). In a similar vein, the jealous person could deny his or her jealousy ("I am not jealous, just upset").

Excuses are used when there is an acknowledgment that the event occurred and that the person assumes some responsibility for its occurrence. In such cases there is a need to minimize the level of perceived responsibility. Schlenker suggests that this may be accomplished by minimizing either foresight of the negative consequences (transgressing partner: "I had no idea it would end up like this"), the person's interest or motivation in the event (partner: "I didn't even like the other person," "She/he kept forcing herself/himself on me"), or by shifting the attribution to extenuating circumstances (jealous person: "I have been under so much pressure lately, any little thing upsets me").

The use of justifications occurs when the event is admitted to and partial responsibility has been assumed, but the consequences are minimized by interpreting them from a different perspective, as when one appeals to a higher set of values. For example, the jealous person could say, "The fact that I'm jealous shows how much I care for this relationship!" A second type of justification mentioned by Schlenker involves two kinds of comparisons. The first refers to the behavior of others (the jealous person: "Other people would react with much more jealousy in similar circumstances than I do"). The second kind involves using this justification to confront the other person's motives for punishing the partner. The transgressing partner could ask: "What's wrong with you that you're so jealous and upset? Do you want to make our life miserable?"

The second major category of responses to predicaments cited by Schlenker is apologies. With an apology, the transgressor accepts blame for the event but attempts to obtain a pardon for the negative consequences. According to Goffman (1971, p. 113), all apologies involve self-splitting, "a gesture through which an individual splits himself into two parts—the part that is guilty of an offense and the part that dissociates itself from the derelict and affirms a belief in the offended rule." An apology can include an expression of guilt, recognition of correct behavior and the endorsement of sanctions for rule violation, attribution of the incorrect behavior to the "bad" self, an assurance that correct behavior will occur in the future, and an offering of penance and compensation (Goffman, 1971).

A final strategy that may be expected from the partner who evoked the jealousy, as well as the jealous person, is ingratiation. Accordingly, both partners may attempt to compliment the other, agree with them, offer to perform favors, and tailor images to the person's liking (Jones, 1964).

Interaction Between Impression Management Strategies

If an interchange between the two partners occurs, then the coping strategies for the jealous person and the partner are intertwined and there is mutual influence. At this point the strategies adopted by each person and perceived in the other person become important to the course of the interaction. Cooperation should increase to the degree that each party has the long-term goal of establishing continued mutual cooperation and the expectation that the other will cooperate (Pruitt & Kimmel, 1975). The expectation of cooperative behavior is referred to as trust (Pruitt & Smith, 1981). The desire to behave cooperatively and the expectation that the partner will also do so are both necessary for the cooperation and the resolution of conflict.

The selection of a particular strategy to produce cooperation is not only dependent on producing the most positive image but also requires weighing the costs of having a tenuously claimed image confronted and questioned. For both partners, the selected strategies can be assumed to be a function of their knowledge of the other person's beliefs and values. Thus, each person "will choose accounts that they believe are fitted to the situation as it appears to be known by the audience" (Schlenker, 1980, p. 151). Similarly, the initial account is subject to negotiation by the couple, with each posing questions and modifying positions until an account is reached that is mutually satisfying. Schlenker posits that the degree to which each person will help the other in providing accounts is a function of the severity of the predicament, with severe predicaments receiving the least assistance in constructing acceptable accounts. Thus, with minor jealousy-evoking events, the jealous person should help the partner with accounts that protect the partner's integrity ("Let's see how we can work this out"). In contrast, with major jealousy-evoking events, such as extramarital relationships, the attitude will be much more distant ("You'd better have a good explanation for this!"). The predicament of a jealousy-evoking event may be more severe for the perpetrator than for the jealous person, because the attribution of responsibility is typically greater and the threat to the self-esteem created by engaging in the extradyadic relationship may be substantial. It would be expected that, in general, the jealous person would receive more assistance from the partner than vice versa.

The strategies adopted by the partners can be influenced by a number of other considerations than "saving face." Their behavior can also be directed at reducing feelings of jealousy. An example is the cathartic release of feelings by the jealous partner or the empathetic understanding by the transgressing partner. Other concerns will often be, for instance, whether or not to change the jealousy-evoking circumstances, how to go about doing so, and how to limit the damage to the relationship. All of these elements may be handled with the most effective strategies, but a given person may focus on one element more than another depending on the given set of circumstances. Furthermore, as Duck (1984) suggests, the most effective strategy will depend on the current phase of relationship breakdown. Duck points out that in the first phase, that of unbalance and dissatisfaction, the emphasis should be on improving communications, while in the second phase, characterized by dissaffection with the partner, the most effective reparative techniques are those that focus on attributions about the partner. In the third phase, where the partners confront their problems, the form of the relationship is the issue for reparative intervention.

There is reason to believe that the direction and affective tone of the negotiated resolution will not be strictly positive, at least not in the short term. In fact, argument, protest, and disagreement may be important steps in resolving the conflict. Studies have shown that totally cooperative behavior following exploitation can increase rather than decrease noncooperative, exploitative responses from the other person (Deutsch, 1973; Kuhlman & Marshello, 1975; Rapaport, 1970). Some noncooperative behavior is assumed to be important to establishing long-term cooperative behavior, as it helps to establish the fact that the offended person will not tolerate being exploited (Pruitt & Kimmel, 1977). This impression of firmness conveys the message that concessions are unlikely and that pressure tactics will not work (Pruitt & Smith, 1981). This is also consistent with the prevention function of the jealous reaction identified by Clanton and Smith (1977) and Hupka (1981). Furthermore, the partial disintegration of the relationship due to noncooperation, seen as a short-term defensive reaction to the partner's exploitative behavior, may be important as it helps to establish an experience of mutual loss of outcomes. This serves to highlight the partners' mutual dependency and the value of subsequent mutual cooperation. Thus, a slow reciprocation of cooperative behavior from the jealous partner, with "things getting worse before they get better," while maintaining the expectation for cooperation, may be a pattern of coping that characterizes couples who are able to work out problems associated with jealousy-evoking events and so remain intact (Bixentine & Gaebelien, 1971; Rapaport & Chammah, 1966). This pattern, which conveys the impression of firmness and trustworthiness (Pruitt & Smith, 1981), may be more successful than complete noncooperation, which does not facilitate resolution, and quick cooperation, which encourages further exploitation.

Conclusion

We have emphasized that jealousy is often a strong, intense emotion controllable only to a limited extent by cognitive effort. It is frequently so overwhelming due to the high value of what is at stake—one's self-esteem and the intimacy and stability of a close relationship. The intensity of jealousy makes people inclined to engage in attributional analyses of the partner's behavior and often in serious arguments. Both the transgressing partner and the jealous person are concerned with protecting their ego, making it difficult to achieve a cooperative attitude. Indeed, jealousy has a paradoxical nature: It is a defensive reaction aimed at protecting one's self-image and one's most valued relationship. Nevertheless, both are likely to be damaged by jealousy. The paradoxical reaction called jealousy and its implications are still only partially understood and rarely described adequately. Additional theoretical work and research are undoubtedly necessary, not only to get more insight into jealousy as such but also because such insight will increase our understanding of some fundamental aspects of intimate relationships, exclusivity, love, trust, and dependency.

REFERENCES

Berscheid, E. (1983). Emotion. in H. H. Kelley, E. Berscheid, A. Christensen, J. H. Harvey, T. L. Huston, G. Levinger, E. McClintock, L. A. Peplau, & D. R. Peterson (Eds.), *Close relationships* (pp. 110-168). New York: Freeman.

Berscheid, E., & Fei, J. (1977). Romantic love and sexual jealousy. In G. Clanton & L. S. Smith (Eds.), *Jealousy* (pp. 101-109). Englewood Cliffs, NJ: Prentice-Hall.

Bixentine, V. E., & Gaebelein, J. W. (1971). Strategies of "real" opponents in eliciting cooperative choice in a prisoner's dilemma game. *Journal of Conflict Resolution, 15,* 157-166.

Bohm, E. (1960). Jealousy. In A. Ellis & A. Abarbanel (Eds.), *The Encyclopedia of sexual behavior I.* New York: Knopf.

Braiker, H. B., & Kelley, H. H. (1979). Conflict in the development of close relationships. In R. L. Burgess & T. L. Huston (Eds.), *Social exchange in developing relationships* (pp. 135-168). New York: Academic Press.

Brickman, P., & Bulman, R. J. (1977). Pleasure and pain in social comparison. In J. M. Suls & R. L. Miller (Eds.), *Social comparison processes: Theoretical and empirical perspectives.* Washington, DC: Halsted Wiley.

Bringle, R. G., & Buunk, B. (1985). Jealousy and social behavior: A review of person relationship and situational determinants. In P. Shaver (Ed.), *Review of personality and social psychology* (Vol. 6, pp. 241-264). Beverly Hills, CA: Sage.

Bringle, R. G., Buunk, B., & Renner, P. (1984). *Attributions and jealousy.* Unpublished manuscript, Indiana-Purdue University, Indianapolis.

Bringle, R. G., Renner, P., Terry, R., & Davis, S. (1983). An analysis of situational and person components of jealousy. *Journal of Research in Personality, 17,* 354-368.

Bryson, J. B. (1976). *The nature of sexual jealousy: An exploratory study.* Paper presented at the annual meeting of the American Psychological Association, Washington, DC.

Bryson, J. B. (1977). *Situational determinants of the expression of jealousy.* Paper presented at the annual meeting of the American Psychological Association, San Francisco.

Buunk, B. (1982). Anticipated sexual jealousy: Its relationship to self-esteem, dependency and reciprocity. *Personality & Social Psychology Bulletin, 8,* 310-316.

Buunk, B. (1980). *Intieme relaties met derden: Een social-psychologische studie.* Alphen a/d Rijn, The Netherlands: Samsom.

Buunk, B. (1981). Jealousy in sexually open marriages. *Alternative Lifestyles, 4,* 357-372.

Buunk, B. (1982). Anticipated sexual jealousy: Its relationship to self-esteem, dependency and reciprocity. *Personality & Social Psychology Bulletin, 8,* 310-316.

Buunk, B. (1984). Jealousy as related to attributions for the partner's behavior. *Social Psychology Quarterly, 47,* 107-112.

Buunk, B., Bringle, B., & Arends, H. (1984). *Jealousy—a response to threatened self concept?* Paper presented at the International Conference on Self and Identity, Cardiff, U.K.

Clanton, G., & Smith, L. G. (Eds.). (1977). *Jealousy.* Englewood Cliffs, NJ: Prentice-Hall.

Constantine, L. L. (1976). Jealousy: From theory to treatment. In D.H.E. Olsen (Ed.). *Treating relationships.* Lakeview, IL: Graphic.

Constantine, L. L., & Constantine, J. M. (1973). *Group Marriage: A study of contemporary multilateral marriage.* New York: Macmillan.

Deutsch, M. (1973). *The resolution of conflict: Constructive and destructive processes.* New Haven, CT: Yale University Press.

Duck, S., & Sants, H. (1983). On the origin of the specious: Are personal relationships really interpersonal states? *Journal of Social and Clinical Psychology, 1,* 27-41.

Duck, S. (1984). A perspective on the repair of personal relationships: Repair of what, when? In S. W. Duck (Ed.), *Personal relationships 5: Repairing personal relationships* (pp. 163-184). London: Academic Press.

Faulk, M. (1977). Men who assault their wives. In M. Roy (Ed.), *Battered women: A psychosociological study of domestic violence* (pp. 119-126). New York: Van Nostrand Reinhold.

Gelles, R. (1972). *The violent home: A study of physical aggression between husbands and wives.* Beverly Hills, CA: Sage.

Goffman, E. (1971). *Relations in public.* New York: Basic Books.

Heider, F. (1958). *The psychology of interpersonal relations.* New York: Wiley.

Hoaken, P. (1976). Jealousy as a symptom of psychiatric disorder. *Australian and New Zealand Journal of Psychiatry, 10,* 47-51.

Hunt, M. (1974). *Sexual behavior in the 1970's.* Chicago: Dell.

Hupka, R. B. (1981). Cultural determinants of jealousy. *Alternative Lifestyles, 4,* 310-356.

Jaremko, M. E., & Lindsey, R. (1979). Stress coping abilities of individuals high and low in jealousy. *Psychological Reports, 44,* 547-553.

Jones, E. E. (1964). *Ingratiation.* New York: Appleton-Century-Crofts.

Jones, E. E., & Davis, K. E. (1965). From acts to dispositions: The attribution process in person perception. In L. Berkowitz (Ed.), *Advances in experimental social psychology* (Vol. 2). New York: Academic Press.

Kelley, H. H. (1979). *Personal relationships: Their structure and processes.* Hillsdale, NJ: Erlbaum.

Kelley, H. H. (1983). Love and commitment. In H. H. Kelley, E. Berscheid, A. Christensen, J. H. Harvey, T. L. Huston, G. Levinger, E. McClintock, L. A. Peplau, & D. R. Peterson (Eds.), *Close relationships* (pp. 265-314). New York: Freeman.

Kelley, H. H., Berscheid, E., Christensen, A., Harvey, J. H., Huston, T. L., Levinger, G., McClintock, E., Peplau, L. A., & Peterson, D. R. (Eds.). (1983). *Close relationships.* New York: Freeman.

Kinsey, A., Pomeroy, W. B., Martin, C. F., & Gebhard, P. H. (1953). *Sexual behavior in the human female.* Philadelphia: Saunders.

Kitson, G. C. (1982). Attachment to the spouse in divorce: A scale and its application. *Journal of Marriage and Family, 44,* 379-394.

Knapp, J. (1976). An exploratory study of seventeen sexually open marriages. *Journal of Sex Research, 12,* 206-219.

Kuhlman, D. M., & Marshello, A.F.J. (1975). Individual differences in game motivation as moderators of preprogrammed strategy effects in prisoner's dilemma. *Journal of Personality and Social Psychology, 32,* 922-931.

Lerner, M. J., & Simmons, C. H. (1966). Observer's reactions to the "innocent victim": Compassion or rejection. *Journal of Personality and Social Psychology, 4,* 203-210.

Leventhal, H. (1980). Toward a comprehensive theory of emotion. In L. Berkowitz (Ed.), *Advances in experimental social psychology* (Vol. 13, pp. 139-207). New York: Academic Press.

Lewin, K. (1948). *Resolving social conflicts.* New York: Harper & Row.

Mathes, E. W., Roter, P. M., & Joerger, S. M. (1982). A convergent validity study of six jealousy scales. *Psychological Reports, 50,* 1143-1147.

Mazur, R. (1977). Beyond jealousy and possessiveness. In G. Clanton & L. Smith (Eds.), *Jealousy* (pp. 181-187). Englewood Cliffs, NJ: Prentice-Hall.

Miller, H. G., & Siegel, P. S. (1972). *Loving: A psychological approach.* New York: Wiley.

Mowat, R. R. (1966). *A psychiatric study of morbidly jealous murderers at Broadmoor.* London: Tavistock.

Orvis, B. R., Kelley, H. H., & Butler, D. (1976). Attributional conflict in young couples. In J. H. Harvey, W. J. Ickes, & R. E. Kidd (Eds.), *New directions in attribution research* (Vol. 1, pp. 353-386). Hillsdale, NJ: Erlbaum.

Passer, M. W., Kelley, H. H., & Michela, J. L. (1978). Multidimensional scaling of the causes of negative interpersonal behavior. *Journal of Personality and Social Psychology, 36,* 951-962.

Pruitt, D. G., & Kimmel, M. J. (1977). Twenty years of experimental gaming: Critique, synthesis and suggestions for the future. *Annual Review of Psychology, 28,* 363-392.

Pruitt, D. G., & Smith, D. L. (1981). Impression management in bargaining: Image of firmness and trustworthiness. In J. T. Tedeschi (Ed.), *Impression management theory and social psychological research.* New York: Academic Press.

Rapoport, A. (1970). Conflict resolution in the light of game theory and beyond. In P. Swingle (Ed.), *The structure of conflict.* New York: Academic Press.

Rapoport, A., & Chammah, A. M. (1966). The game of chicken. *American Behavioral Scientists, 10,* 10-14, 23-28.

Rodgers, M. A., & Bryson, J. B. (1978). *Self esteem and relationship maintenance as responses to jealousy.* Paper presented at the annual meeting of the Western Psychological Association, San Francisco.

Safilios-Rothschild, C. (1969). Attitudes of Greek spouses toward marital infidelity. In G. Neubeck (Ed.), *Extramarital relations.* Englewood Cliffs, NJ: Prentice-Hall.

Schlenker, B. (1980). *Impression management.* Monterey, CA: Brooks/Cole.

Shaw, M. E., & Sulzer, J. L. (1964). An empirical test of Heider's levels in attribution of responsibility. *Journal of Abnormal and Social Psychology, 69,* 39-46.

Shibles, W. (1974). *Emotion, the method of philosophical therapy.* Wisconsin: Language Press.

Weiss, R. (1975). *Marital separation.* New York: Basic Books.

White, G. L. (1981a). Jealousy and partner's perceived motives for attraction to a rival. *Social Psychology Quarterly, 44,* 24-30.

White, G. L. (1981b). Relative involvement, inadequacy and jealousy: A test of a causal model. *Alternative Lifestyles, 4,* 219-309

White, G. L. (1981c). *Coping with romantic jealousy: Comparison to rival, perceived motives, and alternative assessment.* Paper presented to the annual meeting of the American Psychological Association, Los Angeles.

Zajonc, R. B. (1980). Feeling and thinking: Preferences need no inferences. *American Psychologist, 35,* 151-175.

6

Nonverbal Communication
in Marriage

PATRICIA NOLLER

The importance of communication to the quality of the marital relationship has long been recognized (Locke, Sabagh, & Thomes, 1956; Navran, 1967). Only recently, however, have researchers begun to explore and understand the nature of the problems in communication experienced by many couples. Questions such as the relationship of communication accuracy to marital satisfaction and the role of understanding and misunderstanding in marital interaction are now being addressed. Researchers are asking: To what extent is accuracy of communication important in marriage? Do happy and unhappy couples differ in the extent to which they understand or misunderstand each other? Alternatively, are the type of messages couples send each other important? Are particular types of messages sent more frequently by happy couples than by unhappy couples?

Craddock (1980, p. 7) has surveyed a number of marriage therapists and notes: "Clients were described as experiencing considerable difficulty in expressing their goals to one another and discussing constructively the means by which they might be achieved." Much more needs to be learned about the problems experienced by unhappy couples in their marriages if therapists and others working with such couples are to be able to give constructive help in communication and problem solving.

To some extent at least, advances in understanding marital communication have depended on developments in methodology and technology. Kahn (1970), for example, designed an instrument that he called the Marital Communication Scale. This scale consists of a series of ambiguous messages capable of being sent with three different meanings depending on the nonverbal behavior that accompanies the words. An example of an ambiguous message would be the question, "What are you doing?" which could be sent in a neutral curious way, a positive pleased and surprised way, or a negative, angry, or frustrated way.

Kahn designed two separate sets of messages—one to be sent by wives and one to be sent by husbands. The purpose of developing such a scale was to enable the separation of the verbal and nonverbal components of messages: The words are the same for each subject (of the same sex), and each subject is left to use whatever nonverbal behavior seems appropriate in order to get the required intention across to the partner. Of course, the words used are the same across the three different types of messages—positive, neutral, and negative.

The research question for Kahn (1970) was, Are happy couples able to understand one another's nonverbal communication better than unhappy couples? He found clear evidence for happy couples being superior to unhappy couples in their ability to decode each other's nonverbal cues. This was an interesting finding, since studies using self-report questionnaires had shown nonverbal communication (at least as reported by couples) to be relatively unimportant in discriminating between the different marital adjustment groups (Navran, 1967). However, the scale used by Navran, the Primary Communication Inventory (Locke et al., 1956) tends to focus on the types of nonverbal communication that occur without words, and to ignore the fact that nonverbal behavior is a factor in all communication, with nonverbal cues as facial expression or tone of voice frequently being used to modify or qualify the meanings of words.

One of the problems with Kahn's methodology is that subjects are not free to use the words they would normally use in a particular situation. Therefore, the experimental situation could be described as artificial and stylized. Gottman and his colleagues (Gottman, Notarius, Markman, Banks, Yoppi, & Rubin, 1976) developed a methodology for studying differences between communicative intent (the message the spouse wanted to send) and communicative impact (the message the decoding spouse actually received) without the constraint of subjects being able to use only words set by the experimenter. The device they developed was called a "talk-table" and involved married couples facing each other across a specially designed table while they discussed a salient marital problem. After each utterance, the sender of the message was asked to rate his or her intent on a five-point scale from superpositive to supernegative, while the receiver was asked to rate the impact that the message had on him or her on a similar scale.

Although the communication in this talk-table situation should be less stylized than that obtained in the situation devised by Kahn (1970), there are other problems with this methodology. Having to stop after each utterance to make a rating is likely to interfere with the flow of communication. Also, senders are likely to be affected by the social desirability response set and to rate their intentions as less negative than they actually are. The receiver, however, who is rating the other person's communication, not his or her own, is unlikely to be affected in the same way. Yet another problem is that it is no longer possible to separate the verbal and nonverbal aspects of a message (since impact is likely to be affected by both). Finally, as in Kahn's (1970) study, it is not possible to conclude whether differences between communicative intent and communicative impact for a message are related to the encoding process (how the message is sent) or the decoding process (how the message is received).

In fact, Gottman et al.'s (1976) finding—that for unhappy couples impact was more negative than intent, while for happy couples there was no difference between impact and intent—is consistent with several alternative explanations. It is possible that the decoding of unhappy spouses was affected by some kind of negative distortion, with messages being interpreted more negatively than they were actually sent. It is also possible, however, that unhappy spouses, who would presumably be feeling fairly negative toward their partners, actually sent more negative messages than they intended, with underlying resentments affecting the way they encoded their messages (Raush, Barry, Hertel, & Swain, 1974). Duck and Sants (1983) emphasize that relationships are a process over time, and interactions at a point in time are affected by the history of the relationship. At the same time, unhappy spouses may have rated their messages more positively than they actually sent them because of the social desirability response set. Unhappy spouses, who would presumably have more negative comments to make, would be more affected by this particular bias than would other couples.

A further development, this one technological, which provides the possibility for exploring marital communication more fully, is the videotape recorder (Eisler, Hersen, & Agras, 1973). Videotaping can be used to record examples of more natural interaction which can then be viewed over and over again and coded with great detail. For example, Gottman and his colleagues (Gottman, Markman & Notarius, 1977) videotaped couples discussing a marital problem and then coded both the verbal and nonverbal aspects of each utterance.

They were able to demonstrate clearly the importance of nonverbal communication in marriage. While the verbal codes which they used did not discriminate between happy and unhappy couples, such couples could be discriminated in terms of the nonverbal behavior that accompanied the verbal behavior. For example, while most couples used mind-reading (one spouse telling the other what the other thought as though he or she could read the partner's mind), unhappy couples were more likely to mind-read with negative nonverbal behavior.

When videotaping is combined with the methodologies discussed earlier, powerful research techniques result. For example, if subjects were videotaped while sending each other the items of the Marital Communication Scale developed by Kahn (1970), these items could be shown to groups of judges who could be asked to perform the same task as the spouse—decide between three alternative intentions. It would then be possible to decide whether errors in spouse-spouse communication were due to the way in which the message was sent (neither the spouse nor the judge could accurately decode the message) or the way in which it was received (the judges could decode the message but the spouse could not). It also becomes possible to separate the contribution made by each of the sexes, instead of having to assume, as Kahn (1970) did, that each made an equivalent contribution to the accuracy score that the couple received. A similar increase in the power of the methodology could be obtained by combining videotaping with the "talk-table" technique and using judges to rate the messages sent. A number of the questions raised in the earlier discussion could then be answered.

Another important factor in marital communication research has been the development of coding systems designed specifically for coding interaction in the marital situation. The Marital Interaction Coding System (Hops, Wills, Weiss, & Patterson, 1971) and the Couples' Interaction Scoring System (Gottman, Notarius, & Markman, 1976) are examples of the kinds of systems available. One limitation of these systems is that they are primarily designed for coding problem-solving interactions. Problem-solving is an important area of marital communication for study, since couples with problems in communication have been shown to have more problems in areas such as time spent together, conflicting religious views, sex relations, decision making and so on, and to have more difficulty in resolving their problems. However, problem solving is not the only function of communication in marriage, since couples also share experiences with one another and express emotions to one another (e.g., affection, sadness etc.) outside of a context in which problems need to be solved

(Guthrie, 1984; see Noller, 1984, for a more detailed discussion of these systems).

The series of experiments described in this chapter was designed to take advantage of developments in methodology and technology in order to gain increased understanding of problems in marital communication experienced by couples unhappy in their marriages. The studies were designed to answer questions related to accuracy of communication between spouses, awareness of communication, and the types of messages spouses send to one another, as well as how they send them.

A Study of Communication Accuracy

The concept of communication accuracy implies that people can be correct or incorrect in the way that they interpret or send messages, and that some people are more often correct than others (Friedman, 1979). In addition, there is the problem of deciding on a criterion of accuracy—how to decide who is correct and who is incorrect. This study, using a modified version of Kahn's (1970) Marital Communication Scale, explores the effects of marital adjustment level, sex, and type of message on communication accuracy using the decoding of independent judges as the criterion of accuracy. The scale consisted of nine ambiguous messages in each set (one for husbands and one for wives), each with three alternative affect intentions (one positive, one neutral, and one negative). Table 6.1 gives an example of an item, including the information provided for the encoder and the decoder. Each subject sent each of the messages (27 in all) to his or her spouse in random order. The messages were videotaped so that each set of messages could be shown to independent judges who were then asked to make the same decision as the spouse (that is, which message the encoding spouse had intended to send).

The present study replicated Kahn's (1970) finding that happy couples are more successful at decoding one another's nonverbal communication than are unhappy couples. However, because the messages were on videotape and could be shown to independent judges, other questions could also be explored, such as whether misunderstandings in marital communication are primarily related to encoding or decoding; whether husbands and wives differ in their skill at encoding and decoding in the marital relationship; and whether such encoding and decoding differences vary with different types of messages.

TABLE 6.1
Sample Cards Used by Encoder and Decoder

	Encoding Card
Situation	Your wife tells you about the wonderful vacation that one of her friends just took with her husband. She says that she wishes you and she could also take a trip to the same place.
Intention	You feel that a trip to that place is unappealing and would hardly be worthwhile.
Statement	Do you know what a trip like that costs?

	Decoding Card
Situation	Your wife tells you about the wonderful trip that one of her friends just took with her husband. She says that she wishes you and she could also take a trip to the same place.
Intentions	a. You feel that a trip to that place is unappealing and would hardly be worthwhile.
	b. You are pleased that she would want to go with you on such a trip and would like to make serious enquiries about it.
	c. You are interested in finding out if she knows the approximate cost of their trip before committing yourself one way or the other.

Messages were divided into good communications (those that at least two-thirds of the judges were able to decode accurately) and bad communications (those accurately decoded by fewer than two-thirds of the judges). Using this categorization, messages could be classified as either encoding errors (those that both the spouse and the judges had problems decoding) or decoding errors (those that the judges, but not the spouse, were able to decode accurately). There were also some bad communications which spouses decoded accurately. These messages were categorized as idiosyncratic communications, since they are likely to involve ways of communicating which are unique to a couple's private message system. Each person was given a number of different scores which reflected his or her communication accuracy:

(1)   Good communications—the number of messages that were decoded correctly by more than two-thirds of the judges and that could be assumed to be clearly sent;

(2)   Encoding errors—the number of messages that the spouse decoded incorrectly and that fewer than two-thirds of the judges were able to decode correctly (i.e., messages that were generally not clearly encoded);

(3)   Decoding errors—the number of good communications decoded in-

correctly by the spouse. Since only good communications were used here, it could be assumed that these errors were related to decoding rather than encoding;

(4) Idiosyncratic communications—messages that the spouse was able to decode correctly even though the judges could not.

For each of these measures, subjects were given separate scores for each type of message—positive, neutral, and negative.

The results showed that there were differences related to marital adjustment level (as measured by Locke & Wallace's, 1959, self-report marital adjustment scale), sex, and type of message. As already mentioned, happy couples were more accurate than unhappy couples overall, but particularly when the wives were the senders and the husbands the receivers. Of course, this could have been because the happy wives were better message-senders than the unhappy wives, because the happy husbands were better decoders than the unhappy husbands, or because of some combination of these two main possibilities.

Fortunately, the results for encoding and decoding errors shed light on this question. Husbands high in marital adjustment were both more accurate encoders and more accurate decoders than their low marital adjustment counterparts, with no differences between the wives for either variable. Thus the difference in accuracy between the high and low marital adjustment couples when the wife was the encoder are likely to be related to the better decoding of high marital adjustment husbands. Using the Marital Communication Scale in a correlational study, Gottman and Porterfield (1981) have also found evidence for a communication deficit involving the decoding strategies of low marital adjustment husbands. The present study points to both an encoding and a decoding deficit (see Table 6.2)

There were also sex and message-type differences for both encoding errors and good communications. Wives had fewer encoding errors and more good communications than did husbands, especially for positive messages, and it was particularly for positive messages that high marital adjustment husbands were more accurate encoders than low marital adjustment husbands.

The findings (Noller, 1980, 1984) point to the crucial role of the husband's communication accuracy for both encoding and decoding, with the encoding problems especially involving positive messages. Noller (1982a) found that wives low in marital adjustment were particularly concerned about the lack of positive communication from their spouses; these wives wanted more affection, appreciation, and

TABLE 6.2
Summary of Mean Accuracy Scores

Marital Adjustment Level	Males			Females		
	Pos.	Neut.	Neg.	Pos.	Neut.	Neg.
High						
Good communications[a]	38.2	50.7	56.9	52.1	42.4	56.9
Encoding errors[b]	82.7	63.2	69.9	70.3	58.3	51.0
Decoding errors[c]	9.9	14.6	16.8	25.5	27.9	9.3
Moderate						
Good communications[a]	32.6	47.2	50.0	60.4	52.1	61.8
Encoding errors[b]	83.3	68.3	70.9	44.4	62.3	54.2
Decoding errors[c]	21.9	22.7	12.8	13.2	22.5	20.3
Low						
Good communications[a]	25.4	36.5	50.0	51.6	40.5	58.7
Encoding errors[b]	94.2	71.9	58.7	64.0	69.8	57.1
Decoding errors[c]	24.6	27.8	24.2	23.8	17.4	20.2

a. As a percentage of total messages.
b. As a percentage of total errors on a subject's messages.
c. As a percentage of good communications.

attention. These two findings together would seem to indicate that unhappy marriages suffer from a low frequency of positive behavior such as affection and appreciation, but also that husbands, in particular, tend to have problems getting across the positive messages that they do attempt to send.

Two other issues were explored in this study: first, the ways in which decoding was affected by communication channels (e.g., visual or vocal), and second, whether there was any tendency for a bias in decoding (that is, for errors to be made in a positive or negative direction). The first issue was explored by having subjects decode their spouses from the videotape—but using only one channel at a time. Each subject decoded ten items using just the soundtrack and ten items using only the picture. The question was whether spouses were more accurate when decoding from tone of voice or from facial expression. For husband-to-wife messages, the accuracy was similar whichever channel was used, while for wife-to-husband communications greater accuracy was obtained when using the soundtrack than when using the picture. However, correlations between scores for the original decoding task and scores for decoding the visual channel (from the picture) suggest a heavy reliance on the visual channel by low marital adjustment husbands—a procedure that is likely to lead to less accuracy. Such a strategy could well be a factor in the decoding problems of these husbands, since they seem to be depending on the least reliable channel.

As suggested earlier, another important question is whether low marital adjustment subjects systematically distort one another's messages and see them as more negative than they actually are. Such a possibility was suggested by the findings of Gottman et al.'s (1976) talk-table study in which, for unhappy couples, the impact of messages on the spouse was more negative than the intention reported by the sender. To examine this question of bias in decoding, decoding errors were scored according to whether the intention selected by the decoder was more positive or more negative than the correct intention. Positive messages decoded as negative messages were given a score of -2, while positive messages decoded as neutral were given a score of -1. On the other hand, negative messages decoded as positive were given a score of +2, and negative messages decoded as neutral were given a score of +1. Analyses of these scores showed that there was no bias related to marital adjustment level, but there was bias related to sex. Husbands had a bias to decode in a negative direction, decoding messages as more negative than they actually were, while wives had a bias to decode in a positive direction, decoding messages as more positive than they actually were.

A Closer Look at Actual Communication Behavior

A further interest of this series of studies was to examine the encoding process used by married couples for possible explanations of differences in encoding related to sex and marital adjustment level. Therefore, the videotaped messages from the earlier study were analyzed in detail to look for differences in the nonverbal behavior used in each type of message. Each message was coded for the presence or absence of particular nonverbal behavior such as a smile (open or closed), eyebrow raise, eyebrow flash, head down, hand gesture, and so forth. The aim of this study was to see whether there were differences related to sex, level of marital adjustment, or being a good or poor communicator in the behavior that subjects used in the sending of various types of messages. Of course, this procedure would only show up differences related to the visual channel and ignores the possibility of differences in tone of voice.

Overall, there were clear differences between the three types of messages (Noller & Gallois, in press), with smiles (both open and closed) and eyebrow raises occurring more on positive messages and frowns

TABLE 6.3
Mean Number of Items (out of 9)
on Which Relevant Behavior Occurred

	Positive Messages	*Negative Messages*
Males		
Open smile	2.4	
Closed smile	1.3	
Eyebrow raise	4.2	2.2
Eyebrow flash	1.7	1.3
Head up	2.0	
Head down	1.1	
Head tilt	2.5	
Frown		0.7
Females		
Open smile	4.4	
Closed smile	2.1	
Eyebrow raise	2.7	1.1
Eyebrow flash	0.9	0.7
Head up	1.0	
Head down	2.2	
Head tilt	3.7	
Frown		2.7

and eyebrow furrows occurring more on negative messages. However, when husbands and wives were compared for each message type, there were some clear differences between the sexes for both positive and negative messages. Wives used more smiles on positive messages, while husbands used more eyebrows flashes, and wives used more frowns on negative messages, while husbands used more eyebrow raises and flashes. In addition, wives used more of the type of behavior used by good communicators, and more behavior overall. Thus it would seem that wives were more expressive than husbands (used more nonverbal behavior) and also used behavior that best differentiated between message types (i.e., that which is commonly associated with a particular message type and used by good communicators). Husbands, on the other hand, used similar behavior for each message type, relying generally on the eyebrows, particularly eyebrow raises and flashes, whether they were sending positive or negative messages.

Comparing between message types for each of the sexes separately indicated that the differences found were more of degree than kind, since both males and females smiled more on positive messages than negative messages and frowned more on negative messages than on positive messages. Means for the relevant behavior for each of the sexes are provided in Table 6.3. In general, there seem to be clear behavioral reasons that messages from wives are more clearly encoded then those from husbands, particularly for positive messages (where the accuracy difference between the sexes was greatest).

There were few differences in this study related to marital adjustment level. There was a greater degree of pleasantness in the messages from high marital adjustment husbands, as well as a tendency for low marital adjustment subjects to use behavior associated with one message type in conjunction with a different type of message—in other words, to send less clear messages. Such a finding helps to explain the effects for encoding obtained in the accuracy study. Low marital adjustment subjects had more encoding errors because they were using inappropriate behavior in their encoding and giving confused messages.

A Study of Communication Awareness

While the accuracy study described earlier revealed some important factors in marital communication, a further important question is whether husbands and wives are aware of possible problems in communication or whether they assume that the message sent is always the one received (and vice versa). It seemed that the way in which couples dealt with misunderstandings could be related to their marital adjustment in much the same way as the actual level of accuracy. As Sillars and Scott (1983) have pointed out, spouses may have more experience with one another's communication but may be less objective and overconfident in their ability to decode one another accurately (Posavec & Pasko, 1971; Shapiro & Swensen, 1969). Since there is evidence for a greater congruence of perception for high marital adjustment couples (Sillars & Scott, 1983), it would be expected that low marital adjustment couples would suffer more from such biases in decoding and more often feel sure that they have decoded the spouse correctly when they have not.

Encoders, on the other hand, could be expected to put the blame for communication problems on the negative attributes of the spouse (in this case, his or her poor decoding skills) and to assume that misunderstandings are the fault of the spouse. In this case they would be very confident of their own encoding skills, whether the spouse decoded the message correctly or not. It also seemed likely that high and low marital adjustment subjects would differ in their ability to predict correctly whether or not the spouse would accurately decode the message, with low marital adjustment subjects being less accurate than high marital adjustment subjects.

Jenardos (1982) used the Marital Communication Scale with a different group of couples in order to explore this question. Couples sent each other the items of the scale, as in the previous study, but after each item encoders were asked to rate the clarity with which they had sent the message, while the decoders were asked to rate how confident they felt about their decoding. Encoders were also asked to predict whether or not their spouse would correctly decode the message. The expectation was that spouses high in marital adjustment would be more aware than other spouses of the lack of clarity of their messages and would also be more confident about messages they decoded correctly than about messages they decoded incorrectly. It was also expected that high marital adjustment couples would be more accurate in predicting the spouse's response. In other words, we expected high marital adjustment couples to be more aware of the possibility of misunderstandings, of their own communication, and of the spouse's communication.

The results of this study (see Table 6.4) show that in general, subjects did differentiate between their clearly sent and poorly sent messages, although they were less aware of this difference for neutral messages than for other messages. They also rated their negative messages as more clearly sent than other messages. There were no differences related to marital adjustment level or sex for clarity ratings. Thus the expectation that encoders low in marital adjustment would be very confident of their encoding and put the blame for misunderstanding on the decoding spouse was not supported.

Decoders were more confident for messages they decoded correctly than for those they decoded incorrectly and less confident for neutral messages than other messages. While there were no differences between the marital adjustment groups for correct or incorrect messages, subjects low in marital adjustment were as confident for incorrect messages as for correct messages, while those high or moderate in marital adjustment were more confident for correct messages than for incorrect messages—in other words, they were more aware of their decoding. Thus the expectation that low marital adjustment couples would have an unwarranted confidence in their decoding skill was fulfilled, with these subjects feeling that they were decoding correctly when they were actually misunderstanding their spouse.

High marital adjustment subjects, particularly the wives, were better at predicting whether the spouse would correctly decode their

TABLE 6.4
Mean Scores for Awareness Study

Marital Adjustment Level	Males			Females		
	Pos.	Neut.	Neg.	Pos.	Neut.	Neg.
HIGH						
Clarity ratings						
Correct	4.5	4.4	4.7	4.95	4.3	4.9
Incorrect	3.6	3.9	3.9	4.5	4.1	4.4
Confidence ratings						
Correct	4.6	4.97	4.97	4.5	4.4	4.4
Incorrect	4.6	4.3	4.1	3.8	3.4	3.9
% correct predictions	69.2	63.8	80.9	79.1	80.2	84.1
MODERATE						
Clarity ratings						
Correct	4.4	3.9	4.6	4.3	4.2	4.5
Incorrect	4.1	4.1	4.2	3.9	3.6	3.9
Confidence ratings						
Correct	4.4	4.1	4.6	4.4	4.2	4.5
Incorrect	3.7	3.7	3.6	3.98	3.9	4.2
% correct predictions	54.8	56.8	67.1	70.0	68.7	80.9
LOW						
Clarity ratings						
Correct	4.5	4.1	4.6	4.5	3.95	4.7
Incorrect	3.4	3.9	4.5	3.97	3.7	3.7
Confidence ratings						
Correct	4.5	4.2	4.5	4.3	4.2	4.4
Incorrect	4.2	3.8	4.2	4.4	4.1	4.3
% correct predictions	71.6	63.97	76.9	57.6	51.2	76.1

NOTE: Encoders were asked to rate how clearly they thought the message was sent on a 6-point scale ranging from 1 (not at all clear) to 6 (very clear). Decoders were asked to rate how confident they were of the interpretation they had made on a 6-point scale ranging from 1 (not at all confident) to 6 (very confident).

messages than were other wives, and low marital adjustment husbands were worse predictors than other husbands. Predictions were more accurate for negative messages and less accurate for neutral messages. Wives were better predictors than their husbands for the high and moderate marital adjustment groups, while husbands were better predictors than wives for the low marital adjustment group. Again, the results were as predicted, with high marital adjustment subjects being better able to tell whether the spouse would understand their messages.

Thus there were some clear effects for marital adjustment with regard to awareness of communication, and there seem to be some perceptual biases operating (Sillars & Scott, 1983). Low marital adjustment couples tend to assume more understanding of the spouse than they actually have and feel confident they have decoded correctly when in fact they have decoded incorrectly. Their lack of understanding is further emphasized in the finding that they are less able than other subjects to predict whether the spouse will decode the message correctly or not.

A Study of More Natural Interaction

While these studies using standard content messages have provided some interesting information about nonverbal communication in married couples, it is important to see how such findings relate to more natural interaction. For this reason, the same subjects used in the earlier study (Noller, 1980) were asked to fill in several questionnaires about their marriages and were videotaped while discussing issues pertaining to their marriages. The questionnaires focused couples on their own marital relationships and forced them to think about such issues as the extent to which they agreed about a range of issues central to marriage (such as affection, sex, leisure time, dealing with in-laws, etc.) and the amount of change they wanted in each other's behavior (e.g., pay attention to appearance, spend time with me, or pay attention to my sexual needs).

Ten minutes of videotape were obtained for each couple. The conversations were transcribed and the scripts divided into thought units (basically speaker turns; Gottman et al., 1976b). Each unit was then coded four times: using the words as they appeared on the script, using the visual channel of the videotape, using the soundtrack, and using all of the information (words, visual cues, and tone of voice cues). The coders' task was to decide whether a particular unit on a particular channel was conveying positive, neutral, or negative affect.

So far, these tapes have been used to explore three research questions:

(1) Are there differences related to sex and marital adjustment level in the use of particular communication channels and different types of affect (Noller, 1982b)? One would expect high marital adjustment couples to use more positive messages and low marital adjustment couples to use more negative messages.

(2) Are there differences related to sex and marital adjustment level in how negative messages are sent (Noller, 1985)? One would expect negative messages from high marital adjustment subjects to be more clear and direct than those from other subjects, and those from low marital adjustment subjects to be more indirect.

(3) Are there differences related to sex and marital adjustment level in the use of discrepant messages (i.e., messages where one channel is positive and the other negative; Noller, 1982b)? Given some of the work on communication in families with delinquent children (Bugental, Kaswan & Love, 1970; Bugental, Love, & Gianetto, 1971), one would expect low marital adjustment subjects to use more discrepant messages than high marital adjustment subjects.

Use of the Channels

An important overall finding of this study was the large number of messages coded as neutral in the verbal channel (from the script) but coded as either positive or negative in the total channel (see Table 6.5). This finding suggests that a fair amount of marital communication (at least in situations similar to the experimental one) involves neutral words and relies on nonverbal channels for the affective component. Such a result fits with other findings of the significance of nonverbal communication to communication in general (Argyle, Salter, Nicholson, Williams, & Burgess, 1970; Zaidel & Mehrabian, 1969).

Analyses showed that positive messages were especially likely to have neutral words and rely on positive facial expression or tone of voice (or both) to make the message a positive one. Given the finding of the earlier study that husbands, particularly those low in marital adjustment, have problems getting their nonverbal positive messages across, this finding seems to be a cause for concern. Positive messages were also used much more by happy spouses than by unhappy spouses, and the findings from the accuracy study suggest that unhappy husbands have problems communicating even those few positive messages that they do attempt to send.

The main findings for neutral messages, apart from the one already discussed, were that husbands used more neutral messages than wives and that low marital adjustment subjects had fewer messages coded neutral in the total channel. The tendency for husbands to use fewer positive and negative messages, and more neutral ones, than wives would seem to reflect the general inexpressivity of males. However, another important factor was the interaction with marital adjustment

TABLE 6.5
Mean Percentages of Items Coded Positive, Neutral and Negative
for Each Channel

	Type of Coding		
Marital Adjustment Level	*Positive*	*Neutral*	*Negative*
HIGH			
Males			
Verbal channel	7.5	89.1	3.5
Visual channel	30.1	60.0	8.2
Vocal channel	21.7	66.8	11.5
Total channel	31.1	62.9	8.1
Females			
Verbal channel	9.8	87.2	3.0
Visual channel	35.3	53.6	9.7
Vocal channel	25.3	66.3	9.2
Total channel	29.3	59.3	10.1
MODERATE			
Males			
Verbal channel	3.9	86.4	9.8
Visual channel	29.9	53.6	15.5
Vocal channel	22.3	58.9	19.5
Total channel	26.8	56.0	15.2
Females			
Verbal channel	6.9	83.4	9.7
Visual channel	34.2	50.5	15.1
Vocal channel	22.7	58.1	19.3
Total channel	33.2	51.4	16.2
LOW			
Males			
Verbal channel	4.6	79.9	15.5
Visual channel	25.6	59.7	14.6
Vocal channel	16.7	60.4	19.9
Total channel	22.6	53.1	21.9
Females			
Verbal channel	3.4	72.4	24.3
Visual channel	26.9	53.7	18.7
Vocal channel	16.0	49.3	30.9
Total channel	21.7	42.0	35.9

level, with husbands low in marital adjustment having fewer neutral messages than other husbands and low marital adjustment subjects having fewer of their messages coded neutral in the total channel. Such male inexpressivity does not seem to characterize these low marital adjustment husbands, at least when it comes to sending negative messages to their wives. In fact, like their wives, they seemed to be fairly expressive in their negative interactions.

For negative messages, the strong effects were also related to sex and marital adjustment level, with low marital adjustment subjects, particularly wives, using more negative messages than other subjects. Thus, while the low marital adjustment husbands sent fewer neutral messages than other subjects, and low marital adjustment subjects sent fewer positives and more negatives than other subjects, the low marital adjustment husbands sent fewer negative messages than their wives. It does seem, however, as has been suggested, that their expressivity is mainly channeled into negative messages.

There were also some interesting effects related to channel for negative messages: Fewer messages were coded negative in the visual and verbal channel than in the vocal channel, and low marital adjustment subjects had fewer messages coded negative in the visual channel than in the verbal and vocal channels. These findings reflect the tendency for negativity to be carried in the vocal channel (or tone of voice), and for many negative messages to be accompanied by smiles—with the effect for low marital adjustment subjects occurring because these subjects send more negative messages than do other subjects.

Hence, the differences between the marital adjustment groups in how messages are sent seem to be related primarily to the levels of positivity and negativity, while the differences between the sexes seem to be related primarily to expressivity.

Direct Messages

A further analysis was carried out to see whether there were any differences between the groups on the extent to which they used direct messages (i.e., messages on which all channels were coded the same, all positive or all negative). Low marital adjustment subjects used more direct messages than high marital adjustment subjects, although high marital adjustment subjects sent more direct positive messages and low marital adjustment subjects more direct negative messages. There was also a sex difference, with wives sending more direct messages than husbands and low marital adjustment wives sending more direct negative messages than other subjects. These findings seem to contradict the accuracy findings, but it should be remembered that accuracy differences which discriminated between the marital adjustment groups were mainly related to positive messages, and there were no differences on negative messages. In addition, the accuracy findings apply particularly to messages with neutral words, which rely on nonverbal behavior to get the message across.

Indirect Messages

A further type of message which could be isolated was that in which the words were neutral but the nonverbal channels were both the same, either positive or negative. Overall, more positive messages than negative messages were sent with neutral verbal, and this finding confirms the earlier suggestion (on the basis of the small number of messages coded positive in the verbal channel) that positive messages are more likely than negative messages to be sent indirectly (i.e., nonverbally, rather than with words). Again, given the findings for the accuracy study that low marital adjustment husbands have problems sending this type of positive message, it is significant to find that it is particularly positive messages that are sent in this indirect way.

There were also differences between the groups in the ratio of positive to negative indirect messages. High and moderate marital adjustment subjects sent more positives than negatives with neutral verbal, while low marital adjustment subjects sent about the same number of positives as negatives.

Negative Messages

While a clear finding of this study was that low marital adjustment subjects sent more negative messages than other subjects, a further question of interest was whether subjects at different levels of marital adjustment sent their negative messages in different ways. To answer this question, it was necessary to control for the amount of negativity by including in the analysis only messages that were coded negative in the total channel and looking at each type of negative message as a proportion of the number of negative messages sent overall. Three types of negative messages were examined: direct negative messages, those with neutral verbal, and those with smiles. There were no differences between the groups (either by sex or marital adjustment level) with regard to the proportion of negative messages sent in each mode. There was, however, a strong effect for type of negative message, with all groups sending more negative messages with smiles than in either of the other modes.

When the number of subjects using each of the types of negative message was analyzed, a similar result was obtained, with almost all subjects in the high and low marital adjustment groups sending some negative messages with smiles but very few in the high group using

TABLE 6.6
Summary of Negative Messages

Marital Adjustment Level	Males	Females
HIGH		
Channel[a]		
Verbal channel	18.8	14.6
Visual channel	9.4	14.0
Vocal channel	44.4	38.3
Type of negative message[b]		
Direct	1.43	1.13
With neutral verbal	4.52	2.9
With smiles	29.15	34.2
LOW		
Channel[a]		
Verbal channel	29.7	43.5
Visual channel	20.7	23.8
Vocal channel	67.2	68.8
Type of negative message[b]		
Direct	3.01	10.22
With neutral verbal	11.7	6.34
With smiles	22.69	27.97

a. Mean percentage of negative messages coded negative in each channel.
b. Mean percentage of negative messages sent in each mode.

direct negative messages or negative messages with neutral verbal. It seems that, for married couples at least, the favored way for sending a negative message is with a smile. It is likely that such a result is related to Zaidel and Mehrabian's (1969) finding that the verbal channel is interpreted as conveying messages about behavior or deeds, while nonverbal messages are seen as conveying messages about the person. In this case, spouses could be saying, "I don't like your behavior, but I still like you."

A further analysis was designed to look at the percentage of negative messages that were coded negative in each of the channels (verbal, visual, and vocal). There were two main findings: first, that low marital adjustment subjects had a larger percentage of their negative messages coded negative on each of the channels, and second, that negative messages were more likely to be coded negative in the vocal channel than any other (see Table 6.6 for a summary of the data on negative messages). The former finding implies that negative messages from low marital adjustment subjects tend to be more intense (or negative) on more channels than those from other subjects, while the latter finding implies that the tone of voice carries much of the negativity in negative messages—in fact, it seems likely that many negative messages are negative only in the vocal channel. There was also less difference between the marital adjustment groups for the visual channel than for other channels, with the main differences related to the extent to which low marital adjustment subjects used negative words and a negative tone of voice in their negative messages.

Discrepant Messages

Another interest of the interaction study was whether there were differences between the groups with regard to the use of discrepant messages (i.e., messages coded positive in one channel and negative in the other). Since such communications could be discrepant between the words and either of the nonverbal channels, four types of discrepancy were chosen for analysis: those in which the visual channel was negative and the verbal channel positive, those in which the visual channel was negative and the vocal channel positive, those in which the visual channel was positive and the verbal channel negative, and those in which the visual channel was positive and the vocal channel negative.

Discrepancies involving negative messages in the visual channel were relatively rare; the most common involved positivity in the visual channel and negativity in the vocal channel. Wives used more discrepant messages than husbands, and for both groups the percentage of discrepant communications (i.e., the percentage of total communications which were discrepant) increased linearly from the high marital adjustment group to the low marital adjustment group. However, given the results for negative messages, it seems that such a finding mainly reflects the proportion of messages from these wives which were negative.

General Discussion

Each of these studies has revealed differences in communication between couples high and low in marital adjustment. To summarize:

High marital adjustment subjects were more accurate in decoding one another's nonverbal messages, but differences in accuracy for both encoding and decoding occurred particularly for husbands—and for encoding, especially on positive messages.

Low marital adjustment subjects (again, particularly husbands) tended to rely on the least helpful channel when they were decoding, leading to a lower level of accuracy (i.e., low marital adjustment husbands seemed to rely on the visual channel, although the vocal channel gives greater accuracy) when wives were the message-senders.

High marital adjustment subjects were more aware of their decoding than low marital adjustment subjects and better able to predict whether or not their spouse would correctly decode their messages.

Low marital adjustment subjects were more negative in their interactions with one another, and their negative messages were more intense than those of other subjects. For all groups, tone of voice seemed particularly important to negative messages.

Low marital adjustment subjects also sent more discrepant messages with positive visuals and negative verbals/vocals than other subjects, but this mainly reflected the amount of negativity in the interactions of this group. Negative messages were equally likely to be sent with smiles across all groups.

This series of studies, then, has confirmed earlier findings of the importance of nonverbal communication in discriminating between couples high and low in marital adjustment (Gottman et al., 1977; Kahn, 1970). These studies have also increased our understanding of the kinds of communication deficits that may be present in couples where marital adjustment is low.

The overall finding of lower communication accuracy in couples low in marital adjustment confirms Kahn's (1970) finding, but the use of videotapes has enabled a clearer description of problematic communication in marriage. The first important breakthrough was the ability to separate encoding and decoding, and to be able to look at encoding and decoding errors separately. The findings emphasize the importance of encoding in marital communication, with little evidence for the kinds of decoding distortions that have been hypothesized (Kahn, 1969).

Not only were more errors found to be related to the encoding process, but encoding errors also discriminated between the marital adjustment groups, particularly for husbands. Husbands high in marital adjustment were better than other husbands at sending positive messages—that is, they sent them more accurately. The findings of the interaction study—that positive messages were more likely to be sent with neutral words and rely on the nonverbal channels to get the positivity across—confirm the generalizability of this result and suggest that low marital adjustment husbands will generally have problems getting their positive messages across. The findings of the study that looked at the actual nonverbal behavior used by spouses point to the possibility of a "leakage" of negativity in the sending of these messages—that is, underlying feelings of hurt, resentment, disappointment, and so on show through even in attempts to send positive or neutral messages.

Accuracy at sending negative messages did not discriminate between the marital adjustment groups; subjects of both sexes and at all levels of marital adjustment were able to get their negative messages across. Thus the greater intensity found for negative messages in the low marital adjustment group does not seem to be important for accuracy, but it is clearly a sign of the intensification of negativity which occurs in unhappy marriages and families (Patterson & Reid, 1970). Gottman et al. (1977) also point to the importance of negative nonverbal behavior in discriminating between couples high and low in marital adjustment. While there were no differences between clinic and nonclinic couples in their use of various types of verbal behavior (such as agreement or mindreading), the clinic couples were more likely to accompany such behavior with negativity in the nonverbal channels. Further, in a time-series analysis the authors found that clinic couples became involved in cycles of negativity while nonclinic couples did not. Thus a negative message from one spouse led to a further negative message from the other spouse, and so on. Nonclinic couples seemed to be able to deal with negative communications such as criticisms in more constructive ways and without getting caught up in such negative cycles.

The study involving the microanalysis of nonverbal messages points to some further characteristics of the encoding process. The greater degree of pleasantness in the nonverbal messages of high marital adjustment subjects stands in contrast to the intense negativity in the behavior of the low marital adjustment subjects. Such findings tend to give further support to the leakage hypothesis (Ekman & Friesen, 1969)—that high marital adjustment subjects leak their comfortable, happy feelings in their interactions with a spouse, while low marital adjustment subjects leak their unhappiness and resentment.

The study involving the microanalysis of nonverbal messages has also contributed to our understanding of the well-documented finding of greater encoding accuracy for females than males. If females are using the behavior commonly associated with a particular type of message and the behavior used by good communicators, and if they are also discriminating more clearly between the different types of messages and using different behavior for each type, then it is no wonder that females are more accurate encoders. Again, the use of videotapes and microanalysis techniques has given us new understanding of a much researched finding.

The fact that encoding proved to be so important in discriminating between groups of couples does not mean that decoding is irrelevant. Husbands high in marital adjustment were also better decoders of their wive's messages than were husbands low in marital adjustment. Comparisons of accuracy using the different nonverbal channels suggest that these husbands may be relying on the least helpful channel, the visual channel, when greater reliance on the vocal channel would lead to greater accuracy.

An awareness of decoding also discriminated between the marital adjustment groups, while an awareness of encoding did not. High marital adjustment subjects were better able to discriminate between messages they could decode correctly and those they could not than were low marital adjustment subjects. Such a finding suggests that the low marital adjustment subjects had an unwarranted confidence in their ability to decode the messages of a spouse. The finding that these subjects were also less able to predict the decoding of their spouse emphasizes the lack of real understanding of the spouse exhibited by these subjects. Given that awareness of encoding did not discriminate between the marital adjustment groups, prediction is likely to be based on knowledge of the spouse's decoding rather than on awareness of one's own encoding, and it seems that high marital adjustment subjects have a relatively realistic understanding of their spouse's decoding.

Implications

While a number of attempts have been made to design programs in communication skills for married couples (Gottman, Notarius, Gonso, & Markman, 1976; Miller, Nunnally, & Wackman, 1976), there has tended to be a heavy emphasis on verbal communication in such programs. It seems important, however, given the findings of the studies described here, that a program should be designed which emphasizes the total communication, with a much greater emphasis on nonverbal communication. Such a program would need to emphasize both the communication patterns which discriminated between couples high and low in marital adjustment and those which were problematic for all groups, since communication skills training can be an important preventive measure designed to help those whose marriages are going reasonably well but who would like to improve or enrich (Mace & Mace, 1977) those relationships.

Initially, there are some general aspects of nonverbal communication that need to be stressed (Noller, 1984). Couples may particularly need help in understanding the complexity of communication (e.g., that the message sent is not always the message received). They may also need help in understanding the interactive nature of the communication process, with sender and receiver affecting each other throughout the communication cycle and misunderstandings being related to either encoding or decoding or both.

The results of these studies in nonverbal communication point up the need for husbands to be involved in communication skills training, since it seems to be the communication skill of the husband which discriminates best between couples high and low in marital adjustment (Noller, 1980; 1984). There is also a need for such communication skills to be taught in the context of the marital relationship (Gottman & Porterfield, 1981; Noller, 1981; 1984). These latter studies point to the fact that low marital adjustment subjects seem to have more communication skill than they use in communicating with their spouses, with communication with the spouse presumably being affected detrimentally by the level of adjustment in the marriage.

A program aimed at increasing nonverbal skill in married couples would need to focus clearly on encoding skills. All couples need some help in being more aware of their encoding, being more conscious of the nonverbal behavior they are using, and listening to their tone of voice. They may also need some help in identifying the types of behavior that make messages positive and negative, and in understanding the largely unwritten rules and stereotypes that affect communication. Again, videotape playback can be very useful in helping couples gain a greater understanding of how they communicate.

Focusing on nonverbal behavior in this way should help couples become aware of the extent to which their general communication differs from the "rules" and, consequently, why they may have problems getting their messages across. For husbands, focusing on positive messages would be particularly important. While receiving feedback on their nonverbal behavior and training in making it more positive should prove helpful to many couples, another way to deal with this problem is to help couples use the verbal channel more for positive messages (and to actually use positive words to their spouses).

Listening to the tone of voice should aid in the recognition of its potential negativity and in gaining more control over such signals so that they do not leak at inappropriate times. In addition, low marital adjustment subjects may need help in looking at the intensity of their negative messages and learning to express that negativity in more constructive ways (Miller et al., 1976) which lead to understanding and problem solving rather than the destructive cycle of negativity found by Gottman (1979).

Decoding will also need some attention. Couples should learn to discriminate between messages that they can decode correctly and those which they have problems decoding. If they can learn to recognize the messages they are unsure about, they can then seek clarification from the partner and ensure that the message they receive is the one that was intended. As Miller et al. (1976) note, couples need to become more aware of the connection between sense data (what they see, hear, etc.) and their interpretation of such data. For example, how do they interpret an eyebrow raise, furrow, or flash in a particular context? Low marital adjustment husbands may also need help in focusing more on cues from the vocal channel (or tone of voice) rather than relying so heavily on the face.

A further issue is causality—whether communication difficulties cause low marital adjustment or low marital adjustment causes communication difficulties. The findings are equivocal. Research evaluating programs in which couples are taught communication skills (using behavioral marital therapy) tends to show some small effects on general level of marital adjustment (Hahlweg, Revenstorf, & Schindler, 1984; Jacobson et al., 1984). On the other hand, Noller (1981) has found that subjects low in marital adjustment were more accurate with strangers than with spouses. This finding implies that low marital adjustment affects communication accuracy with a spouse. In fact, each is likely to affect the other in a reciprocal or circular fashion.

The series of studies described here has increased our understanding of problematic marital communication, particularly nonverbal communication. Greater understanding of the reasons for sex differences in nonverbal communication has also been achieved. Programs designed to help married couples improve their communication should focus more on total communication rather than on mere words (thereby ignoring the nonverbal aspects of communication). Particular attention should be paid to those aspects of communication which have been shown to be problematic in research studies such as those described here.

REFERENCES

Argyle, M., Salter, V., Nicholson, H., Williams, M., & Burgess, P. (1970). The communication of inferior and superior attitudes by verbal and nonverbal signals. *British Journal of Social and Clinical Psychology, 9,* 222-231.

Bugental, D. E., Kaswan, J. W., & Love, L. R. (1970). Perception of contradictory meanings conveyed by verbal and nonverbal channels. *Journal of Personality and Social Psychology, 16,* 647-655.

Bugental, D. E., Love, L. R., & Gianetto, R. M. (1971). Perfidious feminine faces. *Journal of Personality and Social Psychology, 17,* 314-318.

Craddock, A. (1980). The impact of social change in Australian families. *Australian Journal of Sex, Marriage and the Family, 1,* 4-14.

Duck, S. W., & Sants, H. K. A. (1983). On the origin of the specious: Are personal relationships really interpersonal states? *Journal of Social and Clinical Psychology, 1,* 27-41.

Eisler, M., Hersen, M., & Agras, W. S. (1973). Videotape: A method for the controlled observation of nonverbal interpersonal behavior. *Behavior Therapy, 4,* 420-425.

Ekman, P., & Friesen, W. V. (1969). Nonverbal leakage and cues to deception. *Psychiatry, 32,* 88-105.

Friedman, H. (1979). The concept of skill in nonverbal communication: Implications for understanding social interaction. In R. Rosenthal (Ed.), *Skill in nonverbal communication.* Cambridge, MA: Oelgeschlager, Gunn & Hain.

Gottman, J. M. (1979). *Marital interaction: Experimental investigations.* New York: Academic Press.

Gottman, J., Markman, H., & Notarius, C. (1977). The topography of marital conflict: A sequential analysis of verbal and nonverbal behavior. *Journal of Marriage and the Family, 39,* 461-477.

Gottman, J., Notarius, C., Gonso, J., & Markman, H. (1976). *A couple's guide to communication.* Champaign, IL: Research Press.

Gottman, J., Notarius, C., & Markman, H. (1976). *Couples Interaction Scoring System (C.I.S.S.).* Unpublished manuscript, Department of Psychology, University of Illinois, Champaign.

Gottman, J., Notarius, C., Markman, H., Banks, S., Yoppi, B., & Rubin, M. E. (1976). Behavior exchange theory and marital decision making. *Journal of Personality and Social Psychology, 34,* 14-23.

Gottman, J. M., & Porterfield, A. L. (1981). Communicative competence in the nonverbal behavior of married couples. *Journal of Marriage and the Family, 4,* 817-824.

Guthrie, D. (1984) *Expression of emotion in married couples.* Unpublished paper, University of Queensland, St. Lucia, Australia.

Hahlweg, K., Revenstorf, D., & Schindler, L. (1984). Effects of behavioral marital therapy on couples' communication and problem solving skills. *Journal of Consulting and Clinical Psychology, 52,* 553-566.

Hops, H., Wills, T., Weiss, R. L., & Patterson, G. (1971). *Marital interaction coding system.* Unpublished manuscript, Department of Psychology, University of Oregon, Eugene.

Jacobson, N. S., Follette, W. C., Revenstorf, D., Baucom, D. H., Hahlweg, K., & Margolin, G. (1984). Variability in outcome and clinical significance of behavioral marital therapy: A reanalysis of outcome data? *Journal of Consulting and Clinical Psychology, 52,* 497-504.

Kahn, M. (1969). *Nonverbal communication as a factor in marital satisfaction.* Unpublished doctoral dissertation, Southern Illinois University, Carbondale.

Kahn, M. (1970). Nonverbal communication and marital satisfaction. *Family Process, 9,* 449-456.

Locke, H. J., Sabagh, G., & Thomes, M. (1956). Correlates of primary communication and empathy. *Research Studies of the State College of Washington, 24,* 118.

Locke, H. J., & Wallace, K. M. (1959). Short marital adjustment and prediction tests: Their reliability and validity. *Marriage and Family Living, 21,* 251-255.

Mace, D., & Mace, V. (1977). *How to have a happy marriage.* Nashville, TN: Abingdon.

Miller, S., Nunnally, E. W., & Wackman, D. B. (1976). *Couple communication I: Talking Together.* North Strathfield, NSW: Family Life Movement of Australia.

Navran, L. (1967). Communication and adjustment in marriage. *Family Processes, 6,* 173-184.

Noller, P. (1980). Misunderstandings in marital communication: A study of couples' nonverbal communication. *Journal of Personality and Social Psychology, 39,* 1135-1148.

Noller, P. (1981). Gender and marital adjustment level differences in decoding messages from spouses and strangers. *Journal of Personality and Social Psychology, 41,* 272-278.

Noller, P. (1982a). Couple communication and marital satisfaction. *Australian Journal of Sex, Marriage and Family, 3,* 69-75.

Noller, P. (1982b). Channel consistency and inconsistency in the communications of married couples. *Journal of Personality and Social Psychology, 43,* 732-741.

Noller, P. (1984). *Nonverbal communication and marital interaction.* Oxford, Eng: Pergamon.

Noller, P. (1985). Negative communications in marriage. *Journal of Social and Personal Relationships, 2,* 289-301.

Noller, P., & Gallois C. (1984, July). Nonverbal behaviors in the marital situation. *British Journal of Social Psychology.*

Noller, P., & Venardos, C. (1986). Communication awareness in married couples. *Journal of Social and Personal Relationships, 3,* 31-42.

Patterson, G. R., & Reid, J. B. (1970). Reciprocity and coercion: Two facets of social systems. In C. Neuringer & J. L. Michaels (Eds.), *Behavior modification in clinical psychology.* New York: Appleton Century Crofts.

Posavec, E. J., & Pasko, S. J. (1971). Interpersonal attraction and confidence of attraction ratings as a function of number of attitudes and attitude similarity. *Psychonomic Science, 23,* 433-436.

Raush, H. L., Barry, W. A., Hertel, R. K., & Swain, M. E. (1974). *Communication, conflict and marriage.* San Francisco: Jossey-Bass.

Shapiro, A., & Swensen, C. (1969). Patterns of self-disclosure among married couples. *Journal of Counseling Psychology, 16,* 179-180.

Sillars, A. L., & Scott, M. D. (1983). Interpersonal perception between intimates: An integrative review. *Human Communication Research, 10,* 153-176.

Venardos, C. (1982). *Communication awareness in married couples.* Unpublished honors thesis, University of Queensland, St. Lucia, Australia.

Zaidel, S. F., & Mehrabian, A. (1969) The ability to communicate and infer positive and negative attitudes, facially and vocally. *Journal of Experimental Research in Personality, 3,* 233-241.

7

Attributions in Distressed Relations

How Can We Explain Them?

DONALD H. BAUCOM

The purpose of this chapter is to discuss attributions or causal explanations which spouses make within the context of a relationship, with an emphasis on distressed marriages. In order to approach such a topic, several bodies of literature, thought, and observation must be taken into account. First, the discussion involves a specific application of attribution theory developed within social psychology (Heider, 1958). Kelley and Michela (1980) note that there were more than 900 references focusing on attribution theory from 1970 to 1980. However, most of these studies focused on attributions made by strangers in laboratory settings. Relatively few investigated intimate relationships; fewer still focused on marriages, and even fewer researched distressed marriages. Consequently, the applicability of the many findings from attribution research to the current topic is unclear. Second, the chapter focuses on marriage and marital distress, and selected aspects of our knowledge in this area must be considered. When engaged in marital therapy with distressed couples, one is struck by the immense variability with which different couples explain marital events. A major thesis of this chapter is that this variability results in part because attributions for marital events can serve numerous functions, and interpreting the role of attributions from a single perspective is an oversimplification.

Attributions are made about both partners' behavior within the context of the marriage, and yet they are made by individuals. Consequently, the uniqueness of each individual must be taken into account. This understanding can perhaps be aided by a look at selected aspects of personality theory. Many individuals who are married experience significant individual psychological problems. Although the cause/effect relationship between marital discord and what has typically been labeled "individual psychopathology" is beyond the limits of this discussion, clinical observations and existing data strongly suggest that individual psychopathology can influence the types of attributions an individual makes about marital events (Baucom, Sayers, & Duhe, 1985). Consequently, the maladaptive individual psychological functioning of some individuals must be considered when attempting to understand the attributions they make regarding their marriage. Whereas the literature in each of these fields (attribution theory, marriage, normal adult personality theory, and individual psychopathology) is vast, research attempting to integrate these domains is essentially nonexistent. Therefore, many of the ideas put forth in this chapter are without empirical support but may stimulate further thought and investigation.

This chapter focuses on the various functions served by the attributions that married couples make. First, however, a consideration of basic issues regarding attributions or causal explanations will help to set the stage for that discussion.

When Do People Make Attributions?

A basic question which must be addressed is whether or not people make attributions in their daily lives. The answer appears obvious: People try to give causal explanations for at least some events. However, this has been a more complex issue to investigate than one might expect. In part, the complexity has resulted from the research methodology in attribution investigations. Often subjects are given various rating scales or open-ended questions and are asked to explain why someone has behaved a certain way or why some event has occurred. Subjects are typically able to provide explanations, but the concern is that perhaps they would not have sought explanations naturally without being asked to do so (see Enzle & Shopflocher, 1978). For example, Langer (1978) has suggested that as similar situations are repeated, the individual's response is overlearned and less information is processed. Under such circumstances, the individual may not seek causal explanations but will merely respond in some usual fashion. However, investigations that have used less direct methods to assess attributions without directing the individual to give causal explanations also indicate that persons do initiate attributional processes (see Pyszczynski & Greenberg, 1981; Wong & Weiner, 1981).

Such a conclusion comes as no major surprise, and a more interesting question for understanding couples involves identifying those circumstances which promote the initiation of the attribution process (i.e., what types of marital events couples seek to explain). One might answer that almost any situation which is experienced involves a certain amount of interpretation and explanation. Indeed, Newman (1981, p. 124) discusses the notion of implicit attributions "which are embedded in the very perception and interpretation of communicative messages at the time such messages are experienced." For example, if a husband speaks loudly to his wife, slams the door and leaves, she might say to herself, "Boy, he certainly is angry." That is, her perception of the situation involved the explanation that the reason he behaved this way is due to a given emotional state. Yet attribution investigators are usually referring to something more than the type of explanation just given. Typically, the attribution process has been viewed as a rather explicit, thoughtful analysis of some situation; Newman labels this an "explicit attribution-making process." A more explicit attribution from the wife in the above example would have been, "He's upset because I confronted him about coming home late, and he didn't have a good excuse. He always withdraws when he is on the spot." Whereas most research has focused on more thoughtful, explicit attributions, as will be discussed, implicit attributions are viewed as important in understanding marital distress.

Attribution research has assumed that individuals do not go through this mindful activity to explain everything that occurs. To do so would be extremely time-consuming and would require great amounts of energy. What factors, then, seem to initiate the attribution process? Although this question has not been addressed within the context of marital distress, findings in other aspects of attribution research may be useful in helping to understand when attributions occur within marriages.

When Behavior Is Unpredictable

One type of situation which seems to trigger the attribution process is unpredicted behavior and outcomes (Lau & Russell, 1980; Pyszczynski & Greenberg, 1981; Wong & Weiner, 1981). This is essentially the opposite of the type of situation which Langer proposes leads to mindless behavior. When a person does not behave as one thought the person would act, this is likely to attract the attention of the observer, who will seek to understand this unexpected event. Most nondistressed married couples seem to expect that their spouse will behave positively because of their partner's attributes (Taylor & Koivumaki, 1976). Therefore, persons in nondistressed marriages would be expected to seek attributions when a partner behaves negatively, a somewhat unexpected event in such relationships.

But what about distressed couples—what types of behavior do they predict their partners will exhibit in the marriage? Clinical observation suggests that there is great variability in how maritally distressed partners predict their partners will behave. In part, this seems to be related to how long the couple has been experiencing marital difficulties. Couples who have generally had good relationships but who are beginning to experience marital conflict often feel positively toward each other, are committed to the relationship, are unclear about the reasons for their difficulties, and expect[1] or predict that their partner will behave positively. These couples typically seem to engage in much attribution making when one partner behaves negatively. Such behavior is out of character in terms of the history of the relationship and is likely to initiate the attribution process in an attempt to understand the current problems that the couple is experiencing.

On the other hand, many maritally distressed couples have lived in conflict for years and have behaved toward each other in negative, punishing ways for long time periods. Such couples have stopped viewing the other person as a source of love, support, and encouragement: instead, they come to view the spouse in a generally negative way, predicting negative behavior from the other. This distinction among distressed couples is consistent with Snyder and Regts's (1982) finding that their clearest differentiation among various distressed couples was in terms of the degree of alienation and positive affect withdrawal. Couples who have lived with frequent negative interaction for long time periods would be expected to be less likely to engage in a thoughtful, logical attribution process when a partner behaves negatively. This is not to say that such couples do not make attributions for negative events. They likely make some explicit attributions, but many of these have become implicit, automatic, and simplified. Their very perception of their spouse's behavior seems to involve the interpretation that the spouse is intending to behave negatively to produce hurt, be selfish, or is exhibiting a part of the spouse's negative personality. Thus the extent to which negative behavior is expected among distressed couples is likely to vary widely across couples and influence the initiation of the attribution process. This idea is consistent with Newman's (1981) and Fincham's (in press) assertion that the stage of the marital relationship is likely to influence the attribution process.

When Behavior Is Novel

Closely related to the idea of unexpected behavior is the view that novel behavior from an important person will initiate the attribution process. This novel behavior might result from at least two factors: the stage of the relationship itself and a change in the person's behavior. For example, in the early developmental stages of a relationship, by definition almost all behavior by both persons is novel to that relationship. Consequently, early phases of a relationship would be expected to be a time when the attribution process is active; this is part of the process of forming an impression of the other person.

Important, novel behavior within a long-term marriage would also be expected to initiate the attribution process. For example, a husband and wife might discuss the limited amount of time he spends with the children, with the husband deciding to commit more time to his daughters. Although not surprised by the discussion, the wife might be prompted to seek causal explanations when he gives up watching Sunday afternoon football to spend time with the girls. She is likely to evaluate the motivation for this new behavior and how stable she thinks it will be.

When Behavior Is Negative

In addition to unexpected and novel situations, another circumstance likely to instigate attributional analyses involves negative behaviors, failure, and conflicts of interest (Orvis, Kelley, & Butler, 1976; Schwarz & Clore, 1983; Wong, 1979; Wong & Weiner, 1981). As discussed earlier, at times negative behavior may initiate attributions because such behavior is unexpected. However, there are likely to be factors beyond the unexpected nature of some aversive interactions which lead to attributions. More specifically, the impact of aversive events is likely to attract an individual's attention and disrupt routinized behavior and thought. This can be described as the "splinter phenomenon." With a splinter in the finger, one is unlikely to be thinking about how good the rest of the body feels; attention is drawn instead to the painful finger. Thus couples are likely to be motivated to understand their negative interactions in order to promote changes to alleviate their aversive states. Since there is plentiful evidence that maritally distressed couples engage in significantly more negative communication than nondistressed couples (see Baucom & Adams, in press, for a recent review), distressed couples are likely to be in a position to make more frequent attributions for negative marital events. Also, since this process is likely to interact with the unexpected nature of the event, explicit attributions for negative events seem likely to occur frequently during the early stages of marital distress.

If attributions are particularly likely to be made for negative events, does this mean that positive marital events are likely to receive less thought and attempted explanation? In many cases, probably so. Among nondistressed couples, positive interactions are frequent and expected. Such situations are unlikely to call forth explicit attributions. This may help to explain in part the tendency even among nondistressed couples for spouses to feel unappreciated or taken for granted for their positive behavior. Should such a sense of feeling unappreciated be raised in a nondistressed relationship, the partner is likely to respond: "I *do* realize all of the things you do; I know you work hard to make me happy and I do appreciate your efforts." However, unless called upon to show such appreciation, the partner frequently does not seem to devote great time and energy to interpreting the other's positive behavior. Instead, the attributions are more likely to be implicit, and consequently they are unlikely to be communicated to the other person.

Among distressed relationships, positive behavior may or may not be expected between the two partners, and this would seemingly affect the initiation of attributions. When positive behavior is expected, attributions are less likely to be made for it; when positive behavior is unexpected, attributions might seem more likely. However, on many occasions unexpected positive behavior may occur within the context of frequent negative behavior. Such potent negative behavior may overshadow the positive behavior, resulting in little attention to the positive behavior or in explanations which tend to make it seem unimportant.

When Behavior Is Important

The preceding discussion highlights an important issue—that numerous variables are likely to interact in influencing whether an individual will initiate an explicit, thoughtful attributional analysis. The factors described here are likely to interact with at least one other variable—the importance of the behavior or event. In general, behavior defined by the individual as important is more likely to in-itiate the attribution process than unimportant behavior. That is, most people are unlikely to devote much of their time trying to explain trivia. As Berley and Jacobson (in press) point out, dependence on another person is one factor that is likely to increase the importance of that person's behavior. Thus a relationship in which a spouse looks to the partner for numerous sources of satisfaction is likely to increase the frequency of attributions for that spouse. This suggestion is consis-tent with clinical observations in which highly dependent spouses are hyperalert to their partner's behavior, seeking indications of love or rejection. Exploring the issue of dependency within stranger dyads, Berscheid, Graziano, Monson, and Dermer (1976) found that college students who observed strangers whom they anticipated dating (high outcome dependency) engaged in more attribution analyses of the strangers' behavior than did students who observed the same strangers but did not expect to date them (low outcome dependency).

Attributions, Ambiguity, and Avoidance

The discussion thus far has followed from the proposition that people make attributions because they serve useful functions. As Snyder and Wicklund (1981) point out, the focus of attribution research has been on how people discard some causal explanations and decide on others, with the result that individuals have a clear pic-ture of the world. However, Snyder and Wicklund propose that there may be times when the individual is motivated to arrive at ambiguous attributions or to avoid attributions for one's own or others' behavior. Although their primary focus is not marital relationships, the concept of attributional ambiguity and avoidance seems relevant to marriage.

Assume that a wife did not want to realize that the reason her hus-band frequently came home late was because he was having an affair. In order to avoid this undesirable conclusion, she could remain am-biguous in her explanations and not arrive at any final explanation. Or she could adopt a different strategy: She could avoid thinking about her husband's tardiness as much as possible and simply not make at-tributions. It is not at all atypical for spouses to respond, "I just don't think about it." To accomplish such avoidance, the wife might find other important issues to think about or be away from home or asleep when her husband arrives so that his late arrival and an awkward in-teraction will not be highlighted. The husband's behavior in this ex-ample is an important, negative act to the wife and may be unexpected; generally, these circumstances would be thought to initiate a mindful, attributional process. However, as just described, the wife could be motivated to avoid making attributions because a need to predict and understand is overridden by a need to protect the relationship.

There may be at least one other reason why people are motivated not to arrive at clear attributions. Attribution theory implicitly suggests that the more control and ability to predict an individual has, the more satisfied that person will be; attributions often assist this goal. However, McClelland (1951) and Maddi (1968) propose personality theories that question such assumptions. For example, Maddi, in collaboration with Fiske, suggests that each individual has a customary though variable level of excitation, tension, or activation with which the individual is comfortable. When stimulation is too great, the person will attempt to decrease it; when stimulation is too low, the person will attempt an increase. Although there are multiple ways to alter the level of stimulation, one strategy is to vary the degree of predictability. Consequently, Maddi and Fiske suggest that life can become too predictable, and that a likely result is boredom.

Such logic seems applicable to the marital situation. Indeed, some persons in distressed marriages state that life has become too routine and predictable. It seems unlikely that they would be motivated to make attributions for marital events to further increase predictability. Spouses at times complain, "I know him too well. I know what he is going to do, when he is going to do it, and why he is going to do it. I need something new, a change of pace." Although there seem to be major individual differences in this area, some persons seem to prefer to view the spouse with some degree of mystery, as somewhat unexplainable and unpredictable. Such persons are likely to spend less time attempting to explain the spouse's behavior but instead prefer to experience the partner's unexpected behavior as a welcomed surprise. Although most people may not prefer to lead their lives as a series of surprises, there are probably times when most married persons do not want to be able to predict their spouse's behavior. In such contexts, attributional ambiguity or avoidance may be used to maintain or improve the quality of the relationship.

Attributional Dimensions

Given that persons do try to give causal explanations for certain events, what is a useful way to categorize those attributions?

Typically, attributions have been considered on several dimensions a priori defined by investigators, with different investigators focusing on different dimensions. Perhaps the dimensions that have received the most attention focus on stable/unstable and internal/external attributions. The stability dimension focuses on whether the cause is likely to continue or whether it is changeable (Weiner, 1974). The internal/external dimension involves the "causal source, i.e., who (or what) is responsible for the family conflict" (Doherty, 1981, p. 6). This focus on whether the behavior is attributable to the actor or to circumstances outside of the actor was popularized by Jones and Davis (1965).

Following from the internal/external dimension is a control dimension (Madden & Janoff-Bulman, 1981; Weiner, 1979) that focuses on whether the cause is subject to personal influence. That is, a husband might perceive that some marital event is primarily attributable to his wife. He then might decide that he has a great deal of control or influence over his wife's behavior. Another attributional dimension describes whether the behavior of an actor is voluntary (Heider, 1958) or whether it seems involuntary on the actor's part. Passer, Kelley, and Michela (1978) concluded that this is a frequent dimension used in evaluating the behavior of persons who commit some act.

An additional dimension discussed by Passer et al. (1978) involves the "positive versus negative attitude toward spouse" and focuses on how the behavior reflects an actor's overall evaluation of his or her partner. It is similar to Doherty's intent dimension (i.e., whether the behavior was perceived as intended to be helpful or hurtful, positive or negative). This dimension has not been the subject of extensive research, perhaps because it is less relevant in stranger interaction, which has been the focus of much attribution research. However, whether a husband believes his wife's behavior results from her attempt to be helpful or hurtful, or whether he believes that her behavior reflects that she feels positively or negatively toward him, is likely to be extremely important.

This dimension brings into focus that in attributions within marriage, there is an interpersonal relationship involved. Often the attribution is not merely an explanation of one's own behavior, or one's spouse's behavior in isolation; rather, it is an explanation of that behavior within a relationship. Newman (1981, p. 126) has proposed the idea of an interpersonal attribution for those instances in which the explanation involves a perception of " 'self in regard to other' and 'other in regard to self.' " Examples would include such explanations as, "He did that because he loves me" or "I did that because I wanted to get your attention." Fincham (in press) suggests that it might be useful to distinguish such attributions from what he views as relational attributions, whereas Newman's concept focuses on one person's motivations (e.g., "He did that because *he* wants..."). Fincham proposes that attributing one's behavior to aspects of the relationship is different (e.g., "He left because *we* don't have an effective way to resolve our problems"). Attributions to the relationship place less emphasis on either individual but more on the interaction between the spouses. As such, there might be less anger directed toward the partner for problems when such relationship attributions are made. Although Fincham's differentiation sounds useful, at present there are no data available on couples' use of relationship attributions.

A final dimension that is often discussed is whether a cause is global or specific. In terms of relationships, global causes are those which are likely to affect many aspects of the relationship (e.g., "She did that because she doesn't love me anymore"); specific causes are those which are likely to affect relatively few aspects of the relationship (e.g., "He didn't eat the casserole because he doesn't like casseroles").

Thus these dimensions center on who or what is responsible for some behavior, whether the actor seemed to be behaving in a voluntary manner, whether the actor had positive or negative intentions toward the other person, whether the cause is likely to change in the future, whether the person making the attribution can change the cause, and how many aspects of the relationship will be affected by the cause. Since any attribution can be evaluated on all of these dimensions and probably other useful dimensions, the possible number of types of attributions formed by the intersection of these dimensions is overwhelming. Consequently, no attempt will be made to discuss the combination of all of these dimensions in the current discussion. Instead, dimensions will be considered when they seem particularly pertinent or when there are marital data relevant to a dimension (see Doherty, 1981, for a model that incorporates most of these dimensions into a model of family conflict).

The Functions of Attributions

Thus far, some of the situations that initiate the attributional process have been discussed, and attributional dimensions have been described. One of the most important questions then becomes, Why do people make attributions, and what purposes are served by arriving at causal explanations? For many adults, the marital relationship is of immense importance. Their dreams of happy adult lives often incorporate marriage and a family. Many of one's waking hours are spent either working to make money to support a marriage and family or performing chores in the home to maintain the marriage/family system. Consequently, how people explain their partner's behavior (and their own) within the marriage may be of immense importance to their sense of self. Therefore, one's causal attributions about marital events are likely to serve numerous functions within this broad context.

Understanding and Intimacy

One of the most straightforward reasons for seeking causal explanations is the desire to understand one's world. In recent attribution research, this goal has been deemphasized, with a focus on more complex motivations. Yet the desire to understand should not be neglected, particularly in a marital relationship. Part of developing a close, intimate relationship is coming to know and understand the partner, which certainly involves trying to understand the bases for the other's behavior. For many people this closeness, which includes understanding and causal explanations, is a gratifying, rewarding, and important part of marriage. They do not want to live with someone whose behavior they cannot explain; such a state results in a sense of alienation.

A frequent request from at least one partner in marital therapy involves a desire to feel closer to the other person, to talk more with the other, to understand the person better. When major negative events occur within the marriage, one partner is likely to make the following type of statement: "I just don't understand how you could do that. It just doesn't make sense to me. I've lived with you so long and felt that we knew each other so well. I need to understand what happened. Help me understand." Often this need for causal explanations seems preeminent over solutions to relationship problems. In teaching couples to problem-solve in marital therapy, the therapist will frequently observe that rather than seeking solutions to problems, the couple will focus on why the problem exists. If the immediate goal of the couple were to produce behavior change, the couple would quickly seek solutions to their problems when instructed to do so by the therapist. In essence, finding causal explanations for a married partner's behavior may increase the sense of intimacy, closeness, and oneness with the other person. Whereas this may not be of great importance when studying the behavior of strangers, it is likely to be very important within a marriage.

Control

A major tenet of attribution theory is that people seek attributions for multiple reasons, not just understanding their world. One thesis that has received substantial support is that attributions serve to provide effective control over one's life (Heider, 1958; Kelley, 1967, 1972). As Rothbaum, Weisz, and Snyder (1982) point out, control has often been defined rather narrowly to involve changing the outside world to bring it into alignment with one's desires. Such a definition seems applicable in certain marital situations. If one person is behaving in a way that has negative impact on the partner, the partner is likely to want that behavior changed. In order to accomplish that goal, it is useful to know why the person is behaving in a given way. For example, if a wife begins coming home later and later after work, her concerned husband will probably want to know why so that he can take appropriate steps to influence her behavior. Similarly, if one partner is behaving in some new positive way, the spouse might seek explanations in order to maintain that behavior. Thus, arriving at causal explanations can help the individual develop a set of behavior change or maintenance strategies.

There is a second way in which attributions can be used to alter a partner's behavior. Often one partner's attributions are communicated to the spouse, and this very communication is an attempt to promote change in the spouse. For example, a husband may say to his wife, "You want us to go out with your friends each weekend because you don't really care about me. If you did care, you would want to stay home more with me." In this instance, the husband is attempting to influence his wife to stay home, and he has provided her with a set of explanations in which she must behave as he wishes in order to show she loves him. Of course, she is likely to counter with her own causal explanations to obtain her goal of going out with her friends. Through communicating their attributions, spouses often try to promote change in the other person by, for example, inducing guilt (previous example), issuing a challenge ("You don't get promoted because you just don't have ambition. Why don't you just accept it?") or providing comfort ("It's all right. You were just tired tonight. There's no reason to make a big deal out of it").

Thus, as Orvis et al. (1976) and Knight and Vallacher (1981) point out, the social context within which the attribution is made must be considered. Attributions may serve different purposes and may be altered depending on whether or not they are shared with the spouse (Fincham, in press). Unless this distinction between private versus public attributions is made, confusion can result. For example, in clinical interactions the writer has observed the tendency for many distressed couples to be defensive in making attributions. That is, maritally distressed spouses blame their partners and take little responsibility for their marital problems. By contrast, clinical observation suggests that less distressed and more satisfied couples are less likely to make defensive attributions. Consequently, the author and his colleagues have predicted that the difference between attribution to partner and attribution to self can be correlated with level of marital distress. This hypothesis was based on couples' interactions with each other in which distressed spouses felt a need to defend themselves (i.e., public attributions were being made). However, the hypothesis was tested using a private attributional process in which each spouse completed a self-report attributional inventory during which there was less need to be defensive; hence the hypothesis was not confirmed (Baucom et al., 1985). Nevertheless, this discrepancy between public versus private attributions could easily explain the findings in the study.

Although sharing an attribution with a partner may be oriented toward changing some behavior, other attributions are shared in order to transmit interpersonal or relational information; the person is primarily motivated to produce an emotional impact on his or her partner. Thus a husband may tell his wife, "I did that because you are the most important person in the world to me." Although he might hope that his statement will alter her behavior in a positive way, the primary purpose for this statement might be to make his wife feel good. Similarly, other communicated attributions seem to be motivated by the desire to hurt the other person. Not all marital interaction is oriented toward improving the quality of the relationship. Instead spouses, particularly within unhappy marriages, seem to be motivated on occasion to hurt each other ("I did it because I just don't care about you anymore"). Thus the sharing of attributions may be intended to influence the partner's emotional state and/or behavior.

There are times in distressed marriages when one person is behaving negatively and the partner clings to very stable attributions, emphasizing that the person behaving negatively will never change. On some occasions this may be a challenge to the person to try to change; however, on other occasions this does not seem to be the case. Instead, the person making the stable attributions seems to want to cling to that explanation. Whereas many theories of control would suggest that such an individual experiences a loss of control, Rothbaum et al. (1982) point out that such a person may be exercising a different type of control, which they term "secondary control." Secondary control does not involve changing the outside world but rather in some way involves bringing one's own behavior into "alignment" with that world.

In a marital therapy session, a wife explained, "I don't really expect him to do anything for my birthday anymore. He has never been a thoughtful person, and he never will be. I did expect it the first few years we were married, and each year it broke my heart. So now I don't expect it, and it really doesn't bother me." In essence, through her stable attributions the wife was able to predict her husband's behavior and to control her emotional reaction. Distressed spouses who have been through years of conflict often seem to employ this strategy. After being hurt numerous times, they make attributions that allow them to predict their partner's behavior in order to minimize the negative emotional impact of that behavior. People do not want to become hopeful of a better life and be continually disappointed; therefore, they make attributions to minimize the likelihood of that happening. Such secondary control efforts serve a self-protective function—to lessen the emotional impact of the spouse's behavior.

The preceding discussion involves minimizing the taking of a risk—believing that another person might change and then becoming vulnerable to hurt and disappointment if the change does not occur. Making attributions to accomplish secondary control can be conservative in a second way as well: It lessens the expenditure of effort and physical energy which may not be effective in producing change in the partner or in the marriage. Persons in distressed marriages often describe themselves as being "tired of trying," stating that expending physical energy in an attempt to improve the relationship has left them drained. In such situations these persons often make external, stable, uncontrollable attributions for their marital problems. Such explanations might help to justify their unwillingness to make new efforts.

Thus one broad purpose served by attributions is to increase control within the marriage, and this can occur in numerous ways. First, causal explanations may be sought for a spouse's behavior, so that some strategy can be developed for changing negative behavior and maintaining positive behavior. Second, when attributions are communicated to the partner, those shared attributions may themselves be part of the behavior change strategy. Third, attributions can help an individual obtain a sense of secondary control within the relationship. Such control is often oriented toward conserving personal energy and avoiding the pain that comes with disappointment in the partner's behavior. Therefore, these uses of secondary control can be viewed as attempts at self-protection.

Self-Protection and Enhancement

The use of attributions for self-protection has been construed in a different way as well. Since a person's explanations for success and failure are likely to affect his or her self-esteem, such experiences provide an opportunity for self-serving biases in attributions (see Kelley & Michela, 1980; Miller & Ross, 1975; Zuckerman, 1979 for a review of this literature). That is, by making internal attributions for success and external attributions for failure, the individual can bolster his or her self-esteem. Whereas few data exist pertinent to this issue with couples, the existent findings are consistent with self-serving explanations. For example, Orvis et al. (1976) asked couples to provide explanations for instances of conflict of interest in their relationship. One of their major findings was that persons who behaved negatively tried to justify and excuse their own behavior, while the partner responded with responsibility-placing criticism. These findings were also consistent with Jones and Nisbett's (1972) hypothesis that actors attribute their own behavior more to situational requirements, while observers attribute the same type of behavior more to actors' stable personal dispositions.

Based on the notion of self-serving biases, we would expect a married person to take responsibility for positive marital events and attribute negative happenings to outside factors. At times this logic does seem to apply. Individuals who are maritally distressed often demonstrate a pattern of seeking credit when things go well and blaming the partner for problems. In fact, a cross-blaming pattern is one of the most salient communication patterns observed in maritally distressed couples (Gottman, 1979). Although the basis for this cross-blaming is unknown, it may be related to the need to protect one's self-esteem. As the relationship deteriorates, the person cannot expect to obtain much self-enhancing support from the spouse; unfortunately, the opposite is often true. Therefore, a bolstering of one's self-esteem and protection from accusations must come from within. The person feeling unappreciated and attacked makes self-assuring attributions and attempts to convince the partner that the person is behaving appropriately or at least justifiably.

Attempts to explain or justify one's seemingly negative behavior are often aided by the complexity of the interpersonal interaction. More specifically, little marital behavior occurs in isolation; almost all behavior can be seen as part of a continuing chain of events. How justifiable a spouse's behavior seems can be influenced by the point that person chooses to focus on in the the ongoing flow of events. As Watzlawick, Beavin, and Jackson (1967) note, the person punctuates or divides the chain of activities into segments and selects a beginning point. This beginning point is likely to be viewed as a cause and subsequent behavior as an effect of this cause. Thus a wife may try to justify her negative behavior by explaining it as resulting from her husband's previous actions ("The reason I left the room was because you had been ignoring me"). If he wishes to defend himself, the husband need only punctuate the interaction one step earlier and respond, "The only reason I was ignoring you was that you had just spent fifteen minutes criticizing me, and I didn't want any more of that."

Needs to bolster one's self-esteem are likely to be different among nondistressed and happily married couples. Within nondistressed marriages, individuals may feel secure and not need to make attributions to enhance themselves. This is particularly true if each person behaves and makes attributions so as to enhance the other's self-esteem. In some marriages, each may attribute responsibility for successes to the other and responsibility for failure to self or to factors outside the relationship. Although not within the context of marriage, this reversal of the typical pattern of attributions for success and failure has been noted in situations that call for modesty (Feather & Simon, 1971). A secure marriage, in which the partners build each other's self-esteem, is a situation that could allow one to be modest. Consequently, attributions for self-enhancement and attempts to defend one's self-esteem are likely to be called forth more frequently among distressed than nondistressed relationships.

Partner and Relationship Enhancement

The use of attributions to protect the individual's self-esteem has been discussed. However, the married person is not typically concerned only with self-image; the image of the partner and the relationship are also important. At times, attributions seem to serve the purpose of defending the partner and/or maintaining the relationship. For the sake of maintaining the relationship, spouses at times seem willing to distort the bases for their partner's behavior. For example, a wife gave a rather unbelievable explanation for why her husband came home late at night, although the basis for his behavior seemed apparent to their friends. As she later commented, "I didn't want to see it. I knew once I allowed myself to realize he was having an affair, our marriage would be over. All we have worked for all these years would be for nothing." In essence, people have ideas of how they want their marriages to be, how they think their partners should behave, and they provide attributions in line with those preferences to keep their dreams alive.

Individual Differences in Attributions

The Effects of Depression

The preceding discussion approaches self-serving attributions as a function of the quality of the relationship. However, there are likely to be substantial individual differences which moderate these effects. The stereotype of the distressed couple is one in which each person blames the other for problems. Although this is a prominent pattern, it is by no means universal. There are distressed relationships in which both partners blame the same individual for negative events. Clinical observation suggests that such patterns occur among pronounced dominant/submissive relationships in which the more submissive person is blamed by both partners for the marital problems (at least on a verbalized, communicated level).

A similar pattern is seen when one spouse is experiencing significant individual psychological distress. Clinical observation in marital therapy sessions indicates that depressed persons are often willing to make internal attributions and blame themselves for their marital problems. This observation about attributions for marital problems is consistent with one of the general attributional patterns observed in depressed individuals (Abramson, Seligman, & Teasdale, 1978; Beck, 1973). Frequently, the depressed person's partner attributes many of the couple's problems to the depressed person's lack of energy and motivation, emotional lability, and other depressive behavior. Consequently, couples with one depressed member often exhibit an attributional pattern in which both make attributions for problems to the depressed person.

On the other hand, an individual's individual psychopathology can have the opposite effect. At times, an individual's external attributions for marital problems do not appear to be unique to the marital relationship. Every clinician who has worked with couples has encountered married individuals whose blaming of others and the outside world for problems characterize their general attitude toward life. For a multitude of reasons, some individuals are extremely threatened by assuming responsibility for any problems, and their external attributions within the marriage are part of their broader approach to explaining problems. Such externalization of blame would be expected among individuals with, for example, paranoid features; however, such patterns are also observable in less disturbed individuals.

To attempt to explain an individual's attributions for positive and negative marital events by focusing only on the relationship is an oversimplification. There is great benefit in trying to understand the attributions and behavior of a spouse by considering that person as part of the marital system; however, it would be a mistake to overlook the individual psychopathology and the more normal individual differences of the two persons forming that marriage.

The Effects of Prior Expectations

The previous discussion focuses on instances in which a person's attributions for marital events are part of a broader pattern seemingly related to disturbances in individual psychological functioning which affect many, if not all, aspects of the person's life. In addition, there appear to be individuals who enter marriage with certain beliefs in restricted content areas that nevertheless influence the person's marital attributions. For example, in one troubled marriage the husband explained much of his wife's behavior on the basis that she was planning to leave him. According to the wife and the therapist's perceptions, however, there seemed little reason to believe that the wife was planning to terminate the relationship. Although historical antecedents are not always so clear, in this instance the husband's mother had unexpectedly deserted the family when he was a boy. Perhaps to minimize the pain of a similar surprise in his own marriage, the husband had become conviced that if he ever married, his wife would desert him, too. Unfortunately, as Berley and Jacobson (in press, p. 21) point out, such attributions can take on a life of their own, and the predicted behavior can become fulfilled: "When people test interpersonal hypotheses, they tend to use confirmatory strategies which are likely to constrain others' behavior in ways which support the initial hypotheses." Thus some attributions may be greatly influenced by spouses' long-standing predictions about how their lives will proceed, what their marriages will be like, and so on. It is in this sense that a priori expectations (in this case, the term refers to behavioral predictions) influence attributions.

Marital Adjustment and Types of Attributions—Empirical Status

We have highlighted various functions that might be served by attributions in marital relationships. Most of the preceding comments involve applications from findings in other areas of attribution research or are based on clinical observations from working with distressed couples. Thus far there has been little empirical work which attempts to clarify *why* married couples make various attributions. Instead, the research has been focused on an earlier stage, generally attempting to discern what lawful relationships exist between level of marital adjustment and the types of attributions made.

Perhaps the major finding to date is that married individuals make attributions for their spouses' behavior in a manner that is consistent with the individuals' overall satisfaction with the relationship. That is, compared to nondistressed persons, maritally distressed persons would be expected to blame their partners for negative marital events and to see the causes as stable and global. Baucom et al. (1985) found exactly that. Clinic and nonclinic couples were asked to complete a self-report inventory providing attributions for hypothetical negative behavior which their partners might exhibit. For both husbands and wives, the less maritally distressed persons viewed the causes for their partner's negative behavior as less due to self or partner, more due to factors outside the relationship, less stable, and less global. Using a similar methodology, Fincham and O'Leary (1983) found that distressed couples rated the causes of negative behavior as more global than nondistressed couples. Also as predicted, Madden and Janoff-Bulman (1979) found through interviews that wives low in marital satisfaction were more likely to blame their husbands for marital conflicts than were wives high in marital satisfaction. Jacobson, McDonald, Follette, and Berley (in press) used a laboratory situation to instruct one partner to behave either negatively or positively. They also found that, compared to nondistressed spouses, distressed spouses tended to attribute their partner's negative behavior to factors internal to the partner. Thus, using different research methodologies, investigators have found relationships between attributions (particularly the internal/external dimension) and level of marital adjustment.

Attributions for positive behavior would be predicted to be in the opposite direction: Distressed persons would be less willing than nondistressed persons to give responsibility to their partners for positive behavior and would see the causes for this behavior as less stable and less global. This would be particularly likely among couples who have been distressed for long time periods. Although results are not totally in agreement, several studies have obtained results consistent with these predictions. For example, Fincham and O'Leary (1983) found that, compared to distressed spouses, nondistressed spouses rated the causes of positive behavior as more global and controllable. Similarly, Kelley (1979), Thompson and Kelley (1981), and Jacobson et al. (in press) found that relationship satisfaction was associated with the tendency to give more credit to the partner for positive relationship events. However, Baucom et al. (1985) did not obtain such relationships. Using a methodology very similar to Fincham and O'Leary's, we found attributions for negative behavior and marital adjustment to be related as predicted, but there were no significant correlations between marital adjustment and attributions for positive spouse behavior. At present there is no clear reconciliation of these discrepant findings, but this lack of consistent results parallels findings in the marital communication literature. Whereas almost all studies find that negative communications are correlated with level of marital adjustment, the relationship between frequency of positive communications and marital adjustment is much more inconsistent (see Baucom and Adams, in press, for a review of these findings).

At present there is no clear basis for concluding why the relationships between attributions and marital adjustment exist. First, the attributions could reflect reality. For example, since marital distress is typified by an excess of negative behavior, perhaps it makes sense for distressed spouses to rate the causes of negative events as global and stable. Or it may be that the attributions provide an oversimplification of reality but that the simplification assists in future prediction. Third, the results are also consistent with an interpretation emphasizing the protection of self-esteem, in which distressed spouses blame the partner for negative marital events. Nondistressed spouses, feeling secure in the relationship, are more willing to give responsibility to the partner for positive events. Of course, there is no reason that any single one of these interpretations for the findings has to be correct. Perhaps an effective attribution for a situation is one that is plausible and that serves other useful functions as well. Similarly, for different couples, or the same couple on different occasions, a single attribution may serve different purposes.

Clinical Implications

The purpose of this final section is not to provide a detailed description of specific interventions for dealing with the attributions of couples requesting assistance for their relationships. Instead, a brief overview of some of the goals that the clinician may want to consider is presented along with some strategies for obtaining those goals.

First, to the extent that Langer (1978) is correct that repeated or similar interaction leads to mindless behavior, spouses are unlikely to make explicit attributions for their partner's behavior. Instead, implicit attributions become the norm. One difficulty with implicit attributions is that they are so much a part of the person's perception of the situation that typically they are not questioned or evaluated but merely viewed as part of reality. For many distressed spouses, this implicit attribution process results in the belief that their partners are bad persons who want to hurt them and who are unchangeable. Under such circumstances, the clinician may want to make the attribution process more explicit, having the individual realize that the implicit attribution which was viewed as part of reality actually involves an interpretation that might or might not be appropriate.

Whereas there may be many strategies for accomplishing this end, the current author and his colleagues have been investigating one particular strategy (Baucom, 1981, 1985; Baucom & Lester, 1984). Couples are asked to state a problem in their marital relationship, after which they are asked to discuss how each of the following factors have contributed to the problem: environmental or outside circumstances, husband's behavior, wife's behavior, husband's interpretation of wife's behavior, wife's interpretation of husband's behavior, husband's emotional reaction, and wife's emotional reaction. During this discussion, the husband focuses on his own behavior, thoughts, and emotional reactions, and the wife does likewise.

There are several goals in using this procedure. First, whereas many distressed spouses have developed an automatic attributional process of blaming the spouse, here the couple is asked to recognize the multiple factors that contribute to a problem. Also, each person is focusing on his or her own contributions to the problem, so focus is taken away from blaming the partner. In addition, when each person offers his or her interpretation of the spouse's behavior, it is emphasized that this is only an interpretation, not fact. Each person is asked to check with the partner the appropriateness of that interpretation. Finally, borrowing from the logic of rational emotive therapy (Ellis, 1962), each spouse is shown how his or her emotional reactions follow from the interpretations that he or she has made of the situation. Consequently, the multiple factors contributing to any single problem and the highly subjective, interpretational nature of explaining problem situations is emphasized in order to combat the simplistic, automatic attributional processing in which many distressed spouses engage.

A similar strategy of making the attribution process explicit might be useful in evaluating partners' positive behavior, even in nondistressed relationships. As discussed earlier, in nondistressed marriages many types of positive behavior become routinized, and often little thought goes into evaluating the partner's positive behavior. Instead, the behavior simply becomes expected and is not commented on. Under such circumstances, the person behaving positively begins to feel unappreciated. Having the spouse enter into a more explicit attribution process draws attention to the positive behavior and the actor's good intentions for such behavior. Consequently, one goal of the clinician may be to make implicit attributions for both positive and negative behavior more explicit on selected occasions.

One reason given for attributions was to promote effective prediction and control over one's world. Whereas this is an understandable goal that most, if not all, people share to varying degrees, the concern becomes how the individual attempts to obtain that control. As an example, attributions are frequently communicated to the partner as a way of attempting to alter his or her behavior. If, however, the attributions involve a belittling of the partner and are intended as a punishment for some behavior or as a challenge to change, the therapist must carefully evaluate the individual's behavior change strategy. That is not to say that one partner should never make attributions which reflect negatively on the spouse; however, if such negative attributions are a primary strategy for behavior change, remedial efforts should be considered. For example, one husband made very condemning attributions for his wife's behavior. When the therapist pointed that out, he responded, "Well, I have to do that. First of all, that is the only way to get her attention. Second, she loves to prove me wrong. So if I say these bad things about her, then she might just change, just to prove I'm wrong." Under such circumstances, the therapist may want to teach the couple more positive, effective behavior change strategies such as problem solving and the use of reinforcement.

Another attempt at control which requires intervention involves a situation in which one partner in a distressed relationship comes to believe that no meaningful changes are (realistically) likely to occur. As discussed earlier, this conclusion may be an attempt at secondary control by not becoming vulnerable to disappointment if efforts should be made but fail to improve the relationship. Clearly, little can be accomplished toward improving the relationship while the belief is held. Therapists have developed many strategies to combat this problem, and some attempt must be made early in therapy to convince the individual to take the risk to improve the relationship. Otherwise, the person will demonstrate that, indeed, therapy cannot improve the marriage. What the therapist must realize is that often such persons are not simply lazy. Instead, they are afraid of being hurt and disappointed, and their acknowledgment of this real concern is often a first step in reversing the decision not to work to improve the relationship.

At other times, attributions serve the purpose of protecting or enhancing a person's self-esteem. Again, this does not necessarily call for intervention, but if the attributions are detrimental to the relationship or the spouse, or if they seem greatly distorted, then intervention seems appropriate. One of the most frequent circumstances in which distressed couples seem to feel the need to protect their self-esteem is when they are discussing problem areas of the relationship. This self-protection frequently takes the form of each partner blaming the other for the problem and defending him- or herself. One strategy for reversing the pattern was mentioned above: Have each person speak only about what he or she contributes to the problem, not what the spouse contributes. As each verbally acknowledges some sense of responsibility, there is less need to blame the other or to defend oneself from attack. If the couple can be taught to discuss nondefensively the various factors contributing to any specific problem, then neither person has to be viewed as the villain or the victim. A reversed strategy is often helpful for dealing with positive marital events. Each person can be asked to discuss the other person's contribution to this positive interaction. As each person hears these acknowledgments from the spouse, each is more likely to feel recognized for his or her efforts and to feel appreciated.

Intervention is also needed when a spouse's a priori predictions of how the partner will behave lead to attributions to confirm that prediction. An example was given earlier of a husband who was convinced before he even met his wife that if he ever married, his wife would desert him. He then interpreted much of her behavior as signs of her impending separation from him. Often such attributions and the underlying predictions are difficult to change within the context of marital therapy. At times, feedback from the therapist—in this case that the partner seems unlikely to leave—may effectively challenge the individual's beliefs. However, individual psychotherapy might also provide a more fruitful avenue for exploring such predictions in detail. Otherwise, one spouse can become the focus of the marital sessions while the partner sits quietly and listens.

Again, it must be realized that there are insufficient data to validate the effectiveness of the above interventions; instead, they are based on this therapist's clinical experience and limited treatment outcome data. Although existing data are encouraging, treatment outcome studies evaluating the effectiveness of cognitive restructuring, including a focus on attributions with distressed couples, are extremely limited (Baucom, 1985; Baucom & Lester, 1984; Epstein, Pretzer, & Fleming, 1982; Margolin & Weiss, 1978). Baucom and Lester (1984) compared the effectiveness of (1) behavioral marital therapy alone and (2) behavior marital therapy plus cognitive restructuring, including a focus on inappropriate attributions and unrealistic relationship expectations. Whereas both treatments improved the marital adjustment of the couples, only the treatment that included cognitive restructuring produced relevant cognitive changes in the couples. In a larger but similar study still in progress, the same pattern of results is evident (Baucom, 1985). Similarly, Epstein et al. (1982) compared the effectiveness of (1) cognitive restructuring, including a focus on attributions and unrealistic relationship expectations, with (2) a communications training approach to marital distress. They found that the cognitive restructuring approach was more effective in producing relevant cognitive changes. In the first treatment study explicitly attempting to augment behavioral marital therapy with cognitive restructuring, Margolin and Weiss (1978) employed a four-week analog marital treatment. They found that helping the couple to realize that many of their martial problems were due to a lack of relationship skills rather than a bad partner (a less damaging attribution) improved the effectiveness of their intervention (see Baucom & Hoffman, in press, for a more detailed evaluation of these studies). Whereas these investigations indicate that procedures are being developed which can successfully change a couple's cognitions, each of these cognitive treatments actually includes a number of specific interventions. Consequently, which particular techniques are of use to the couples and which couples benefit from these procedures are as yet unknown.

Within the next few years, we can expect (predict) that our knowledge of the role of attributions in marital relationships will increase significantly. At present there are numerous basic research investigations underway. Several theoretical papers have been developed which may help to guide questions for investigation and which can provide a framework for interpreting isolated findings (Berley &

Jacobson, in press; Doherty, 1981; Fincham, in press), and treatment outcome studies applying these concepts with distressed couples are in progress (e.g., Baucom, 1985). It is hoped that the present study will assist both the researcher and the clinician in considering various purposes served by attributions for marital events to help bring clarity to this complex phenomenon.

Summary and Conclusions

We have addressed several issues, but the major focus has been on the functions served by attributions within the context of the marital relationship. Although making attributions for the sake of understanding per se may be less important in interactions among strangers, among married couples the desire to understand and feel close to one's mate is quite important. The often-cited goal of obtaining or maintaining control as a motivation for making attributions was also discussed within the context of marital relationships. Appropriate attributions can help, rather straightforwardly, to control a partner's behavior by leading to effective behavior change and maintenance strategies. Control can also be obtained by communicating attributions to the spouse with an attempt to influence him or her. Consistent with Rothbaum et al.'s (1982) notion of secondary control, one can attain a sense of control by bringing oneself into alignment with the existing outside world. More specifically, certain attributions can assist individuals in controlling their own emotional responses to a partner or in conserving their own energies in a situation that appears stable.

The usefulness of attributions for self-protection and enhancement in marriage was also discussed. It was suggested that the need for self-protection is probably related to the level of marital adjustment that the married person is experiencing. Similarly, not only is the image of the individual frequently at stake, but the image that the person wants to maintain of the partner and the relationship also influence the attributions that are made. At times, when one is attempting to maintain a certain image of the partner or the marriage, attributions might be left vague or not made at all if the partner's behavior seems contrary to the preferred image.

Individual differences also seem to influence the attribution process. Since attributions often appear to provide a sense of predictability and control, an individual's preference for level of predictability tends to affect whether or not attributions will be sought. Individual differences also appear to influence the types of attributions made, and certain types of psychopathology may be consistent with certain types of attributions. Finally, expectations or predictions of how a spouse will behave are developed at various times in one's life, even prior to marriage, and these a priori expectations may influence one's attributions for subsequent marital interaction.

Whereas the functions of the attributions discussed earlier are consistent with both attribution research outside of the marital area and clinical observation, there is little empirical investigation of these functions within the context of marriage. Clearly, additional investigation is needed to either substantiate, refute, or modify these impressions. Further study should also address the interaction of the various attribution dimensions discussed in this chapter. Almost all investigations in this area consider several attribution dimensions, but these are typically investigated separately, one at a time. That is, global/specific attributions are correlated with level of marital distress, and then stable/unstable attributions are correlated with level of marital distress. Whereas the interaction of these dimensions is discussed on a theoretical level, our data analytic strategies to date fail to reflect this level of complexity.

Furthermore, nearly all of our studies thus far have focused on attributional dimensions, almost to the exclusion of the content of the attributions. As Epstein, Pretzer, and Fleming (1985) point out, ignoring the content of attributions may omit important information, since different attributions can receive similar dimensional ratings but have very different effects. For example, the attributions, "My husband ignores my birthday because he is a thoughtless person" and "My husband ignores my birthday because he doesn't love me" might both be viewed as stable, global attributions. However, the former attribution might result in a sense of frustration and/or anger, whereas the latter is more likely to result in sadness or depression. There may be important content themes in couples' attributions, and these should not be excluded in favor of investigators' a priori assumptions of the appropriate dimensions to assess.

Finally, one guiding principle of most marital researchers and therapists is that marriage is an ongoing, interactive process between husband and wife. Empirical investigations exploring couples' communications substantiate that both positive and negative communications from one spouse influence the partner to respond in a similar manner; that is, positive and negative reciprocity does exist (see Gottman, Notarius, Markman, Banks, Yoppi, & Rubin, 1976; Margolin & Wampold, 1981). As discussed earlier, when attributions are shared with the partner, they become a type of communication. With the exception of Gottman's (1979) study of cross-blaming among couples, there are almost no empirical investigations of how attributions made by one spouse influence subsequent attributions from the other spouse. In order to understand more fully the communicated aspects of attributions, this interactive, sequential process must be explored.

Thus we are truly in our infancy of investigating the role of attributions in marriage. Creative research designs and assessment strategies will have to be developed to address many of the issues described here. In addition, if we as investigators and therapists are to increase our understanding of couples, improve our control over the therapeutic process, and thus bolster our own self-esteem, an increased explicit focus on couples' attributions appears to be a fruitful avenue to pursue.

NOTE

1. The term *expectations* is used in at least two different ways in discussing marital relationships. First, it is used to refer to behavior predictions of what will occur. For example, a wife might say, "He has forgotten our wedding anniversary for thirty years and I expect him to forget it again this year." On the other hand, the term also refers to what should occur—what is deemed appropriate and acceptable (e.g., "I expect a marriage to involve mutual respect, care, and thoughtfulness"). Clearly, these two meanings are not the same; in fact, much marital discord involves discrepancies between how one partner believes the spouse should behave versus how the partner predicts the spouse will behave. In this chapter, the reader can expect that the meaning will be made clear whenever the term *expectation* is used.

REFERENCES

Abramson, L. Y., Seligman, M.E.P., & Teasdale, J. F. (1978). Learned helplessness in humans: Critique and reformulation. *Journal of Abnormal Psychology, 87*, 49-74.

Baucom, D. H. (1981, November). *Cognitive behavioral strategies in the treatment of marital discord.* Paper presented at the 15th Annual Convention of the Association for the Advancement of Behavior Therapy, Toronto.

Baucom, D. H. (1985). *Can BMT be improved? The utility of cognitive restructuring and emotional expressiveness training.* Unpublished manuscript, University of North Carolina, Chapel Hill.

Baucom, D. H., & Adams, A. (in press). Assessing communication in marital interaction. In K. D. O'Leary (Ed.), *Assessment of marital discord.* New York: Erlbaum.

Baucom, D. H., & Hoffman, J. A. (in press). The effectiveness of marital therapy: Current status and application to the clinical setting. In N. S. Jacobson & A. Gurman (Eds.), *Handbook of marital therapy.* New York: Guilford Press.

Baucom, D. H., & Lester, G. W. (1984, November). *Augmenting behavioral marital therapy with cognitive restructuring.* Paper presented at the 18th Annual Convention of the Association for the Advancement of Behavior Therapy, Philadelphia.

Baucom, D. H., & Sayers, S. L., & Duhe, A. (1985). *Assessing couples' attributions for marital events.* Unpublished manuscript, University of North Carolina, Chapel Hill.

Beck, A. T. (1973). *The diagnosis and management of depression.* Philadelphia: University of Pennsylvania Press.

Berley, R. A., & Jacobson, N. S. (in press). Causal attributions in intimate relationships: Toward a model of cognitive behavioral marital therapy. In P. Kendall (Ed.), *Advances in cognitive-behavioral research and therapy* (Vol. 3). New York: Academic Press.

Berscheid, E., Graziano, W., Monson, T., & Dermer, M. (1976). Outcome dependency: Attention, attribution, and attraction. *Journal of Personality and Social Psychology, 34,* 978-989.

Doherty, W. J. (1981). Cognitive processes in intimate contact 1: Extending attribution theory. *American Journal of Family Therapy, 9,* 3-13.

Ellis, A. (1962). *Reason and emotion in psychotherapy.* New York: Lyle Stuart.

Enzle, M. E., & Shopflocher, D. (1978). Instigation of attribution processes by attributional questions. *Personality & Social Psychology Bulletin, 4,* 595-599.

Epstein, N., Pretzer, J., & Fleming, B. (1982, November). *Cognitive therapy and communication training: Comparison of effects with distressed couples.* Paper presented at the 16th Annual Convention of the Association of the Advancement of Behavior Therapy, Los Angeles.

Epstein, N., Pretzer, J., & Fleming, B. (1985). *Marital Attitudes Questionnaire.* Unpublished manuscript.

Feather, N. T., & Simon, J. G. (1971). Attribution of responsibility and valence of outcome in relation to initial confidence and success and failure of self and other. *Journal of Personality and Social Psychology, 18,* 173-188.

Fincham, F. D. (in press). Attributions in close relationships. In J. Harvey & G. Weary (Eds.), *Contemporary attribution theory and research.* New York: Academic Press.

Fincham, F. D., & O'Leary, K. D. (1983). Causal inferences for spouse behavior in maritally distressed and nondistressed couples. *Journal of Social and Clinical Psychology, 1,* 42-57.

Gottman, J. M. (1979). *Marital interaction: Experimental investigations.* New York: Academic Press.

Gottman, J. M., Notarius, C., Markman, H., Bank, S., Yoppi, B., & Rubin, M. E. (1976). Behavior exchange theory and marital decision making. *Journal of Personality and Social Psychology, 34,* 14-23.

Heider, F. (1958). *The psychology of interpersonal relations.* New York: Wiley.

Jacobson, N. S., McDonald, D. W., Follette, W. C., & Berley, R. A. (in press). Attribution processes in distressed and nondistressed married couples. *Cognitive Therapy and Research.*

Jones, E., & Davis, K. (1965). From acts to dispositions: The attribution process in person perception. In L. Berkowitz (Ed.), *Advances in experimental social psychology* (Vol. 2). New York: Academic Press.

Jones, E. E., & Nisbett, R. E. (1972). The actor and the observer: Divergent perceptions of the causes of behavior. In E. E. Jones, D. E. Kanouse, H. H. Kelley, R. E. Nisbett, S. Valins, & B. Weiner (Eds.), *Attribution: Perceiving the causes of behavior* (pp. 79-94). Morristown, NJ: General Learning Corporation.

Kelley, H. H. (1967). Attribution theory and social psychology. In D. Levine (Ed.), *Nebraska symposium on motivation.* Lincoln: University of Nebraska Press.

Kelley, H. H. (1972). Causal schemata and the attribution process. In E.E. Jones, D. E. Kanouse, H. H. Kelley, R. E. Nesbitt, S. Valins, & B. Weiner (Eds.), *Attribution: Perceiving the causes of behavior* (pp. 151-174). Morristown, NJ: General Learning Corporation.

Kelley, H. H. (1979). *Personal relationships: Their structures and processes.* Hillsdale, NJ: Erlbaum.

Kelley, H. H., & Michela, J. L. (1980). Attributional theory and research. In M. R. Rosenzweig & L. W. Porter (Eds.), *Annual review of psychology* (Vol. 31). Palo Alto, CA: Annual Reviews.

Knight, J. A., & Vallacher, R. R. (1981). Interpersonal engagement in social perception: The consequences of getting into the action. *Journal of Personality and Social Psychology, 40,* 990-999.

Langer, E. J. (1978). Rethinking the role of thought in social interaction. In J. H. Harvey, W. J. Ickes, & R. F. Kidd (Eds.), *New directions in attribution research* (Vol. 2, pp. 35-58). Hillsdale, NJ: Erlbaum.

Lau, R. R., & Russell, D. (1980). Attributions in the sports pages: A field test of some current hypotheses in attribution research. *Journal of Personality and Social Psychology, 39,* 311-328.

Madden, M. E., & Janoff-Bulman, R. (1981). Blame, control, and marital satisfaction: Wives' attributions for conflict in marriage. *Journal of Marriage and the Family, 44,* 663-674.

Maddi, S. R. (1968). *Personality theories: A comparative analysis.* Homewood, IL: Dorsey Press.

Margolin, G., & Wampold, B. E. (1981). Sequential analysis of conflict and accord in distressed and nondistressed partners. *Journal of Consulting and Clinical Psychology, 49,* 554-567.

Margolin, G., & Weiss, R. L. (1978). Comparative evaluation of therapeutic components associated with behavioral marital treatments. *Journal of Consulting and Clinical Psychology, 46,* 1476-1486.

McClelland, D. C. (1951). *Personality.* New York: Dryden.

Miller, D. T., & Ross, M. (1975). Self-serving biases in the attribution of causality: Fact or fiction. *Psychological Bulletin, 82,* 213-225.

Newman, H. M. (1981). Interpretation and explanation: Influences of communicative exchanges within intimate relationships. *Communication Quarterly, 6,* 123-132.

Orvis, B. R., Kelley, H. H., & Butler, D. (1976). Attributional conflict in young couples. In J. H. Harvey, W. Ickes, & R. F. Kidd (Eds.), *New directions in attribution research* (Vol. 1, pp. 353-386). Hillsdale, NJ: Erlbaum.

Passer, M. W., Kelley, H. H., & Michela, J. L. (1978). Multidimensional scaling of the causes for negative interpersonal behavior. *Journal of Personality and Social Psychology, 36,* 951-962.

Pyszczynski, T. A., & Greenberg, J. (1981). Role of disconfirmed expectancies in the instigation of attributional processing. *Journal of Personality and Social Psychology, 40,* 31-38.

Rothbaum, F., Weisz, J. R., & Snyder, S. S. (1982). Changing the world and changing the self: A two-process model of perceived control. *Journal of Personality, 42,* 5-37.

Snyder, D. J., & Regts, J. M. (1982). Factor scales for assessing marital disharmony and disaffection. *Journal of Consulting Psychology, 50,* 736-743.

Snyder, M. L., & Wicklund, R. A. (1981). Attribute ambiguity. In J. H. Harvey, W. Ickes, & R. F. Kidd (Eds.), *New directions in attribution research* (Vol. 3), Hillsdale, NJ: Erlbaum.

Schwartz, N., & Clore, G. L. (1983). Mood, misattribution, and judgments of well-being: Informative and directive functions of affective states. *Journal of Personality and Social Psychology, 45*, 513-523.

Taylor, S. E., & Koivumaki, J. H. (1976). The perception of self and others: Acquaintanceship, affect, and actor-observer differences. *Journal of Personality and Social Psychology, 33,* 403-408.

Thompson, S. C., & Kelley, H. H. (1981). Judgments of responsibility for activities in close relationships. *Journal of Personality and Social Psychology 41,* 469-477.

Watzlawick, P., Beavin, J. H., & Jackson, D. D. (1967). *Pragmatics of human communication.* New York: W. W. Norton.

Weiner, B. (1974). *Achievement motivation and attribution theory.* Morristown, NJ: General Learning Press.

Weiner, B. (1979). A theory of motivation for some classroom experiences. *Journal of Educational Psychology, 71,* 3-25.

Wong, P.T.P. (1979). Frustration, exploration, and learning. *Canadian Psychological Review, 20,* 133-144.

Wong, P.T.P., & Weiner, B. (1981). When people ask "why" questions, and the heuristics of attributional search. *Journal of Personality and Social Psychology, 40* 650-663.

Zuckerman, M. (1979). Attribution of success and failure revisited, or: The motivational bias is alive and well in attribution theory. *Journal of Personality, 47,* 245-287.

PART III

The Deterioration and Reorganization of Relationships

Relationships begun in enthusiasm and hope don't always work out. One recent U.S. Census Bureau projection estimated that four out of every ten marriages end in divorce. The image often prompted by such statistics is to think of the relationships as being over. In fact, however, this is not the case. Like it or not, as social scientists are increasingly coming to realize, our intimate and pseudo-intimate relationships persist.

Each of the chapters in Part III examines how people deal with ongoing relationships that have gone awry. Rusbult provides a typology of responses to dissatisfaction. We can leave (exit); try to make improvements (voice); patiently wait, hoping that things will improve (loyalty); or just let things fall apart (neglect). Rusbult describes responses in detail and identifies both structural and individual determinants of each.

Chapters 9 and 10 focus on family reorganization following divorce. Working within a sociological tradition, Rodgers (Chapter 9) brings four theoretical perspectives to bear on postmarital family relations. From these theories, he is able to derive 68 specific propositions. Ahrons has conducted a major longitudinal study of ex-partners. Ahrons and Wallisch's chapter extends previous publications based on this project in two ways: It reports interaction patterns three years postdivorce (rather than one year postdivorce), and it explores in greater depth the correlates of postmarital interaction.

These last two chapters dovetail nicely. Rodgers uses Ahrons's notion of the binuclear family and incorporates her systems viewpoint into his theoretical integration. Both chapters note the limitations of treating divorce as a deviant, pathological form of behavior. Both imply the need to treat postmarital family interaction as a normal, developmental aspect of relationships. Finally, both emphasize the stages (or processes) of divorce rather than the causes or consequences which have traditionally been the focus of attention.

In a sense, postmarital relations bring us full cycle. Deterioration leads to reorganization and new beginnings. Thus, two parting questions become: How, if at all, is the development of subsequent courtships different from the path leading to first marriages? And how is reorganizing an old relationship similar to (or different from) initiating a new romantic bond? We believe that more complete answers to these questions are needed; we hope that the reader will be prompted to think about these and other personal relationship issues. These chapters constitute the last major section of this book. However, like the relationships they describe, they may also serve as a catalyst for new beginnings. In our view, social science contributions are best when they both answer questions and contribute to an upward, ever-widening spiral of knowledge.

8

Responses to Dissatisfaction in Close Relationships

The Exit-Voice-Loyalty-Neglect Model

CARYL E. RUSBULT

One of the most important goals in the study of close relationships is to gain an understanding of the manner in which people react to periodic decline in their involvements. No close relationship, no matter how ideal for both partners, maintains uniformly high satisfaction; no close relationship is without its "ups and downs." But while social scientists have developed a variety of theories intended to explain the development of close relationships (Altman & Taylor, 1973; Huesmann & Levinger, 1976; Murstein, 1970; Rusbult, 1983), the manner in which individuals react to periodic deterioration in their relationships has not been as systematically addressed.

This is not to say that there is no extant research or theory on relationship deterioration; social scientists have developed numerous models designed to account for the dissolution of close relationships (Altman & Taylor, 1973; Baxter, 1984; Johnson, 1982; Lee, 1984; Levinger, 1979; Miller & Parks, 1982). However, the goal of most of this work has been to describe the manner in which relationships terminate; that is, the implicit assumption in most of this work is that the couple eventually splits up. Very little of this work has the more general goal of accounting for the variety of reactions to dyadic stress—of describing the manner in which couples react to periodic, perhaps reparable declines in relationship quality. An approach that encompasses a wider range of reactions to decline—including not only

AUTHOR'S NOTE: I would like to express my gratitude to Drs. Steve Duck and Daniel Perlman for their helpful comments on an earlier draft of this chapter.

termination but also a broader range of alternative responses to relationship stress, both destructive and constructive—might advance our understanding of behavior in close relationships.

In addition to the work on the process of relationship dissolution, social scientists have also studied a variety of single responses to relationship decline—separation or divorce (Baxter, 1984: Bentler & Newcomb, 1978; Hill, Rubin, & Peplau, 1976), conflict resolution style (Billings, 1979; Gottman, Notarius, Markman, Bank, Yoppi, & Rubin, 1976), and extrarelationship affairs (Glass & Wright, 1977; Jaffe & Kanter, 1976). Others have examined related phenomena in close relationships such as communication style (Birchler, Weiss, & Vincent, 1975; Fineberg & Lowman, 1975; Krain, 1975), self-disclosure processes (Critelli & Dupre, 1978), attributional behavior (Harvey, Wells & Alvarez, 1978; Orvis, Kelley, & Butler, 1976), and power relations (Peplau, 1979, Raven, Centers, & Rodrigues, 1975). By and large, this work explores a single mode of reaction—communication *or* termination *or* cognitions about the partner and relationship, and so on—and does not simultaneously examine alternative modes of response. Those few investigations that have examined multiple responses to dissatisfaction have not done so within the context of a more general typology of reactions to relationship problems.

While the literature on reactions to relationship stress identifies a variety of important types of interpersonal behavior, and while it explores the characteristics, determinants, and consequences of numerous responses to relationship decline, its focus on single responses in isolation of one another may undermine the development of theoretical typologies sufficient to describe the full range of possible reactions to dissatisfaction. While work on each of the various reactions to relationship problems is important in promoting our understanding of the particular response under consideration, a broader, typological approach has much to recommend it. In the absence of a typology of responses to dissatisfaction, we may forget that the single response under consideration is but one of many possible reactions to decline, and thus we may fail to examine partners' interdependent patterns of problem solving. Without a more general typology, we are unlikely to explore important phenomena such as the relationships among various reactions to relationship stressors or the temporal sequencing of responses to relationship problems. In short, without a more general typology of responses to dissatisfaction, it is difficult to develop a comprehensive, theory-based understanding of decline processes.

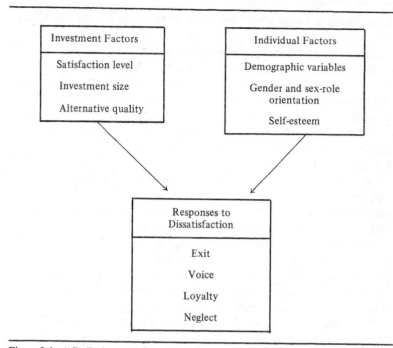

Figure 8.1 A Preliminary Model of Responses to Dissatisfaction in Close Relationships

This chapter describes a program of research designed to develop an integrated typology of responses to dissatisfaction in close relationships. The goal in developing such a typology is to outline a comprehensive model of responses to dissatisfaction that describes a broad range of reactions to relationship stress. This model should serve an integrative function by pointing out the relationships among the variety of individual responses that have been explored in the literature on close relationships. The chapter begins with a discussion of the typology itself—the exit-voice-loyalty-neglect model of responses to dissatisfaction—along with research designed to assess the validity and comprehensiveness of this typology. Appropriate methods for exploring reactions to relationship stressors are then considered. Several hypotheses regarding the determinants of each category of response are advanced, and research conducted to date to test these predictions is reviewed (Figure 8.1 provides a preliminary schematic representation of responses to dissatisfaction and their main determinants). Finally, directions for future research are discussed, and potential applications of the model are considered.

Exit, Voice, Loyalty, and Neglect

On the assumption that there exist a variety of modes of response to periodic decline in relationships, the exit-voice-loyalty-neglect typology was developed. This model is based loosely on the work of Hirschman (1970). In his *Exit, Voice, and Loyalty: Responses to Decline in Firms, Organizations, and States*, Hirschman describes three characteristic ways of reacting to deterioration in economic/political domains: (1) *exit*—ending or threatening to end the relationship; (2) *voice*—actively and constructively expressing one's dissatisfaction, with the intent of improving conditions; and (3) *loyalty*—passively but optimistically waiting for conditions to improve. Hirschman's typology appears on the face of it to capture a diverse range of reactions to deterioration in relationships and thus seems to be an excellent starting point for an exploration of modes of response to dissatisfaction in close relationships.

To demonstrate that there are in fact a diverse range of reactions to decline, and to assess the ability of the Hirschman typology to cover the range of reactions to decline in romantic involvements (i.e., to assess the comprehensiveness of the model), we performed a multidimensional scaling analysis of individuals' responses to dissatisfaction in their close relationships. In two three-phase studies (Rusbult & Zembrodt, 1983), we explored the close relationships of two populations: those of adults residing in the local community, and those of college students. The two studies proceeded as follows: In Phase 1 we collected a representative sample of individuals' reactions to relationship problems. In Phase 2 we asked judges to assess the degree of similarity among the various responses and computed the most accurate and parsimonious "picture" of the relations among the responses. In Phase 3 we obtained data to enable us to label the primary clusters of response and to identify the dimensions on which the various categories of response differed from one another.

We found that Hirschman's three categories effectively characterize behavior in romantic relationships and also identified a fourth important response to dissatisfaction: *neglect*—passively allowing one's relationship to atrophy. The exit category includes actions wherein the individual actively harms his or her relationship, the voice category includes active and constructive attempts to improve the relationship, the loyalty category includes behavior wherein the individual passively "hangs in there," waiting for conditions to improve without doing much to change things, and the neglect category includes passive behavior that results in the slow deterioration of the relationship. These four categories—exit, voice, loyalty, and neglect—thus appear to provide a fairly comprehensive, yet simple, description of the domain of reactions to deteriorating satisfaction. The following are examples of behavior representative of each response category:

Exit—formally separating, moving out of a joint residence, deciding to "just be friends," thinking or talking about leaving one's partner, threatening to end the relationship, actively destroying the relationship, or getting a divorce;

Voice—discussing problems, compromising, seeking help from a therapist or member of the clergy, suggesting solutions to problems, asking the partner what is bothering him or her, and trying to change oneself or the partner;

Loyalty—waiting and hoping that things will improve, "giving things some time," praying for improvement, supporting the partner in the face of criticism, and continuing to have faith in the relationship and the partner;

Neglect—ignoring the partner or spending less time together, refusing to discuss problems, treating the partner badly emotionally or physically, criticizing the partner for things unrelated to the real problem, "just letting things fall apart," chronically complaining without offering solutions to problems, *perhaps* developing extrarelationship sexual involvements (whether extrarelationship involvement is exit or neglect depends on the individual's intentions—to end the relationship or to stick with it and inadvertently cause it to deteriorate).

From the outset, it should be noted that the category labels are mere symbols for a broad set of interrelated reactions. For example, "voice" refers to active and constructive reactions, not to all behavior involving vocalization. While belligerent complaints involve vocalization, they do not constitute behavior intended to address relationship problems constructively. And many behaviors falling in the voice category do not involve actual vocalization (e.g., attempting to change one's own behavior). Thus the voice category is not synonymous with vocalization. Similarly, "exit" refers to active and destructive behavior, including not just actual relationship termination but also, and more important, other behavior intended to actively harm the relationship.

Although these response categories are characterized as "pure" types—each response independent of all other categories—the categories are in fact continuous and overlapping to some degree. Weak forms of exit verge on neglect, strong forms of loyalty verge on

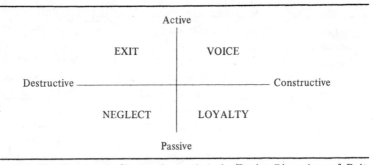

Figure 8.2 The Constructive/Destruction and Active/Passive Dimensions of Exit, Voice, Loyalty and Neglect Behaviors

voice, and so on. Also, while the four responses frequently occur in their pure form, an individual's reponse to problems in his or her relationship may on some occasions be a blend of two or more categories. For example, the response, "I swallowed my pride and asked for another chance," combines voice and loyalty. Finally, we should point out that during the course of a period of dissatisfaction, the individual may engage in a sequence of responses (see Lee, 1984). For example, a dissatisfied individual might initially react to relationship problems with loyalty, then move to voice, engage in neglect if problems persist, and finally resolve the problem with exit. Despite these caveats, however, the extant research on this model has demonstrated that the four categories of response are statistically distinguishable. For example, although measures of exit and neglect are weakly correlated (r's of .20 or so), the various responses are consistently sufficiently independent to be treated as discrete modes of reaction to dissatisfaction.

As shown in Figure 8.2, the four responses differ from one another along two dimensions. The first is constructiveness/destructiveness: Whereas voice and loyalty are constructive responses that serve to (or are at least intended to) maintain and/or revive the relationship, exit and neglect tend to be relatively more destructive to the future of the relationship. It should be noted that constructive/destructive refers to the impact of the response on the relationship. For the individual, any of the four responses might be equally constructive. That is, for a given individual in a given relationship, it might be that the most constructive thing to do would be to exit. But the exit response is certainly destructive to the relationship.

The second dimension on which the four responses differ from one another is activity/passivity: Exit and voice constitute active behavior (i.e., the individual is doing something about the problem), whereas loyalty and neglect are relatively more passive responses. In the most extreme cases, of course, loyalty and neglect would be "nonresponses," or the complete absence of activity, and would be behaviorally indistinguishable. But recall that we are speaking of a continuous dimension, from completely active to completely passive, and that most responses will involve some degree of action. It should also be noted that the term "passive" refers to the impact of the response on the problem at hand, and may not necessarily be descriptive of the behavior itself. For example, a neglectful response such as destructive criticism may be overtly active, but it is passive and destructive in regard to the future of the relationship. Thus both constructiveness/destructiveness and activity/passivity refer to the impact of a response on the relationship. Is the effect good or bad, and does the behavior actively address relationship problems or not?

Prior research (e.g., Rusbult, Johnson, & Morrow, in press) has confirmed that the four modes of response bear the predicted relations to one another: Responses that are theoretically opposite one another in the model—exit and loyalty, voice and neglect—are moderately negatively correlated with one another (r's of -.15 to -.30), while responses that are in contiguous quadrants are either weakly or not at all correlated with one another (r's of .00 to .25).

The exit-voice-loyalty-neglect typology can be used to distinguish among various specific responses to specific relationship problems, or it can be used as a way of characterizing individuals' generalized responses to relationship problems. That is, we can use the typology to study situationally determined problem-solving behavior that is relatively independent of individual differences (e.g., situations that routinely promote exit reactions). Alternatively, the model can be used to study generalized problem-solving styles or individual differences in response tendencies (e.g., persons who chronically react to problems by threatening to leave). In this chapter we review research on the determinants of both specific and generalized exit-voice-loyalty-neglect responses.

How does this model relate to other work on responses to dissatisfaction in close relationships? First, as noted earlier, the model describes a diverse range of possible reactions to relationship stressors rather than focusing on a single mode of response. And while some investigators have explored multiple responses, they have not based their work on a formal typology that specifies the relations among the variety of possible reactions to dissatisfaction. Second, whereas a variety of extant models effectively account for the process by which individuals disengage from and dissolve relationships (e.g., Baxter, 1984; Duck, 1982; Johnson, 1982; Lee, 1984; Miller & Parks, 1982), the present model attempts to describe reactions to potentially reparable lapses in relationship quality. Rather than assuming that the relationship is on the road to dissolution, the exit-voice-loyalty-neglect approach deals with reactions to problems at whatever point they emerge, discussing factors promotive of each mode of reaction.

Methods for Studying Responses to Dissatisfaction

Due to limited space, detailed accounts of the methods utilized in our research on exit, voice, loyalty, and neglect behavior cannot be provided. However, a general discussion of the methodologies employed is in order before summarizing that work. First, the reader will note a dearth of laboratory experimentation in the following summary. We believe that laboratory experimentation can be of great use in the study of close relationships in two respects: (1) to study attraction between strangers (i.e., first impressions); and (2) to obtain detailed information regarding the processes governing a specific category of responses to dissatisfaction (e.g., communication patterns in dyads). We further believe that to adequately explore problem solving in close relationships, one must study real close relationships. Thus we favor the maximization of construct and external validity (see Cook & Campbell, 1979), even at the occasional loss of some degree of internal validity.

Second, we have routinely and deliberately made use of the notion of converging operations; that is, much of our work combines, in a complementary fashion, survey data and experimentation, simulation research, or multidimensional scaling. No single method is without flaws, but through the judicious use of complementary techniques, it is possible to make relatively confident inferences about relationships among model variables (see McGrath, 1981).

Third, in most of our research we have utilized multiple modes of measurement. Typically, we used 20-35 structured Likert-type items to measure exit, voice, loyalty, and neglect behavior—five or more nine-point items per category, with each set of items possessing demonstrated reliability and both convergent and discriminant validity. For example, "I threatened to end the relationship" is an exit item, while "I suggested that we talk things over" is a voice item. In addition, we typically asked respondents to write an essay in response to an open-ended question (e.g., "How did you react to this problem, if at all?'') and have pairs of trained raters code each essay for degree of exit, voice, loyalty, and neglect. These measures, too, possess demonstrated interrater reliability and validity. (Further information regarding specific measurement issues and information regarding the reliability and validity of our measures is presented in each of the articles cited). We believe that these three principles—maximizing construct and external validity, using converging operations, and employing multiple operations—are critical methodological "values" in the study of relationships. Accordingly, we have attempted to apply these principles in our program of research on exit, voice, loyalty, and neglect responses to dissatisfaction.

Structural Determinants of Exit-Voice-Loyalty-Neglect

In the search for powerful determinants of the four behavior types, we began by asking what it is about relationships that leads to a greater or lesser probability of reacting to problems with exit, voice, loyalty, and neglect. Rusbult's (1980a, 1983) investment model of commitment in close relationships served as our starting point. The investment model variables of satisfaction, investment size, and alternative quality have been shown to be predictive of level of commitment to close relationships as well as to actual stay/leave behavior. Greater commitment and lesser probability of ending a relationship occurs under conditions of high satisfaction, high investment size, and poor quality alternatives (Rusbult, 1980a; Rusbult, 1983; Rusbult, Johnson, & Morrow, in press); the model has also been shown to predict job commitment and turnover [Farrell & Rusbult, 1981; Rusbult & Farrell, 1983], as well as commitment to friendships [Rusbult, 1980b]). The investment model seemed to be a reasonable starting point in that it has been demonstrated to be powerful in predicting two types of response to dissatisfaction—exit (low commitment) and loyalty (high commitment).

Beginning with investment model predictors had an added advantage: The model is based on interpersonal interdependence theory (Kelley & Thibaut, 1978; Thibaut & Kelley, 1959) and employs traditional exchange theory constructs (see Blau, 1964; Homans, 1961). Thus it should be relatively easy to connect this work to other research and theory sharing this general orientation (e.g., that of Altman & Taylor, 1973, Levinger, 1979, and others). Before proceeding, we should note that this approach is nomothetic in character; that is, our goal was to identify a simple set of predictors that could effectively predict specific response tendencies to specific relationship problems. This is not to deny the complex nature of reactions to decline, nor to deny the process by which relationships deteriorate (see Baxter, 1984; Duck, 1982; Lee, 1984). We do not wish to argue that global features of relationships simplemindedly predict uniform styles of coping. Rather, we wish to identify several basic features of relationships that exert general pressures toward one or another category of response across individuals and across relationships.

We reasoned that satisfaction, investment size, and alternative quality might equally well predict exit, voice, loyalty, and neglect behavior. First, level of satisfaction with a relationship prior to the relationship's decline should determine whether the individual reacts to problems in a constructive or a destructive manner. Given high prior satisfaction, the individual is likely to believe that it is desirable to restore the relationship to its previous state, and that constructive responses are more likely than destructive ones to produce "payoffs." Thus, greater prior satisfaction should induce voice and loyalty while discouraging exit and neglect.

The extant research on the correlates of marital satisfaction and adjustment support the assertion that satisfaction is positively associated with voice-like behaviors such as superior communication, greater perceptual accuracy, and expressions of love and affection (in some of this work, we merely know that happy couples engage in these types of behavior at higher levels; we do not know that they are engaging in such behavior in response to relationship problems; Davidson, Balswick, & Halverson, 1983; Rands, Levinger, & Mellinger, 1981; Sporakowski & Hughston, 1978). For example, in a comparison of the communication styles of couples who report low versus high marital happiness, happily married couples have been found to evidence more relaxed, friendly, open, and attentive communication behavior (Honeycutt, Wilson, & Parker, 1982). Conversely, marital satisfaction has been found to be negatively associated with neglect responses such as hostility, belligerent complaints, and the enjoyment of fewer shared recreational actvities (Billings, 1979; Gottman et al., 1976; Hawkins, 1968; Rands et al., 1981). Specifically, Birchler et al. (1975) gathered data from home and laboratory interactions to compare distressed and nondistressed couples and found that distressed couples emit "fewer pleases and more displeases" (p. 349) and engage in fewer recreational activities together. In addition, marital satisfaction—as well as factors predictive of satisfaction—has been shown to be promotive of more stable, durable relationships (i.e., loyalty), whereas dissatisfaction and distress are related to divorce and separation (Cutright, 1971; Hill et al., 1976). In a longitudinal study of dating couples, Rusbult (1983) found that declining satisfaction was associated with decreases in reported commitment to relationships and increases in the probability of exit. Fineberg and Lowman (1975) found that in comparison to maladjusted couples, adjusted couples showed greater affection and submission (i.e., loyalty).

Second, increases in investment size should promote constructive behaviors while inhibiting destructive responses. "Investments" are the resources the individual has put directly into the relationship that are then intrinsic to that involvement—such as time, self-disclosures, or emotional investments—or resources that were originally extrinsic but became indirectly connected to the relationship (e.g., shared material possessions, shared recreational activites, or mutual friends). Individuals who have invested highly in their relationships have much to lose if the relationship suffers or ends, and so should be more likely to enact constructive responses intended to maintain or revive their relationships (i.e., voice or loyalty). Persons who have invested little in their relationships have nothing to lose if their involvements deteriorate further or end, and should thus be more likely to react to problems with exit or neglect. Unfortunately, few researchers have explored the phenomenon of investment, although there is some indirect evidence that greater investments in relationships lead to higher levels of voice and loyalty and lower levels of exit and neglect (Bloom, Hodges, Caldwell, Systra, & Cedrone, 1977; Rubin & Brockner, 1975; Staw, 1976). For example, Rusbult (1980a) carried out two studies to demonstrate that greater investment size is associated with stronger commitment to remain in relationships and reduced intentions to end them. Krain (1975) studied premarital couples at three stages of dating and found that communication (voice) developed linearly with greater involvement.

Third, alternative quality should determine whether an individual's response to dissatisfaction will be active or passive. Good alternatives (an alternative relationship, spending time with friends or relatives, or solitude) provide the individual with the motivation to do something (be active, voice, or exit; "shape up or ship out") and give him or her a source of power for effecting changes in the relationship. Thus the threat posed by an attractive alternative can serve as a source of power. In the absence of a good alternative, the more probable reaction is to passively wait for the relationship to improve (i.e., remain loyal) or passively allow it to die (i.e., neglect it). When individuals believe that they have nowhere else to go, they should be more likely to passively let the relationship take its own course. Once again, there is indirect evidence to support these predictions; factors associated with alternative quality appear to promote exit and voice while inhibiting loyalty and neglect (Glass & Wright, 1977; Jaffe & Kanter, 1976). For example, White (1980) found that greater physical attractiveness relative to one's partner (i.e., superior alternatives) is associated with breakups. Also, Rusbult (1980a) has shown that persons with poorer alternatives to their current relationships report stronger commitment to maintaining their involvements.

We argue that three predictors—satisfaction (SAT), investments (INV), and alternatives (ALT)—should exert independent and additive effects on responses to dissatisfaction. For example, persons should be more likely to voice to the degree that they have invested much in their relationships. To the degree that they also possess good alternatives, voice should become even more probable, but to the degree that alternatives are poor, level of voice should be reduced to some degree. These predictions can be expressed as follows, with " − " representing a main effect wherein lower levels of the predictor promote the response, and " + " representing a main effect wherein higher levels of the predictor promote the response:

Exit   − SAT, − INV, + ALT
Voice   + SAT, + INV, + ALT
Loyalty + SAT, + INV, − ALT
Neglect − SAT, − INV, − ALT

To empirically test these predictions, we designed four studies of college-age dating relationships—two role-playing experiments and two cross-sectional surveys (Rusbult, Zembrodt, & Gunn, 1982). In the role-playing studies, subjects were asked to imagine themselves in the position of the protagonist of an essay and to indicate how they would respond in that situation. The essays described persons who were dissatisfied with their relationships; eight versions of the essays orthogonally manipulated satisfaction, investments, and alternatives. The two cross-sectional survey studies obtained measures of each relevant model variable. In general, and consistent with predictions, we found that to the extent that prior satisfaction was high, voice and loyalty were more probable, whereas exit and neglect were less probable. Similarly, increases in investment size encouraged voice and loyalty, whereas lower levels of investment appeared to inspire exit or neglect responses. Finally, more attractive alternatives promoted exit while hampering loyalist behavior. However, there appeared to be no (or at best a weak) relation between alternative quality and voice or neglect reactions to dissatisfaction.

In addition to studying the relationships of college students, we explored the power of this model to predict responses to dissatisfaction in a more heterogeneous adult population (Rusbult, Johnson, & Morrow, 1986). We designed a questionnaire to obtain measures of each model variable and conducted a large-scale mailed survey of individuals residing in the Lexington, Kentucky, area. The findings of this study paralleled those just reported, although the effects were not as strong: Greater prior satisfaction encouraged voice responses while discouraging exit and neglect reactions; greater investment size was associated with higher levels of voice and lower levels of exit; and higher quality alternatives promoted exit and inhibited loyalty.

In this large-scale survey, we also examined the impact of problem severity on each of the four responses to dissatisfaction. We found that when faced with more severe relationship problems, individuals were more likely to report high levels of each of the four responses. Furthermore, greater problem severity was especially powerful in promoting the active responses, exit and voice. Finally, this study explored the consequences of exit, voice, loyalty, and neglect. Using as outcome measures individual reports of immediate consequences (favorable or unfavorable), as well as reports of later levels of satisfaction and commitment, voice and loyalty resulted in more favorable outcomes whereas exit and neglect produced less favorable immediate and longer-term consequences.

Individual-Level Determinants of Exit-Voice-Loyalty-Neglect

In addition to examining the impact of relationship qualities on tendencies to respond to dissatisfaction with each of the four responses, we also conducted studies to examine the relationship between numerous individual-level characteristics and generalized tendencies toward exit, voice, loyalty, and neglect responses. In this section we review the results of this research.

Demographic Variables

First, in the large-scale survey mentioned earlier, we studied the relationship between several demographic variables and exit-voice-loyalty-neglect responses (Rusbult, Johnson, & Morrow, 1986). In this regard, the study was frankly exploratory; we had no a priori predictions regarding the connection between demographic factors and the four responses. Rather, we wished to determine the degree to which our model was generalizable across a wide range of individuals and relationships. Indeed, the model outlined earlier, including the variables of satisfaction, investments, alternatives, and problem severity, effectively predicted choice of problem-solving behavior in a wide range of relationships—those of married and single persons, in shorter- and longer-term relationships, among better- and less well-educated persons, and so on.

We observed the following relationships between demographic characteristics and problem-solving style: We found that older persons are more likely than younger persons to respond to problems passively, with loyalty or neglect. Individuals with higher incomes are less likely to engage in any of the four responses—exit, voice, loyalty, or neglect. Level of education is not strongly related to type of response, but greater education appears to be weakly promotive of the active responses of exit and voice, while persons with less education are more likely to react to problems with loyalty. Those involved in relationships of longer duration are less likely to react to dissatisfaction with exit or voice and are somewhat more likely to react passively, with loyalty or neglect. Finally, compared with single persons, married persons are less likely to engage in exit, somewhat less likely to voice, and somewhat more likely to engage in loyalty or neglect.

Thus the profile of the person engaging in active behaviors—exit or voice—includes youth, lower income, greater education, brief involvement, and single marital status. In contrast, passive loyalty or neglect responses are more common among older married persons with lower incomes and less education who are involved in more long-standing relationships. One striking finding is that greater education and lower income are associated with active responses. The reader may wonder why lower income and greater education were not collinear, producing parallel effects on responses. It may be that our younger, well-educated respondents were in earlier stages of their careers and had not yet reached their full earning power. It should also be noted that some of the demographic characteristics described above may be highly collinear. Furthermore, it is unclear what impact history and maturation may have on type of response. Older persons in long-standing marriages may simply have fewer stressors in their relationships or may have learned over years of involvement to respond to dissatisfaction more quietly; younger, single persons in relationships of briefer duration may have more serious problems to confront and may believe that it is more appropriate to confront them head-on with voice or exit. Such speculations remain to be explored in future work.

Gender

In every close heterosexual relationship—and at least 90% of the close relationships in Western nations are heterosexual—we find one male and one female. This statement seems to belabor the obvious, but we feel that it is important to highlight the fact that gender differences in interpersonal behavior must have a tremendous impact on the course of heterosexual involvements. To explore the role of gender in affecting problem-solving in close relationships, several of our studies have explicitly assessed sex difference in generalized tendencies toward exit, voice, loyalty, and neglect. Based on prior research on sex differences in interpersonal behavior, we can characterize the behavior of females, relative to that of males, as showing greater direct communication, a more contactful and less controlling style, greater emphasis on maintenance/social-emotional behavior, greater awareness of relationship problems, a desire to confront and discuss problems and feelings, lesser tendencies toward conflict avoidance, a greater desire for affectional behavior, less emphasis on instrumental behavior, and higher levels of intimate self-dislosure (Hawkins, Weisberg, & Ray, 1980; Kelley, Cunningham, Grisham, Lefebvre, Sink, & Yablon, 1978; Kitson & Sussman, 1982; Morgan, 1976).

Given the female's generally greater affiliative/communal orientation, we expected that in comparison to males, females would evidence more tendencies to respond constructively and fewer tendencies to respond destructively to relationship problems. We advanced this prediction despite evidence that females are actually more likely to terminate relationships (Hagestad & Smyer, 1982; Hill et al., 1976). Not all relationships terminate, and final termination is but one form of exit (the others being thinking about leaving, threatening to leave, or engaging in other actively destructive responses); there are many ways to exit other than actually ending one's relationship, and actual termination is a relatively low-frequency response (relative to other ways of reacting to problems in relationships). Given the large body of literature suggesting that throughout the bulk of a relationship the female is more oriented toward maintenance than the male, it seems reasonable to expect that in general, males will engage in fewer constructive and more destructive responses. In a sense, the female's greater concern for the affective quality of relationships—her emphasis on personalism, self-disclosure, and mutual support—makes her automatically more heavily invested in them. Her greater investment should naturally move her toward the constructive end of the constructiveness/destructiveness dimension.

In the large-scale survey described earlier, Rusbult, Johnson, and Morrow (1986) found that females are somewhat more likely than males to react to dissatisfaction with loyalty. In a second study, Rusbult, Zembrodt, & Iwaniszek (in press) examined the impact of gender and sex-role orientation on responses to dissatisfaction in two cross-sectional surveys using a college sample and a community sample. We found neglectful behavior to be more common among males (at least among college-age males). In a third study, a cross-sectional survey designed to assess the problem-solving behavior of lesbians, gay males, and heterosexual males and females, Rusbult and Iwaniszek (1986) found that males, homosexual or heterosexual, exhibited greater tendencies toward exit and marginally greater tendencies to behave in a neglectful manner.

Finally, Rusbult, Johnson, and Morrow (in press-a) carried out a study designed to obtain information from both partners in college-age dating relationships concerning individuals' own problem-solving behaviors, perceptions of a partner's problem-solving style, and reactions to exit, voice, loyalty, and neglect behavior from partners. In this study of couple patterns of problem solving, we found that females showed higher levels of voice and loyalty and lower levels of neglect than males. This study also demonstrated that the female's propensity to voice more than her male partner is particularly evident in response to less severe problems, in response to her partner's attempts to voice, and in response to her partner's loyalist responses. She is more likely than her male partner to engage in loyalist behavior in response to both mild and severe problems, and in response to her partner's exit and neglect behavior. Moreover, her weaker tendencies toward neglect are evident across the entire range of problem situations, mild or severe.

In support of our predictions, it appears that there are relatively consistent, if weak, gender differences in tendencies toward exit, voice, loyalty, and neglect: Females show greater propensities to react to problems with voice and loyalty, whereas males react to relationship problems in a more neglectful manner (and perhaps with higher levels of exit). We might note that this pattern of results is congruent with the findings of Kelley and his colleagues (1978, p. 473), who characterize the behavior of males and females in close relationships as "the interaction between a conflict-avoidant person (the male) and his partner (the female), who is frustrated by the avoidance and asks that the problem and the feelings associated with it be confronted."

Sex-role Orientation

Several pieces of research were also designed to examine the relationship between sex-role orientation and problem-solving behavior. Most sex-role researchers and theorists characterize psychological femininity as a communal orientation, one associated with greater interpersonal warmth and a greater concern with the maintenance of stable interpersonal relations. In contrast, psychological masculinity is generally described as an agentic orientation, one associated with a greater focus on instrumental behavior (e.g., career, task completion) than on interpersonal relations (Bakan, 1966; Bem, 1974; Berzins, Welling, & Wetter, 1978; Heilbrun, 1976; Wiggins & Holzmuller, 1978). Therefore, we reasoned that psychological femininity might be associated with our constructiveness/destructiveness dimension, with highly feminine persons showing more constructive and less destructive problem-solving behavior. We further reasoned that masculinity might be associated with our activity/passivity dimension, with highly masculine persons showing more active and less passive problem-solving behavior. In support of this line of reasoning, Wiggins and Holzmuller (1978) found that femininity is associated with Wiggins's (1980) warmth/coldness interpersonal trait dimension (i.e., constructiveness/destructiveness), and that masculinity is associated with his dominance/submission interpersonal trait dimension (i.e., activity/passivity). Accordingly, we predicted that androgynous persons, who possess both high masculinity and high femininity, would be most likely to solve problems with voice; that feminine-type persons, who possess high femininity and low masculinity, would be most likely to engage in loyalty; that masculine-type persons, who possess high masculinity and low femininity, would be most likely to exit; and that undifferentiated persons, who are low on both masculinity and femininity, would behave in a neglectful manner.

In fact, in several studies designed to explore the associations between psychological masculinity and femininity and generalized tendencies toward exit, voice, loyalty, and neglect, our predictions were not confirmed. We found much simpler relationships among these variables than we had expected. Rusbult et al. (in press) study (described earlier) found that persons with higher psychological femininity evidence greater tendencies to respond to problems constructively; high femininity is associated with higher levels of voice and loyalty and lower levels of neglect. Rusbult and Iwaniszek (1986) also found high femininity to be associated with higher levels of voice and loyalty. In Rusbult et al. (in press) study, high psychological masculinity was found to be related to tendencies to respond to problems in relationships in a destructive manner; highly masculine individuals report greater generalized tendencies to react to problems with exit and neglect and show lower levels of voice and loyalty. Thus the relationship between psychological masculinity, psychological femininity, and generalized tendencies toward exit, voice, loyalty, and neglect is really quite straightforward: Greater masculinity is associated with greater destructiveness and less constructiveness, while greater femininity is associated with greater constructiveness and less destructiveness.

Self-esteem

We have also explored the relationship between self-esteemed and response tendencies. In research reported earlier designed to study the effects of relationship factors on problem solving, we found that although alternative quality was predicted to exert a strong impact on active/passive responding, in fact good alternatives merely promoted exit (one active response) and inhibited loyalty (one passive response).

Our original hypothesis was advanced on the assumption that good alternatives would serve as a source of power and motivation to do something. Instead, it may be that the sense that one has acceptable alternatives to one's relationship—and the attendant tendency to respond actively to relationship problems—might be a more stable quality or a trait residing relatively permanently within the individual. Accordingly, we decided to examine the relationship between self-esteem and exit, voice, loyalty, and neglect responses, arguing that persons with strong self-esteem should have a greater sense that they are worthwhile individuals with acceptable options should their relationships end (i.e., that they have good alternatives). We reasoned that higher self-esteem should be associated with greater tendencies toward active responding (i.e., exit and voice) and weaker tendencies toward passive responding (i.e., loyalty and neglect). Although little prior research has examined the impact of self-esteem on interpersonal behavior, there is some indirect evidence in support of our predictions: Persons with stronger self-esteem are more willing to self-disclose, more interpersonally receptive and less defensive, and less dependent and jealous (Berger, 1973: Dion & Dion, 1975; Ellison & Firestone, 1974; White, 1981).

We carried out two cross-sectional surveys that obtained measures of self-esteem as well as self-reports of tendencies to respond to relationship problems with exit, voice, loyalty, and neglect, using a college sample and a community sample (Rusbult, Morrow, & Johnson, 1986). We found that individuals with high self-esteem show greater tendencies toward exit and lesser tendencies toward loyalty and neglect than do low self-esteem persons (although the effect on loyalty was significant in only one sample). Low self-esteem persons reported a greater tendency toward passive responding, while high self-esteem persons revealed a greater likelihood of active responding. Variations in self-esteem did not significantly affect voice responses in either sample.

A Summary of the Findings to Date

It is important to pause for a moment and attempt to pull together these diverse findings. We now attempt to characterize the conditions under which we are likely to see exit, voice, loyalty, and neglect problem-solving behaviors in reponse to dissatisfaction in close relationships. What follows is a brief portrait of the conditions promotive of each response category.

Exit

In a sense, people exit when they have little to lose by doing so and believe that what they've got is not worth saving. Individuals are most likely to exit when they have not been satisfied with their involvements, when they have invested little in their relationships, when they believe that they have good alternatives to their relationships, and when they are faced with what they regard as serious relationship problems. Tendencies toward exit are more common among younger persons with lower incomes and (perhaps) greater education who are single and involved in relationships of shorter duration. Finally, several personality traits are associated with exit tendencies: Persons are more likely to exit to the degree that they possess greater psychological masculinity, lesser psychological femininity, and higher self-esteem.

Voice

Voice is an attempt to rescue something of value that is in danger of being damaged. It is the more probable response to relationship problems among persons who have high prior satisfaction with their relationships, who have invested heavily in their involvements, and who are faced with relatively serious problems in their relationships. The voicer appears to be, on average, younger, with lower income and greater education, single, and involved in relationships of briefer duration. The voicer is also more likely to be female and to have high psychological femininity and low psychological masculinity.

Loyalty

Loyalty is a conservative response, one that serves primarily to maintain the status quo (i.e., why mess with a [basically] good thing?). The loyalist response is most likely to occur when the individual has high overall satisfaction with his or her involvement, has invested much in the relationship, has poorer quality alternatives to the involvement, and believes that his or her relationship problems are relatively minor. The loyalist tends to be an older person with lower income and lesser education who has been married for some time. Finally, loyalty is much more common among females and among persons with high femininity, low masculinity, and (perhaps) lower self-esteem.

Neglect

Neglect is basically an ineffectual response, one likely to occur when the individual doesn't really know what to do about a troubled relationship and isn't motivated to do much of anything about it. Neglectful behavior occurs under conditions of low prior satisfaction, low investment of resources in one's relationship, and/or in response to problems that are relatively trivial. Neglect appears to be more probable among males, older persons, persons with lower incomes and less education, and among individuals who have been married for some time. Neglectful behavior is also associated with the personality traits of high psychological masculinity, low psychological femininity, and low self-esteem.

Current Work and Directions for the Future

At present, we are extending the exit-voice-loyalty-neglect typology in several respects. First, we should note that our research to date has been much more effective in predicting differentiation along the constructive/destructive dimension than along the active/passive dimension. This is not to say that we have failed completely in our attempts to predict active/passive response differences, but that differences along this dimension have not been as strong, clear, or consistent as those along the constructive/destructive dimension. Therefore, we are devoting much of our current effort to explorations of this dimension.

In this regard, two variables seem quite promising: Morrow, in his thesis research, is examining the role of potential for control of the problem and the personality trait of internality/externality in affecting active/passive responses. He reasons that persons who have high control over the problem solution are most likely to react actively to problems, with those with low prior commitment and relatively serious problems reacting with exit. Given less control over the problem, loyalty or neglect should become more likely reactions to dissatisfaction. Morrow also argues that the trait of internality/externality should exert powerful effects on response tendencies. Persons with internal orientations believe that they control events in their lives, that an individual's outcomes in life result from his or her own actions. Therefore, internally oriented persons should be more likely to respond to problems in an active manner, taking charge of the situation and the outcome of the problem, and doing something about the problem. The externally oriented individual, who believes that events in life are determined by external forces, should be more likely to react to problems in a passive fashion (i.e., with loyalty or neglect), allowing other persons or situational forces to "take care of" the problem.

In addition, we believe that through further explorations of the interdependence of partner reactions to problem situations we may gain insights into the determinants of active/passive responding. It is crucial that we recognize that the individual's reaction to a given problem does not occur in a vacuum; a person decides how to react to a given problem in light of his or her partner's actions. It may be that we choose to react more passively when our partner has taken a more active role in dealing with relationship problems. Alternatively, it could be that we react actively to problems when we perceive that our partner has engaged in behavior that is destructive to the future of our relationship. We are currently conducting research on such issues.

Finally, we believe that the temporal sequencing of problem-solving behavior may be critical in affecting active/passive responses. To date, we have dealt with exit, voice, loyalty, and neglect behavior in a static manner, as though the individual recognizes a problem in his or her relationship and elects to react to that problem with a single response (or with a reaction that simultaneously combines two or more response categories). In fact, most relationship problems are extended over time and are probably reacted to in several different manners over their course. We are presently conducting research to determine which sequences of response are most probable and what qualities of relationships and of individuals render one or another sequence more or less likely. Such work is especially important in light of arguments that responses to dissatisfaction must be understood as a process (e.g., Baxter, 1984; Duck, 1982). Furthermore, research on patterns of disengagement from relationships suggests that there may be important differences across couples in patterns of response to dissatisfaction (see Baxter, 1984; Lee, 1984).

Acknowledging possible couple-level differences in sequence/pattern, one might speculate that the following sequence would occur with some frequency: The individual becomes aware of a problem in his or her relationship and decides to "hang in there" for a bit and see if the problem persists or goes away. If the problem persists, the individual may move from loyalty to voice, taking action aimed at solving the problem. If such actions are unsuccessful—if the partner continues to behave in an undesirable manner or the two are unable to work out a satisfactory solution—the individual may begin to engage in neglectful actions, allowing the relationship to deteriorate out of despair or insufficient courage to exit. Finally, when it becomes apparent that the problem is a permanent and irreparable one, the individual may decide to exit the relationship. Thus it may be that problem-solving behavior follows a sequence moving simultaneously from constructive to destructive and from passive to active. This proposed sequence is congruent with the models of relationship termination advanced by Baxter (1984) and Lee (1984), although neither of those models includes all four of the modes of response included in the present typology. Beyond the simple pattern outlined here, it is also logical to assume that the duration of a sequence and the time spent on a given response will differ as a function of overall satisfaction and investment size (greater time spent on the constructive portion of the sequence given greater satisfaction and investments), the severity of a problem (greater time spent on active behavior given more severe problems), and a host of other relational and individual characteristics.

A second issue in our plans for the future concerns cross-situational consistency in exit, voice, loyalty, and neglect response tendencies. Given that there are individual-level characteristics that are reliably predictive of generalized reactions to relationship problems, one may reasonably ask whether these generalized tendencies are relationship-specific or more general. Do persons who react to problems in their romantic relationships with voice react to problems with parents or friends in a similar manner? Is the loyalist at home a loyalist at work?

We might note that we have utilized the exit-voice-loyalty-neglect typology not only to examine problem solving in close relationships but also to study work-related behavior. Researchers in the areas of personnel and organizational behavior have typically explored examples of worker behavior such as turnover, grievance-filing, job commitment and attachment, good citizenship behavior, effort expenditure, obstructionism, and chronic absenteeism and lateness in isolation as though they were independent of one another. In fact, we have found that all of these behavior types are related to one another and cluster in the categories of exit, voice, loyalty, and neglect (Farrell, 1983). We have also begun to study the impact of job satisfaction, investments, and alternatives on exit-voice-loyalty-neglect responses and have found support for the predictions that were confirmed in our work on close relationships (Farrell & Rusbult, 1985).

A third direction for future work concerns the functional value of exit, voice, loyalty, and neglect behavior. In this regard, some critical questions are: Are the constructive responses more adaptive than the destructive responses? Do the constructive responses yield "healthier" and more gratifying close relationships? Are there interdependent patterns of responding that yield better consequences for the individual and the relationship? Are there sequences of responding that are more functional than other sequences? At present, we have some indirect evidence that tendencies toward voice and loyalty produce better immediate and longer-term consequences than do exit and neglect response tendencies (Rusbult, Johnson, & Morrow, 1986). However, we believe that we must address these issues more directly and carefully before we can make confident statements regarding the functional value of the four responses. The classic test of such questions involves the comparison of distressed and nondistressed marriages (i.e., couples in marital counseling and couples not in counseling; see Billings, 1979; Birchler et al., 1975; Fineberg & Lowman, 1975; Gottman et al., 1976). Accordingly, we are presently undertaking a study of the response tendencies of both partners and the interdependent response patterns of partners in distressed and nondistressed marriages.

Finally, it should be noted that the model outlined herein is one that assumes that reactions to relationship stressors are essentially rational, in that persons in general act so as to protect investments and maximize outcomes (current relationship relative to alternative involvements) in light of returns (satisfaction). With respect to arguments that behavior in close relationships is also strongly driven by emotions and feelings (see Duck, 1982), it may be fruitful to explore the less rational forms of response to dissatisfaction. For example, in addition to the constructiveness/destructiveness and activity/passivity dimensions of response of decline, there may be an additional rational/irrational dimension. There may be circumstances that reliably elicit irrational rather than rational responses, and there may be individuals who routinely react with greater spontaneous emotion and less rational thought to relationship problems.

Applications of the Exit-Voice-Loyalty-Neglect Model

Can this model be used to improve the quality of marital relations and other close relationships? We believe that the model has obvious utility in this regard. If our research on distressed and nondistressed marriages reveals reliable differences in problem-solving styles, a next obvious step would be to design intervention strategies to help couples in distressed marriages develop more adaptive mechanisms for solving problems in their involvements. Such intervention strategies would need to take into consideration not just the consequences for the couple of various patterns of problem solving but also the consequences for the individual of different types of responses. It is possible, for example, that loyalist responses are effective in maintaining stable functioning in the relationship while producing stress or other deleterious consequences for the individual loyalist.

The exit-voice-loyalty-neglect model could also be used to develop organizational policies for promoting positive worker membership behavior and discouraging destructive membership behavior. The art of developing a retention program that is tailored to the specific circumstances of a given firm lies in finding appropriate means of maintaining high employee satisfaction and encouraging employee investments, especially among valued employees who may be at risk of exit and/or neglect. Policies designed to maintain strong employee satisfaction will need to address issues such as compensation, supervision, worker autonomy, co-worker relations, and so on. Employee intrinsic investment could be encouraged in many ways, including the adoption of shared-cost training programs, through fostering the development of firm-specific skills (i.e., nonportable training) or through incentives that increase community involvement or help to link employees' families to the employing organization. Such personnel policies should not only help to encourage positive membership behavior but should also produce a work setting that is more gratifying for the individual employee.

Conclusions

The exit-voice-loyalty-neglect model describes a complex, comprehensive set of possible reactions to relationship decline. The program of research that we have conducted to date demonstrates that there is a wide range of qualities of both relationships and individuals that powerfully and reliably predict the four responses. The model is capable of integrating previously unrelated research on such diverse behavior as marital communication and conflict resolution, separation and divorce, romantic satisfaction and commitment, spouse abuse and neglect, and extrarelationship sexual involvements. However, the model is not intended to replace research on each of these individual responses. Such research, involving detailed analyses of the causes and consequences of individual responses, is of critical importance in its own right. The major utility of the model may lie in its integrative function, in its ability to point out the relationships among various responses to dissatisfaction, and in its focus on the interdependence of various categories of reaction. We believe that the exit-voice-loyalty-neglect typology shows great promise in promoting the development of a comprehensive, theory-based understanding of the manner in which individuals react to periodic decline in their close relationships.

REFERENCES

Altman, I., & Taylor, D. A. (1973). *Social penetration: The development of interpersonal relationships*. New York: Holt, Rinehart & Winston.

Bakan, D. (1966). *The duality of human existence*. Chicago: Rand McNally.

Baxter, L. A. (1984). Trajectories of relationship disengagement. *Journal of Social and Personal Relationships, 1,* 29-48.

Bem, S. L. (1974). The measurement of psychological androgyny. *Journal of Consulting and Clinical Psychology, 47,* 155-162.

Bentler, P. M., & Newcomb, M. S. (1978). Longitudinal study of marital success and failure. *Journal of Consulting and Clinical Psychology, 47,* 1053-1070.

Berger, C. E. (1973). Attributional communication, situational involvement, self-esteem and interpersonal attraction. *Journal of Communcation, 23,* 284-305.

Berzins, J. I., Welling, M. A., & Wetter, R. E. (1978). A new measure of psychological androgyny based on the Personality Research Form. *Journal of Consulting and Clinical Psychology, 46,* 126-138.

Billings, A. (1979). Conflict resolution in distressed and nondistressed married couples. *Journal of Consulting and Clinical Psychology, 47,* 368-376.

Birchler, G. R., Weiss, R. L., & Vincent, J. P. (1975). Multimethod analysis of social reinforcement exchange between maritally distressed and nondistressed spouse and stranger dyads. *Journal of Personality and Social Psychology, 31,* 349-360.

Blau, P. M. (1964). *Exchange and power in social life.* New York: Wiley.

Bloom, B. L., Hodges, W. F., Caldwell, R. A., Systra, L., & Cedrone, A. R. (1977). Marital separation: A community survey. *Journal of Divorce, 1,* 7-19.

Cook, T. D., & Campbell, D. T. (1979). *Quasi-experimentation: Design and analysis issues for field settings.* Boston: Houghton Mifflin.

Critelli, J. W., & Dupre, K. M. (1978). Self-disclosure and romantic attraction. *Journal of Social Psychology, 106,* 127-128.

Cutright, P. (1971). Income and family events: Marital stability. *Journal of Marriage and the Family, 33,* 291-306.

Davidson, B., Balswick, J., & Halverson, C. (1983). Affective self-disclosure and marital adjustment: A test of equity theory. *Journal of Marriage and the Family, 45,* 93-102.

Duck, S. (1982). A topography of relationship disengagement and dissolution. In S. Duck (Ed.), *Personal relationships 4: Dissolving personal relationships* (pp. 1-30). New York: Academic Press.

Dion, K. K., & Dion, K. L. (1975). Self-esteem and romantic love. *Journal of Personality, 43,* 39-57.

Ellison, C. W., & Firestone, I. J. (1974). Development of interpersonal trust as a function of self-esteem, target status, and target style. *Journal of Personality and Social Psychology, 29,* 655-663.

Farrell, D. (1983). Exit, voice, loyalty, and neglect as responses to job dissatisfaction: A multidimensional scaling. *Academy of Management Journal, 26,* 596-607.

Farrell, D., & Rusbult, C. E. (1981). Exchange variables as predictors of job satisfaction, job commitment, and turnover: The impact of rewards, costs, alternatives, and investments. *Organizational Behavior and Human Performance, 27,* 78-95.

Farrell, D., & Rusbult, C. E. (1985). Understanding the retention function: A model of the causes of exit, voice, loyalty, and neglect behaviors. *Personnel Administrator, 30,* 129-140.

Fineberg, B. L., & Lowman, J. (1975). Affect and status dimensions of marital adjustment. *Journal of Marriage and the Family, 37,* 155-160.

Glass, S. P., & Wright, J. L. (1977). The relationship of extramarital sex, length of marriage, and sex differences on marital satisfaction and romanticism: Athanasiou's data reanalyzed. *Journal of Marriage and the Family, 39,* 691-703.

Gottman, J. M., Notarius, C., Markman, H., Bank, S., Yoppi, B., & Rubin, M. E. (1976). Behavior exchange theory and marital decision making. *Journal of Personality and Social Psychology, 34,* 14-23.

Hagestad, G. O., & Smyer, M. A. (1982). Dissolving long-term relationships: Patterns of divorcing in middle age. In S. Duck (Ed.), *Personal relationships 4: Dissolving personal relationships* (pp. 155-184). London: Academic Press.

Harvey, J. H., Wells, G. L., & Alvarez, M. D. (1978). Attribution in the context of conflict and separation in close relationships. In J. H. Harvey, W. Ickes, & R. F. Kidd (Eds.), *New directions in attribution research* (Vol. 2, pp. 235-260). Hillsdale, NJ: Erlbaum.

Hawkins, J. L. (1968). Association between companionship, hostility, and marital satisfaction. *Journal of Marriage and the Family, 30,* 647-650.

Hawkins, J. L., Weisberg, C., & Ray, D. W. (1980). Spouse differences in communication and style: Preferences, perception, behavior. *Journal of Marriage and the Family, 42,* 585-593.

Heilbrun, A. B., Jr. (1976). Measurement of masculine and feminine sex-role identities as independent dimensions. *Journal of Consulting and Clinical Psychology, 44,* 183-190.

Hill, C. T., Rubin, Z., & Peplau, L. A. (1976). Breakups before marriage: The end of 103 affairs. *Journal of Social Issues, 32*(1), 147-168.

Hirschman, A. O. (1970). *Exit, voice, and loyalty: Responses to decline in firms, organizations, and states.* Cambridge, MA: Harvard University Press.

Homans, G. C. (1961). *Social behavior: Its elementary forms.* New York: Harcourt Brace.

Honeycutt, J. M., Wilson, C., & Parker, C. (1982). Effects of sex and degrees of happiness on perceived styles of communicating in and out of the marital relationship. *Journal of Marriage and the Family, 42,* 395-406.

Huesmann, L. R., & Levinger, G. (1976). Incremental exchange theory: A formal model for progression in dyadic social interaction. In L. Berkowitz & E. Walster (Eds.), *Advances in experimental social psychology* (Vol. 9, pp. 191-229). New York: Academic Press.

Jaffe, D. T., & Kanter, R. M. (1976). Couple strains in communal households: A four-factor model of the separation process. *Journal of Social Issues, 32*(1), 169-191.

Johnson, M. P. (1982). Social and cognitive features of the dissolution of commitment to relationships. In S. Duck (Ed.), *Personal relationships 4: Dissolving personal relationships* (pp. 51-73). London: Academic Press.

Kelley, H. H., Cunningham, J. D., Grisham, J. A., Lefebvre, L. M., Sink, C. R., & Yablon, G. (1978). Sex differences in comments during conflict within close heterosexual pairs. *Sex Roles, 4,* 473-492.

Kelley, H. H., & Thibaut, J. W. (1978). *Interpersonal relations: A theory of interdependence.* New York: Wiley.

Kitson, G. C., & Sussman, M. B. (1982). Marital complaints, demographic characteristics, and symptoms of mental distress in divorce. *Journal of Marriage and the Family, 44,* 87-101.

Krain, M. (1975). Communication among premarital couples at three stages of dating. *Journal of Marriage and the Family, 37,* 609-618.

Lee, L. (1984). Sequences in separation: A framework for investigating endings of the personal (romantic) relationship. *Journal of Social and Personal Relationships, 1,* 49-73.

Levinger, G. (1979). A social exchange view on the dissolution of pair relationships. In R. L. Burgess & T. L. Huston (Eds.), *Social exchange in developing relationships* (pp. 169-193). New York: Academic Press.

McGrath, J. E. (1981). Dilemmatics: The study of research choices and dilemmas. *American Behavioral Scientist, 25,* 179-210.

Miller, G. R., & Parks, M. R. (1982). Communication in dissolving relationships. In S. Duck (Ed.), *Personal relationships 4: Dissolving personal relationships* (pp. 127-154). London: Academic Press.

Morgan, B. (1976). Intimacy of disclosure topic and sex differences in self-disclosure. *Sex Roles, 2,* 161-166.

Murstein, B. I. (1970). Stimulus-value-role: A theory of marital choice. *Journal of Marriage and the Family, 32,* 465-481.

Orvis, B. R., Kelley, H. H., & Butler, D. (1976). Attributional conflict in young couples. In J. H. Harvey, W. J. Ickes, & R. F. Kidd (Eds.), *New directions in attribution research* (Vol. 1, pp. 353-386). Hillsdale, NJ: Erlbaum.

Peplau, L. A. (1979). Power in dating relationships. In J. Freeman (Ed.), *Women: A feminist perspective* (2nd Ed., pp. 106-121). Palo Alto, CA: Mayfield.

Rands, M., Levinger, G., & Mellinger, G. D. (1981). Patterns of conflict resolution and marital satisfaction. *Journal of Family Issues, 2,* 297-321.

Raven, B. H., Centers, R., & Rodrigues, A. (1975). The bases of conjugal power. In R. S. Cromwell & D. H. Olson (Eds.), *Power in families* (pp. 217-232). New York: Wiley.

Rubin, J. Z., & Brockner, J. (1975). Factors affecting entrapment in waiting situations: The Rosencrantz and Guildenstern effect. *Journal of Personality and Social Psychology, 31,* 1054-1063.

Rusbult, C. E. (1980a). Commitment and satisfaction in romantic associations: A test of the investment model. *Journal of Experimental Social Psychology, 16,* 172-186.

Rusbult, C. E. (1980b). Satisfaction and commitment in friendships. *Representative Research in Social Psychology, 11,* 96-105.

Rusbult, C. E. (1983). A longitudinal test of the investment model: The development (and deterioration) of satisfaction and commitment in heterosexual involvements. *Journal of Personality and Social Psychology, 45,* 101-117.

Rusbult, C. E., & Farrell, D. (1983). A longitudinal test of the investment model: The impact on job satisfaction, job commitment, and turnover of variations in rewards, costs, alternatives, and investments. *Journal of Applied Psychology, 43,* 304-317.

Rusbult, C. E., & Iwaniszek, J. (1986). *Problem-solving in male and female homosexual and heterosexual relationships.* Unpublished manuscript, University of Kentucky, Lexington.

Rusbult, C. E., Johnson, D. J., & Morrow, G. D. (in press-a). The impact of couple patterns of problem-solving on distress and nondistress in dating relationships. *Journal of Personality and Social Psychology.*

Rusbult, C. E., Johnson, D. J., & Morrow, G. D. (in press-b). Predicting satisfaction and commitment in adult romantic involvements: An assessment of the generalizability of the investment model. *Social Psychology Quarterly.*

Rusbult, C. E., Johnson, D. J., & Morrow, G. D. (1986). Determinants and consequences of exit, voice, loyalty, and neglect: Responses to dissatisfaction in adult romantic involvements. *Human Relations, 39,* 45-63.

Rusbult, C. E., Morrow, G. D., & Johnson, D. J. (1986). *Self-esteem and problem-solving behavior in close relationships: A research note.* Unpublished manuscript, University of Kentucky, Lexington.

Rusbult, C. E., & Zembrodt, I. M. (1983). Responses to dissatisfaction in romantic involvements: A multidimensional scaling analysis. *Journal of Experimental Social Psychology, 19,* 274-293.

Rusbult, C. E., Zembrodt, I. M., & Gunn, L. K. (1982). Exit, voice, loyalty, and neglect: Responses to dissatisfaction in romantic involvements. *Journal of Personality and Social Psychology, 43,* 1230-1242.

Rusbult, C. E., Zembrodt, I. M., & Iwaniszek, J. (in press). The impact of gender and sex-role orientation on problem-solving in closed relationships, *Sex Roles.*

Sporakowski, M. J., & Hughston, G. A. (1978). Prescriptions for happy marriage: Adjustments and satisfactions of couples married for 50 or more years. *Family Coordinator, 27,* 321-327.

Staw, B. M. (1976). Knee-deep in the big muddy: A study of escalating commitment to a chosen course of action. *Organizational Behavior and Human Performance, 16,* 27-44.

Thibaut, J. W., & Kelley, H. H. (1959). *The social psychology of groups.* New York: Wiley.

White, G. L. (1980). Physical attractiveness and courtship progress. *Journal of Personality and Social Psychology, 39,* 660-668.

White, G. L. (1981). Some correlates of romantic jealousy. *Journal of Personality, 49,* 129-147.

Wiggins, J. S. (1980). Circumplex models of interpersonal behavior. In L. Wheeler (Ed.), *Review of personality and social psychology* (Vol. 1, pp. 265-294). Beverly Hills, CA: Sage.

Wiggins, J. S., & Holzmuller, A. (1978). Psychological androgyny and interpersonal behavior. *Journal of Consulting and Clinical Psychology, 46,* 40-52.

9

Postmarital Reorganization of Family Relationships

A Propositional Theory

ROY H. RODGERS

The purpose of this chapter is to present the theoretical basis for a propositional approach to the study of the processes of separation, divorce, and remarriage. I also present a specification of the propositions intended to guide research which might be undertaken. The analysis begins with an assessment of the current state of theorizing in the area of divorce as reflected in the literature. Space does not permit a detailed treatment of the extensive body of literature available. Rather, my purpose is to deduce from this literature the character of theorizing which is implicit or explicit.

Following this brief review, I turn to four theoretical approaches which appear to hold promise for a new approach to the study of family reorganization following marital disruption. The overarching theory selected is the family developmental approach and its specific incorporation of the work of Ahrons on binuclear family system reorganization (see chapter 10). Included in this comprehensive model are theories dealing with social networks as reflected in the work of McLanahan, Wedemeyer, and Adelberg (1981), family problem solving as presented by Klein and Hill (1979), and family stress theory as conceptualized by McCubbin, Patterson, and their co-workers (see McCubbin & Patterson, 1983).

A theoretical integration of these four formulations is developed. By reviewing the issues and variables addressed in each conceptualization, it is proposed that the problem-solving process set forth by Klein and Hill may be seen as part of the overall coping process in the McCubbin and Patterson model. Similarly, the characteristics of social networks among divorced women identified by McLanahan and associates may be logically placed in the existing and new resources category of the McCubbin double ABCX model. This model in turn feeds logically into the overall model of binuclear family reorganization, both as a part of the explanation of the quality of binuclear family relationships and as a part of the explanation of the final level of reorganization in the binuclear family.

As a way of demonstrating the efficacy of the integrated model, a set of generic propositional statements of relationships between the key variables of the model are set forth. Finally, I identify further work which might incorporate other extant theories into the model. A word of warning: The space limitations imposed on the presentation prohibit a detailed review of the supportive literature from which the key concepts are derived. It has not been possible to provide definitions and discussions of all of them, nor to present possible operational measures of these concepts. (Most of the variables in the propositional inventory, however, are taken from the four aforementioned theoretical models. Therefore, readers can turn to these earlier theorists for conceptual, and sometimes operational, definitions.) The work presented is in process. The objective of this presentation is to stimulate others to participate in that process and to test its efficacy for a fuller understanding of postmarital family reorganization.

Theory is rarely explicit in the study of divorce processes. Several research foci appear in the literature on divorce, most of which may be roughly divided into two kinds—that concerned with the causes of divorce and that concerned with the consequences of divorce. However, a third focus is emerging, one that deals with the processes that occur in the family during and after marital breakup. This chapter deals with this latter focus. Ultimately, a "general theory of divorce" may incorporate the causes and consequences of divorce into the understanding of the family during marital disruption. The strategy for the moment is to omit these from this analysis.

The research on divorce includes a large number of studies which might be categorized as descriptive in nature. This somewhat older literature tends to carry a "problems" focus (i.e., it is concerned with the impact of divorce as a negative influence on the individual and the group). The literature frequently has as its goal some sort of therapeutic strategy for curing the problem. Also typical of this research is the use of clinical and/or "availability" samples for carrying out the research. Thus, while the older research literature has provided a considerable body of description, it is vulnerable on the grounds that there are potential distortions in that description. Such research has been valuable, nevertheless, in helping to gain a perspective on the theoretical problem.

In more recent work an explicit attempt has been made to introduce explanatory theory. It was in connection with this literature that I began to attempt to systematically develop a propositional theory of the processes of divorce and remarriage (Rodgers, 1984). In the course of this work it has become clear that the theory should be addressed not only to the processes of divorce and remarriage but to that of marital separation as well. Indeed, there appears to be no significant theoretical difference in the group and interpersonal processes that carry these separate labels.

One might question whether remarriage is, in fact, in this same domain. The key reason for including it lies in the understanding of the dependent variable to which the theory is addressed. My focus is on the postmarital family reorganization process, not on the dissolution of the marital relationship. My interest in remarriage, as with separation and divorce, is the impact of these independent variables on the dependent process of postmarital family reorganization. Remarriage is interesting, therefore, because of its implications for the processes that take place in the structure of the *original* family unit which has experienced marital disruption. I am not interested in the process of remarriage per se, which is undoubtedly a much happier experience for the new spouses than was the preceding divorce. That is a separate (though related) area of investigation, as is the study of the processes of marital separation and divorce. Throughout the remainder of this chapter, the shorthand "SDR" will be used when referring to the common processes. The specific terms "separation," "divorce," and "remarriage" will be used only when focusing on that particular area.

It is clear that characteristics of the institutional structure of a society relate to certain SDR processes and that the processes of SDR have relationships to institutional characteristics in the society. The development of propositions in this area has intriguing implications for an understanding of SDR in a society. Similarly, there are some fascinating consequences for individuals, and individuals have some provocative effects on the SDR processes. Beguiling as these areas are, this chapter is concerned chiefly with the relationships between SDR processes and the group-interactional level of analysis—namely, the processes of SDR in the family group. It also deals in a minimal way with the individual-psychological realm in following Ahrons's (1979, 1980a, 1980b, 1981) Wisconsin research. Thus there are several areas in which individual aspects of the effects of SDR are explored for former spouses and for new partners.

Concentrating on the relationship between the processes of SDR and the family group is deceptively simple. The bulk of the existing research has not used the family as the unit of analysis, but rather the individual. In this chapter, consequently, I capitalize on a range of research and theory that does not always use the family as the unit of analysis and/or does not always have a focus on SDR. Since the theory-building effort is concerned ultimately with an understanding of family behavior in general, bringing to bear theoretical and empirical work not directly related to SDR demonstrates that these phenomena belong in a general theory of the family. This is so despite a general tendency to treat them as extra-family, or at least as "deviant" family behavior. The implicit pronuclear family value position of much family research becomes quite apparent in the treatment of SDR. While total freedom from the influence of this value position is not claimed, the approach attempts to place these phenomena solidly in the area of normal—indeed, normative—family behavior. It is to be emphasized that the approach conceptualizes SDR as processes, not events. The fact that SDR can be viewed as stressful critical life transitions ought not to mask the organizing, as well as the disorganizing, elements of these processes. With this view of the nature of SDR in mind, then, can we conceptualize postmarital family reorganization in developmental terms?

Developmental Theory and Separation/Divorce/Remarriage

Interest in family development theory makes theorizing in the SDR area a special challenge. In a formulation of developmental theory written over a decade ago, the author attempted to incorporate divorce/remarriage (Rodgers, 1973). It was a minimal attempt, however, and one that tended to treat divorce as a disruption of the family career and/or the individual life course rather than focusing on the continuity that might also be characteristic of the experience. Like cohabitation, divorce is an embarrassment to a conceptual approach that emphasizes the centrality of the nuclear family unit progressing from formation at marriage to dissolution upon the death of one of the partners. Remarriage, of course, only further complicates matters, especially if one or both partners bring dependent children to the new union. Nevertheless, it is argued that none of these phenomena are outside the purview of the developmental perspective.

The emphasis on continuity contained in the ideas of family career and individual life course need not be a conservative influence. Indeed, these concepts can have the effect of requiring attention to the fact that individual and family roles must continue to be played and that family relationships continue beyond SDR. The research efforts of Hetherington, Cox, and Cox (1976, 1978, 1979) and of Wallerstein and Kelly (1980) using longitudinal designs have helped focus on this continuity.

Hagestad and her colleagues (1981, 1982, 1984) have theorized on the divorce process and its impact on the family unit. Because of her particular focus on the intergenerational consequences of life events, Hagestad (1981, p. 49), has been exploring a methodology that attempts to trace the impact on family lineages. In discussing this particular approach, she says:

> Neither traditional life course analysis nor a family development perspective can capture the intimate interconnections of life matrices in the family. ... We now need to ... recognize that people's coping abilities and available supports are influenced not only by a constellation of events but also by a *family* (emphasis added) constellation of events, affecting individuals and their significant others. For example, an older woman might become widowed at a time when her son has had a heart attack and another child is going through a divorce. ... An experience of overload among the middle-aged is likely to be produced by factors in three or four generations: the needs of one or two generations of elderly, the needs and resources of the young, and the number of available siblings in the middle generations as well as their tangible and intangible resources. [Hagestad, 1981, pp. 34-35]

By focusing on midlife divorce, Hagestad has been able to concentrate on the "bridge generation" in which the family lineage consequences of divorce are most clearly identified. She observes that while past research has dealt with the effect of divorce on young children, it has neglected to deal with the effect of their parents' divorce on grown children or of the effect on parents whose grown children divorce (1982, pp. 5-6). The consequence of this theoretical perspective is the expansion of the yield over that usually found in divorce data analysis.

A major piece of research which takes the family as the unit of analysis and focuses on the processes of divorce and remarriage on the family unit is the longitudinal project being carried out by Ahrons in Dane County, Wisconsin. The chapter in this volume by Ahrons and Wallisch provides details of that investigation. My particular interest in Ahrons's work lies in the fact that it is guided by a systems developmental theoretical perspective. This perspective develops a conceptualization of the postdivorce family as a "binuclear family system" (Ahrons, 1979, 1980a, 1980b, 1981) undergoing a process of reorganization. Ahrons (1979, p. 500) notes:

> The reorganization of the nuclear family through divorce frequently results in the establishment of two households, maternal and paternal. These two interrelated households, or nuclei of the child's family of orientation, form one family system—a BINUCLEAR FAMILY SYSTEM. The centrality of each of these households will vary among postdivorce families. Some families make very distinct divisions between the child's primary and secondary homes, whereas in other families these distinctions may be blurred and both homes have primary importance. Hence, the term BINUCLEAR FAMILY indicates a family system with two nuclear households, whether or not the households have equal importance in the child's life experience.

Ahrons (1980a) outlines five transitions that are part of the family's change "from nuclearity to binuclearity." Individual cognition represents the internal psychological process that a spouse undergoes in recognizing dissatisfaction with the marriage and in moving toward its dissolution and termination. The "topography of relationship disengagement and dissolution" set forth by Duck (1982) is directly relevant to this transition and to some of the later transitions. Family metacognition deals with the process in the family of determining that something is wrong in the marriage and beginning interpersonal processes that bring that fact into the open. Systemic separation is the explicit process of physical and emotional separation of the family into its binuclear form. Systemic reorganization is the process through which the binuclear family establishes new patterns for relating in the absence of the marital bond. Family redefinition is the ongoing process of consolidating and revising these new patterns and of developing a new sense of family identity, internally and externally.

Ahrons (1980a, p. 535) sees each transition, including social role transitions, as encompassing a complex interaction of overlapping experiences. This conceptualization, then, provides a fruitful foundation within a developmental model for exploring the processes of divorce and remarriage in the family. In theorizing on family SDR reorganization, this chapter has depended heavily on Ahrons's initial formulation. While profiting from her pioneering efforts, this chapter attempts to extend her views.

In setting forth a model of SDR processes, I have followed Burr's strategies for developing propositional theory. This approach involves six steps (Burr, 1979, pp. 8-9): (1) Clarify conceptually the major dependent variable to be explained; (2) review theories pertaining to the phenomenon of interest capable of being rendered context-free; (3) formulate a limited number of general context-free propositions; (4) deduce context-specific propositions at lower orders of abstraction; (5) scan research for empirical support, if any, for the deduced propositions; and (6) incorporate all of these propositions into an accounting model format. Not all that is called for in this list has been accomplished in this chapter, nor has the order called for by Burr necessarily been followed. However, the ultimate objective is to develop a theory that generally meets these criteria.

Propositional theory building appears to me to have several benefits. First, like most systematic approaches to theory building, it introduces a disciplined approach to the process of developing an explanatory approach to a particular area of human behavior. Using a propositional approach requires the clear and explicit identification of variables and the relationships between those variables. Furthermore, in the process of combining several theoretical approaches, the propositional process assists in making clear those points at which the selected theories—or subtheories—are analogous and at which each contributes something new. The development of an inventory of propositional statements provides for broadening the explanatory and predictive power of the theory by the logical process of producing new combinations of variable relationships. Finally, the propositional inventory, when operationalized, provides a broad range of hypotheses for testing the power of the theory.

The rest of this chapter will discuss the author's integrative theoretical scheme for analyzing postmarital family reorganization. First, the four component models will be introduced briefly. This introduction will highlight the main ideas of each position and show how they are interrelated. A set of propositions will then be derived from the overall integrated model, and the commentary will move through the various phases in the binuclear family reorganization process. In a series of four tables, 68 specific propositions are offered. It is in this section of the chapter that the four component theories are used fully as the basis for predictions about the process of family reorganization.

Further Theorizing

Basic Variables from Binuclear Family Reorganization Theory

In this analysis, SDR processes will be treated as the dependent variable in the theory. The dependent variable name selected is the "level of binuclear family reorganization," which is derived from Ahrons's work. Similarly, a number of independent variables are drawn from Ahrons. Because her research is specifically on families with dependent children, a major independent variable is the quality of coparenting relationship in the postdivorce family. The quality of several other relationships must also be considered in SDR. These are: the non-coparenting relationship, spouse/new partner relationship, new partner/former spouse relationship, parent/child relationship, new partner/child relationship, sibling relationship, and the extended family relationship. These variables are certainly implicit (and often explicit) in Ahrons's treatment of the binuclear family reorganization process. Each is analytically distinct, and all contribute to the final level of reorganization in the binuclear family.

Three predivorce variables related to the quality of the coparenting relationship are role clarity in the parental/spousal roles, marital history, and divorce history. For example, there are indications in the empirical literature that former spouses who deal effectively in their coparental relationships are those who, during their marriage, had established clear boundaries between their spousal roles and their parental roles. Thus, after separation and/or divorce, such couples are much more competent at distinguishing between controversial issues which are chiefly related to their own dyadic relationship and those which are relevant to parenting. They are less likely, therefore, to entangle their children in conflicts that are rooted in their couple relationship rather than in their approach to their roles as parents. Similar kinds of influences on the coparenting roles may be found in the way the couple related over their marital careers and the manner in which they moved through the separation and divorce process.

Postdivorce variables in the coparenting relationship chain include custody type, type of binuclear family structure, clarity of postdivorce role models, and clarity of postdivorce community norms. One example of how one of these variables influences coparenting is the empirical evidence that joint custody appears to be associated with more effective coparenting than either split custody or sole custody. The causal direction of this relationship, however, remains unclear. One may reason that ex-spouses who enter into a joint custody agreement— either voluntarily or as a result of a court order—may have already been more effective parents than those who are involved in split or sole custody agreements. Alternatively, one can argue that joint custody provides for a more effective coparental relationship than the other types. To date we do not have adequate data to determine which of these two may be the better interpretation.

The variables treated in Ahrons's model as postdivorce variables can also be used in the postseparation period. These variables focus on the normative structure by which the family functions once there is an actual marital severance. As such, they provide the basis for the role behavior that family members exhibit in the postmarital period of the family career.

Figure 9.1 provides a paradigm of the relationships between the variables derived from Ahrons's conceptualization. This paradigm does not include all of the variables that Ahrons sees as explanatory. Some of these will eventually need to be incorporated as the theory extends out to the societal and individual levels.

Social Networks and Postmarital Family Reorganization

Families that experience SDR do not do so in a social vacuum. Family and friends are involved in a variety of ways. Thus an important aspect of the process is the effect of social networks on the binuclear family reorganization. McLanahan, Wedemeyer, and Adelberg (1981) provide the basis for some propositional statements in their analysis of divorced mothers' social networks. Drawing on the social network literature for a basic conceptual approach, these researchers found four distinct types of social network patterns among their divorced mothers—family of origin, extended, and two types of conjugal networks. These conjugal networks were distinguished chiefly by the presence of a "key male or spouse-equivalent." Otherwise, they differed in that one type ("A") focused on involving relatives and close old friends similar to the family of origin network. The other type ("B") was composed chiefly of new friends, as was the extended network. Two of the types, family of origin and conjugal type A, were "close-knit." The other two types, extended and conjugal type B, were "loose-knit" networks. Close-knit networks are those in which the various members have interlocking ties to each other as well as to ego. Loose-knit networks are characterized by dyadic ties between the individual members and ego only.

The outcome of the research resulted in three hypotheses (McLanahan et al., 1981, pp. 609-610):

(1) Loose-knit networks are supportive for women who are attempting to establish a new identity.

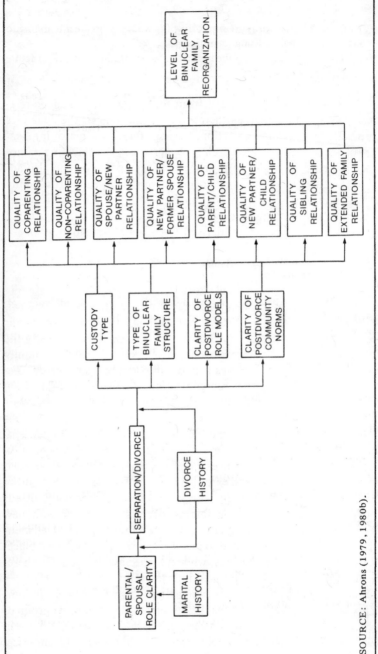

SOURCE: Ahrons (1979, 1980b).

Figure 9.1 A Paradigm of Postmarital Variable Relationships Based on Ahrons's Conceptualization

(2) Close-knit networks are supportive for women who are attempting to maintain their existing identities.
(3) The role orientation of the mother and, in turn, her network structure may change over time.

This treatment may be extended from the rather individualistic relationships stated in these hypotheses to ones that suggest the dynamics of binuclear family reorganization. Perhaps one of the major implications of the McLanahan research is to alert us to the changing nature of social networks in the SDR process. At this point we can also anticipate joining the impact of social networks on binuclear family reorganization as set out by McLanahan with some of the work of McCubbin on family stress with which I deal shortly. Figure 9.2 presents a detailed paradigm derived from the McLanahan work.

Family Problem-Solving Variables

A third major theoretical area relevant to binuclear family reorganization is the problem-solving ability of the family. One can incorporate the work of Klein and Hill (1979) directly into our ultimate model, since they have not been content-specific about the kinds of problems to be addressed. The level of binuclear family reorganization clearly involves a particular level of problem-solving competency as part of that reorganization. I have focused on Klein and Hill's point that problem-solving effectiveness is a combination of solution quality and solution acceptability (1979, pp. 519-520). As they emphasize, a solution may be of high quality but low acceptability. Similarly, a highly acceptable solution may be of low quality. Family problem-solving involves a delicate balance between these two factors. It might be pointed out also that the factors included in the Klein and Hill model fit nicely with several factors already discussed. Thus it represents a genuine joining of existing theory with new theory—one of the major goals of theory building. Variables identified by Klein and Hill related to member characteristics, social placement, and cultural orientations, while not specifically dealt with here, should eventually be incorporated into the model.

Klein (1983) has published a comparison between the work in family problem solving (PS) and that being carried out by another group of theorist/researchers on family stress, crisis, and coping (SCC). Klein (1983, p. 85) develops the point that "the theories and empirical research in these areas have come to take on mutually independent status, with the result that the two streams of work have failed to

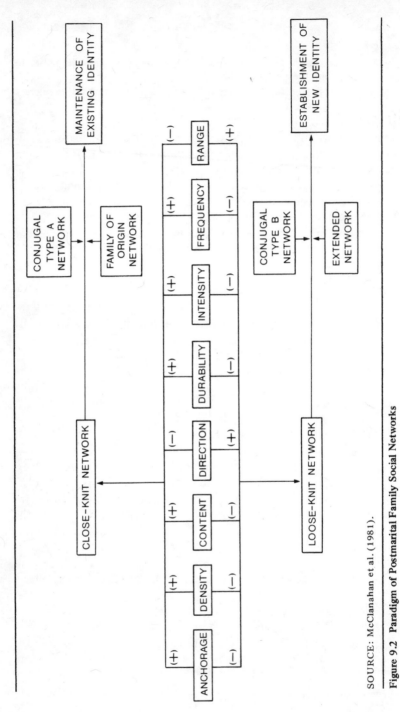

SOURCE: McClanahan et al. (1981).

Figure 9.2 Paradigm of Postmarital Family Social Networks

benefit from one another in ways which would be advantageous to both and to the field as a whole" (p. 85). At the end of his comparative analysis, Klein concludes, somewhat pessimistically (pp. 108-109):

> While the search for an overarching framework which can deal equally well with SCC and PS is worthwhile, we expect no resolution in the immediate future. Different frameworks remain useful for different purposes and our commitments as social scientists, conditioned by our intellectual ecologies, affect the choices we make. . . . Although the momentum is currently on the side of those who are troubled by the family's ability to cope with the crises and stresses of the modern world, one expects problem solving behavior to continue to be relevant, and for the two streams of research to become increasingly integrated in the years ahead.

While not claiming to have solved the difficulties of integration which Klein identifies, both PS and SCC will be incorporated into the model. We turn, therefore, to a consideration of family stress and crisis coping.

Stress and Crisis Theory

A major aspect of the SDR theory of binuclear family reorganization is the nature of these processes as crises or stressful events. As Ahrons (1980a, pp. 533-534) points out, "Family stress theory (Burr, 1973) provides constructs for identifying and explaining the relationships between major stressors in the divorce process and their impact on the family and allows the further clarification of a model for clarifying normative family transitions that result from the divorce process." It thus becomes clear that the theory must include conceptualization that can deal with the stress/crisis coping process.

There would appear to be no better theoretical attack on this problem than the extension of Hill's (1949) ABCX model by McCubbin and Patterson (1983), which they have labeled the "double ABCX" model of family adjustment and adaptation. The authors make an important distinction between a stressor and a crisis. There are many stressors in the lives of all families. A stressor is a life event or transition "which produces, or has the potential of producing, change in the family social system" (McCubbin & Patterson, 1983, p. 8). A crisis "is characterized by the family's inability to restore stability and by the continuous pressure to make changes in the family structure and patterns of interaction. In other words, stress may never reach crisis proportions if the family is able to use existing resources and define the situation so as to resist systemic change and maintain family stability" (p. 10). Whether a particular stressor (e.g., SDR) becomes a crisis or not, and the maladaptation/bonadaptation outcome, is determined by a highly complex process. This process includes the interplay of the particular stressor and the possible pile-up of other stressors; existing and new family and/or individual resources; and familial perceptions of the stressors, resources, coping styles, and the crisis itself (McCubbin & Patterson, 1983, pp. 8-17). (We should note the parallel of the concept of pile-up with Hagestad's idea of "overload" cited earlier.)

The key significance of the McCubbin work is its specific view of the family response to any particular stressor or set of stressors as a process that takes place over time, not an event with no time dimension. This idea, of course, is highly compatible with the family development approach, the Hagestad family lineages idea, and with Ahrons's binuclear family notion. To date no explicit attempt has been made to apply family stress theories in a systematic manner to the SDR processes (McCubbin & Patterson, 1983, p. 152). We turn now to an attempt to make such an application.

In their model, McCubbin and Patterson identify three phases of the stress/crisis coping process in families. These are adjustment and two phases of accommodation—restructuring and consolidation. Adjustment involves the initial attempts of the family to cope with the stressors without falling into crisis. Restructuring is called for when, having failed to adjust, the family moves to crisis and must change the manner of interacting in a significant way. Consolidation involves the processes of incorporating the changes arrived at in the restructuring phase into the daily life of the family system. During consolidation, additional modifications—a sort of "fine-tuning"—to these changes occur.

In each of these phases it is possible for the family to develop appropriate coping mechanisms and move on to the next phase. However, failure to do so results in moving again into the crisis state or one of the other phases in the process, depending on the degree of maladjustment that results. At each phase new variables are introduced, as well as elements of variables already encountered in an earlier phase or phases. While the representation of this process on a printed page (see Figure 3) necessitates its depiction as if it were circular, it is in fact an ongoing process. "Returning" to crisis does not represent precisely the same condition in the family after an attempt at adjustment, restructuring, or consolidation. This is not a cyclical model but rather one that sets forth the family career in linear chronological and processual terms.

In adjustment there are a set of attempts by the family to deal with the stressor either by avoidance, elimination, or assimilation. Depending on the impact of prior strains and the hardships that the stressor may produce—and on existing resources and the definition and appraisal of the situation—the family can successfully resist allowing the stressor to become a crisis. Their adjustment will lie along a continuum between maladjustment and bonadjustment—with maladjustment, of course, leading into crisis.

The restructuring phase of accommodation involves some of the same elements found in adjustment which combine to explain the degree of success in handling the crisis. A new element is introduced, however. Pile-up indicates the salient fact that stressors do not occur in isolation. Thus other stressors and events may combine to make the crisis even deeper than it might have been or, indeed, to precipitate additional crises. Again, depending on the way these factors operate, the family may be unsuccessful in attaining a level of adaptation that allows them to move on to consolidation. Rather, they enter a new level of crisis and begin again to attempt to cope with the situations that face them. They remain in crisis if the resources available are inadequate, if they cannot arrive at mutually acceptable solutions of adequate quality to their difficulties and implement them, and/or if maintenance of the system fails. It is also possible that, having used up their energies in attempting to cope, they fall into exhaustion.

Should the restructuring process lead to a certain (as yet undefined) level of adaptation, the family may move to the consolidation level of accommodation. Here the available resources and the shared definitions and problem solutions arrived at are further defined and refined so as to reach an adaptive level lying along the continuum from maladaptation to bonadaptation. Two measures of this adaptation level are identified: member to family fit and family to community fit. It is also possible, of course, that the consolidation process breaks down for some reason or reasons. In this event, the family may move to either the restructuring level or into crisis—and, possibly, to exhaustion.

This paradigm of the stress/crisis coping process provides a useful way of approaching the SDR processes. Each of these—separation, divorce, and remarriage—may be seen as stressors. Thus it is not particularly relevant to deal with each process as being theoretically distinct. The paradigm provides a way of dealing with the distinctive aspects of each while at the same time addressing the more theoretically interesting issue of how families reorganize themselves as a result of them. Indeed, depending on where we wish to inject ourselves into the family career, we can see any of the preceding or succeding processes as moving through one or more of the phases in the McCubbin and Patterson paradigm. Separation may indeed be the means of responding to marital stress, and the family may consolidate in the separated state. Or, having successfully reorganized at the separated state, the family may move to divorce and find that the stresses introduced produce a new crisis with which they must cope. Similarly, successful adaption to divorce does not preclude the necessity of dealing with the stress brought on by the remarriage of either or both of the former spouses—which may or may not develop to the crisis level.

Figure 9.3 represents a minor redrawing of McCubbin and Patterson's (1983) paradigm. There is no essential modification in this redrawing. Space prohibits placing the concepts from the other theoretical work I have discussed in their appropriate locations.

What is required at this point is specification of the relationships between the variables that the theory might use to examine these processes in detail. In what follows I combine the work of McCubbin and Patterson, Ahrons, McLanahan, and Hill and Klein.

Deriving Generic Propositions
From A Theoretical Framework

The paradigm shown in Figure 9.3 provides a useful "map" for moving systematically through the binuclear family reorganization process. Readers are encouraged to refer frequently to this map in the discussion that follows. It is possible to begin to set out generic propositions of relationships between variables in the paradigm. What follows is not intended as an exhaustive listing of such propositions. "Generic" is intended to indicate that they are those most immediately deduced from the background of theory and research available. They are relatively simple, they vary in their level of abstraction, and they are relatively weak in explanatory power. Perhaps most important, however, they point the direction to other propositions which may yield higher explanatory power. Tables 9.1-9.4 list the propositions developed.

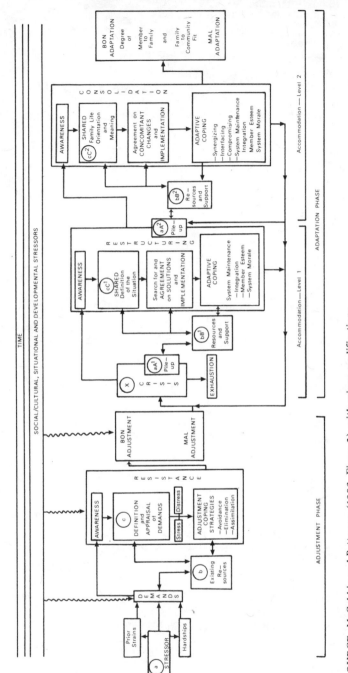

SOURCE: McCubbin and Patterson (1983, Figure 2), with minor modifications.

Figure 9.3 Binuclear Family Reorganization Following Separation/Divorce/Remarriage

255

TABLE 9.1
Generic Propositions Derived from Theory:
Demands and Resources

Demands and Hardships:

P1.   The greater the conflict in the marital/separation/divorce history, the greater the probability of the stressor (a) becoming a crisis (x).

P2.   The presence of any hardships is positively related to the stressor (a) becoming a crisis (x).

P3.   The presence of more than one of the hardships or strains that accompany the stressor (a) increases the probability of the stressor (a) becoming a crisis (x) by a multiplicative function of an undetermined nature which includes interaction.

Resources:

P4.   The greater the quality of any of the existing relationships, the less the probability of the stressor becoming a crisis.

P5.   The greater the family strengths, the less the probability of the stressor becoming a crisis.

P6.   A loose-knit social network is negatively related to the stressor becoming a crisis for individuals who wish to change their role definitions.

P7.   A loose-knit social network is positively related to the stressor becoming a crisis for individuals who wish to maintain their role definitions.

P8.   A tight-knit community network is negatively related to the stressor becoming a crisis.

P9.   The greater the psychological well-being, the less the probability of the stressor becoming a crisis.

P10. The greater the financial well-being, the less the probability of the stressor becoming a crisis.

P11. The greater the dependability of sources of financial support, the less the probability of the stressor becoming a crisis.

P12. The greater the diversification of sources of financial support, the less the probability of the stressor becoming a crisis.

P13. The greater the stability in the occupational history, the less the probability of the stressor becoming a crisis.

P14. The greater the stability in the occupational status, the less the probability of the stressor becoming a crisis.

P15. Age has an indeterminate relationship to the probability of the stressor becoming a crisis.

P16. The greater the education, the less the probability of the stressor becoming a crisis.

P17. The greater the homogeneity of family composition, the less the probability of the stressor becoming a crisis.

P18. The greater the homogeneity of household composition, the less the probability of the stressor becoming a crisis.

P19. The number of previous marriages is indeterminately related to the stressor becoming a crisis.

P20. The greater the housing mobility, the greater the probability of the stressor becoming a crisis.

P21. The greater the housing adequacy, the lower the probability of the stressor becoming a crisis.

P22. The greater the number and diversity of existing resources utilized by the family, the less the effect of prior strains and hardships on the probability of the stressor becoming a crisis.

Demands and Resources

Demands. We begin at the left of the model with those aspects that make up the general "a" factor of demands, which include not only the stressor but also prior strains and hardships associated with the stressor or independent of it. The stressor, of course, can be any of the three SDR processes. Or, in a more longitudinal analysis, we can envision seeing any combination of them. Included under the prior strains category are the following variables: marital history, separation history, and divorce history. In the hardships category fall economic hardships, interpersonal hardships, employment hardships, and supporting services hardships. Generic propositions 1-3 in Table 9.1 are stated to begin the theoretic chain.

Existing Resources. Moving to the next point in the model, we encounter the "b" factor, "existing resources." The Ahrons independent variables listed on the left side of Figure 9.1 are included in this factor. Additional variables are specified by McCubbin and Patterson and by McLanahan, as well as others that have been shown to be important in previous research: family strengths—esteem and communiction, family strengths—mastery and health, social network (i.e., the primary group network of the individual), community network (i.e., the broader network of secondary relationships beyond the primary group network), psychological state, attitudes, financial well-being, sources of financial support, occupational history/status, and such demographic statuses as family composition, age, education, household composition, and previous marriages.

Generic propositions derived from the "b" factor include propositions 4-21 (Table 9.1). By examining the relationship between the demands and existing resources, an additional proposition (P22) presents itself.

Awareness and Resistance to Change

Awareness. Continuing right in the paradigm, we reach the third aspect of the process, one that McCubbin and Patterson have termed "awareness"—the "c" factor. Here we encounter the set of variables that capture how families define and appraise demands and develop particular adjustment coping strategies. Under the definition and appraisal of demands would fall such variables as attitudes, perceptions, custody arrangements, impact of SDR on the child, role clarity in family

TABLE 9.2
Generic Propositions Derived from Theory:
Awareness and Resistance to Change

Awareness:

P23. The greater the demands present, the less likely are attitudes that will support resistance to change.

P24. The greater the demands present, the less likely are perceptions that will support resistance to change.

P25. The greater the demands present, the less resistance to change in custody arrangements.

P26. The greater the demands present, the more the stressor will be defined as having an impact on the child(ren).

P27. The more the stressor is defined as having a negative impact on the child(ren), the less resistance to change.

P28. The greater the demands present, the less resistance to change in clarifying family role boundaries.

P29. The greater the demands present, the less resistance to perceiving family/social/community networks as facilitating change.

P30. The greater the demands present, the more clarity is required in community definitions of SDR roles as a means for accomplishing change.

P31. The greater the demands present, the more clarity is required in SDR role models as a means for accomplishing change.

Awareness and Resistance to Change:

P32. The more custody arrangements are perceived as satisfactory, the less resistance to change.

P33. The more role clarity in family roles, the less resistance to change.

P34. The more clarity in family role boundaries, the less resistance to change.

P35. The more family/social/community networks are perceived as being supportive, the less resistance to change.

P36. The more clarity in community definitions of SDR roles, the less resistance to change.

P37. The more clarity in SDR role models, the less resistance to change.

---

roles, clarity of family role boundaries, perceptions of the family/social/community networks, clarity of community definitions of SDR roles, and clarity of SDR role models.

McCubbin and Patterson (1983, p. 25) state:

> The family resistance response begins with an awareness of the *demands* which is shaped by the intensity of the stressor (a factor), the extensiveness of related hardships, and the extensiveness of unresolved prior strains. The family arrives at a definition of the demands (c factor) and makes an appraisal of what needs to be done to manage the situation.

TABLE 9.3
Generic Propositions Derived from Theory: Coping

Coping Strategies:

P38.   The more clarity of role definitions, the greater the probability of selecting the elimination or assimilation strategies over the avoidance strategy, holding existing resources constant.

P39.   The greater the existing resources, the greater the probability of selecting the elimination or assimilation strategies over the avoidance strategy, holding clarity of role definitions constant.

P40.   When clarity of role definitions is high and existing resources are low, the probability of selecting the avoidance coping strategy is high.

P41.   The greater the combined occurrence of clarity of role definitions and greater existing resources, the greater the probability of selecting the elimination or assimilation strategies over the avoidance strategy.

P42.   Loose-knit networks are negatively related to the clarity of role definitions.

P43.   The fewer existing resources and the less clarity of role definitions, the more probable the failure of any of the coping strategies selected to provide a satisfactory level of family functioning.

Pile-up:

P44.   The greater the pile-up (aA1), the greater the crisis (x) experienced by the family.

P45.   The greater the pile-up (aA1), the less the family's ability to bring resources and sources of support (bB1), either preexisting ones or newly discovered ones (as a result of the restructuring process), to bear on the crisis (x).

P46.   The lower the pile-up (aA1) and the greater the resources and support (bB1) in combination, the greater the shared definitions of the situation.

Problem Solving:

P47.   The more the family reaches a shared definition of the situation, the greater the solution quality.

P48.   The more the family reaches a shared definition of the situation, the greater the solution acceptability.

P49.   The greater the solution quality and solution acceptability, the greater the agreement on implementation of solutions.

Problem Solving and Coping:

P50.   The greater the problem-solving ability, the more integration in the system.

P51.   The greater the problem-solving ability, the more member esteem.

P52.   The greater the problem-solving ability, the more system morale.

It is not clear from this statement whether the shaping of awareness through these three conditions is additive or multiplicative or, more likely, a combination of both. What is quite certain is that the relationships are complex. Generic propositions 23-31 (Table 9.2) reflect the impact of these demands on awareness. Propositions 32-37 state some direct relationships between the awareness variables and resistance to change.

Coping

As a consequence of the definitions and appraisals, some level of stress occurs. Stress is an actual or perceived demand-capability imbalance in the family's functioning. Distress is seen as unpleasant or undesirable stress (McCubbin & Patterson, 1983, p. 9). The coping strategies identified are avoidance, elimination, and assimilation. There does not appear to be any reason that one of these strategies is likely to be used more frequently than any of the others, or as a first alternative. It may be that by examining carefully the relationships between the variables that some propositions may appear which would explain the selection of one strategy over another. As initial attempts at this kind of propositional formulation, propositions 38-42 (Table 9.3) are stated. Ultimately, propositions that will explain the relationship between the variables in the three aspects of the process and the onset of crisis must be formulated. Beyond those already stated, proposition 43 is offered.

Accommodation Level 1—Restructuring

If the family coping processes in the adjustment phase are unsuccessful in either avoiding, eliminating, or assimilating the stressor, the family moves to crisis—the "X" factor. Patterson and McCubbin posit two possible routes. One of these is to move to the "adaptation phase," and the other is to move to exhaustion. The propositions related to exhaustion will be left until later, since this outcome can occur in several different sequence positions. It will be recalled that the adaptation phase is conceptualized further as having two levels—the restructuring level and the consolidation level. Prior to entering the restructuring process, however, it is important to recognize that the crisis will probably be exacerbated by pile-up—the "aA" factor. Thus it is unlikely that any crisis is experienced in its "pure" form without other stressors or events intensifying the crisis. In view of this, proposition 44 (Table 9.3) is offered.

In approaching the restructuring process, the family brings to bear the resources and support structures available to it. It can be recognized that the process which has moved the family from encountering the stressor to the level of crisis has the possibility of having also identified some new resources that may be called upon. It must also be noted that the restructuring itself may reveal other existing resources, not previously identified, or may produce some new resources as part of the process. Thus the paradigm indicates "loops" that move in both directions between the bB and the aA and cC factors (shown in Figure 9.3), as well as a loop back to the "c" factor.

The specific variables related to the factor aA, pile-up, are essentially the same as those which appeared as demands at the outset. We must add, of course, the new strains and hardships that may have been introduced by the process which has occurred up to this point, as well as any newly experienced stressors that have arisen in the passage of time. Similarly, the bB resources and support variables include those variables found under b, existing resources, as well as any new resources identified. Proposition 45 (Table 9.3) reflects this process.

By the same token, the cC restructuring process focuses on variables first encountered in the c factor. It is to be noted here that, having overcome the resistance to change, we expect the primary processes to focus on problem solving (Klein & Hill, 1979). We should expect a process of developing shared definitions of the situation. Thus we will focus in the family problem-solving process on solution quality and solution acceptability. Clearly the combination of the level of pile-up and the level of resources and support affect the problem-solving process. Thus proposition 46 (Table 9.3) is stated. Furthermore, there are a series of relationships between the problem-solving variables in the restructuring process. Generic propositions 47-49 (Table 9.3) attempt to capture these elements.

In the area of coping, we will examine integration, member esteem, and system morale. Generic propositions 50-52 are set down to identify the relationships between problem-solving effectiveness and coping.

Accommodation Level 2—Consolidation

Finally, as we move from successful restructuring to the consolidation level, we again see the process of pile-up (aA) and the effect of the resources and support (bB). As can be seen in the paradigm, the newly introduced variables are those which capture the process of "settling in" to a new level of binuclear family reorganization. These include shared family life orientation and meaning, level of agreement on concomitant changes, level of agreement on implementation of changes, synergizing (efforts to coordinate and pull together as a unit), interfacing with the community, and compromising as a result of a realistic appraisal of the situation and a willingness to accept and support a less-than-perfect resolution. Several generic propositions (P53-P61, Table 9.4) identify relationships between these variables.

A New Level of Family Reorganization

Assuming successful consolidation, the family reaches a new level of binuclear family reorganization which involves some level of bonadaptation in McCubbin and Patterson's terms. This level need not be as great as that prevailing before the crisis, but it is a level that represents the adequate functioning of family processes. Two propositions apply (P62 and P63).

Exhaustion

If the family is not successful in reaching a satisfactory level of reorganization, they move to one of the less organized levels. There they begin again to address the crisis and to attempt to work through the family's coping with it. It is possible that the family may have depleted its resources to such an extent that it is no longer able to cope. In this situation, we posit a movement into the condition of exhaustion. Here we find the family unable to begin to address the issues facing it with an adequate level of competency. I set forth propositions 64-68 concerning the movement to exhaustion.

A major advantage of a longitudinal design such as the one proposed here is that it is possible to identify the various paths that families may take in SDR and to identify the individual and group characteristics that accompany any particular pattern.

Summary

This discussion has attempted an integration of the four main theoretical streams identified. Figure 9.4 is a representation of this integration. It becomes clear that we already have a highly complex model at this point, despite the limitation placed on it to deal only with the family group level of analysis. The original decision to treat the level of binuclear family reorganization as a dependent variable was useful for establishing the original paradigm. Now it is possible to recognize, however, that the level of binuclear family reorganization itself feeds back on the system to affect how almost all of the "in-

TABLE 9.4

Generic Propositions Derived from Theory: Outcomes

Consolidation:

P53.   The lower the pile-up (aA2) and the greater the resources and support (bB2) in combination, the greater the shared family life orientation and meaning (cC2).

P54.   The greater the shared family life orientation and meaning, the more agreement on concomitant changes that the family identifies as required to accomplish consolidation.

P55.   The greater the agreement on concomitant changes required, the more agreement on implementation of those changes.

P56.   The greater the agreement on concomitant changes required and the greater the agreement on implementation of those changes, the more synergizing in the family.

P57.   The greater the agreement on concomitant changes required and the greater the agreement on implementation of those changes, the more interfacing in the family.

P58.   The greater the agreement on concomitant changes required and the greater the agreement on implementation of those changes, the more compromising in the system.

P59.   The greater the synergizing, interfacing, and compromising, the more integration in the system.

P60.   The greater the synergizing, interfacing, and compromising, the more member esteem in the system.

P61.   The greater the synergizing, interfacing, and compromising, the greater the system morale.

P62.   The greater the consolidation (cC2), the greater the binuclear family reorganization as measured by member to family fit.

P63.   The greater the consolidation (cC2), the greater the binuclear family reorganization as measured by family to community fit.

Exhaustion:

P64.   The greater the pile-up (aA1 or aA2), the greater the probability of moving to exhaustion.

P65.   The greater the restructuring (cC1) achieved, the less the probability of moving to exhaustion.

P66.   The greater the consolidation (cC2) achieved, the less the probability of moving to exhaustion.

P67.   The more accommodation achieved prior to failure, the greater the probability of moving to exhaustion. That is, if the family has moved successfully through restructuring to consolidation but is unsuccessful at that level, they are more likely to fall into exhaustion than if they had failed at the restructuring level.

P68.   The greater the number of times the family has attempted and failed to restructure (cC1) and/or consolidate (cC2), the greater the probability of moving to exhaustion.

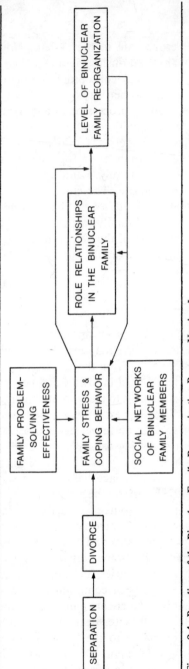

Figure 9.4 Paradigm of the Binuclear Family Reorganization Process: Version I

dependent" variables operate in the system. Not surprisingly, the covariate nature of the relationships is revealed clearly.

Returning to the original conceptual foundation of the family development approach, another way of viewing this covariate system is to recognize the ongoing process of family dynamics. The family career as a set of mutually contingent individual careers (life courses)—or, in Hagestad's terms, family lineages—deals continually with past experience as a foundation for present functioning and for the future direction of the family. Families who experience SDR are no exception to this principle. The changing membership constellations, which have been used as the basic means for developing analytical categories of the family career ("family life cycle stages"), remain an important aspect of the binuclear family career just as they do of the "normal" nuclear family.

Future Directions

The future work on this propositional theory of the processes of SDR seems quite clear. One major task is to glean the available research-based propositions from the existing literature, as well as to design research that can assist in identifying new propositional statements. Yet another strategy is to incorporate other existing theories into the current paradigm. For example, it would appear that the work of Boss (1979, 1980, 1982) on father absence assists in a particularly appropriate way in analyzing family crises that involve the loss of members. Similarly, the theory of Lewis and Spanier (1979) on the quality and stability of marriage has some direct relevance to this model. Adams's (1979) work on the mate selection process would also appear to be an important source for further understanding the processes occurring both prior to divorce and after divorce in the remarriage process. Aspects of Reiss and Miller's (1979) model of heterosexual permissiveness have some transferability to this model, not only in terms of their substantive focus but as a way of beginning to explain some of the aspects of community/societal influence on the SDR process. In addition, there are a number of theoretical pathways to be explored which will better deal with the individual life course variables as they contribute to the binuclear family reorganization process. Hagestad's (1981) approach to interweaving life careers appears to have some promise in this respect.

Finally, the appearance of this chapter in this volume represents a major crossing of theory boundaries for this writer. It has introduced an entirely new (to him) body of thought which has major implications for the study of the family processes precipitated by marital dissolution and termination. Recent publications on the topic of relationship dissolution by Baxter (1984), Duck (1982, 1984), Duck and Sants (1983), and Lee (1984) all have intriguing potential for their application to further theorizing. The rather extensive literature that lies behind these pieces only whets the appetite further. Incorporating this theory represents further potential growth in the explanation of postmarital family reorganization. My interest in this literature is its potential to identify the way in which the process of marital dissolution and termination contributes to an explanation of the process of binuclear family reorganization. There are many parallels in the conceptualizations and process mappings that appear in this work which make it most compatible for incorporation into an extended theory. It is hoped, as well, that the exposure of this work to that group of thinkers will stimulate them to venture into new intellectual territory.

This detailing of the work that lies ahead once again demonstrates the high "job security" of those committed to theory building.

Acknowledgments

This chapter is a revision and extension of papers presented at the annual meeting of the National Council on Family Relations (Rodgers, 1982b) and at the American-Scandinavian Research Seminar: Parent-Child Relationships Post-Divorce in Copenhagen, Denmark, June 1983 (Rodgers, 1984). A number of individuals contributed to those efforts as well as to this version. The author acknowledges the assistance of F. Ivan Nye, C. R. Ahrons, C. L. Martin, and a number of unidentifiable conference participants who gave helpful critical suggestions during its development. Acknowledgment is also given to the University of British Columbia, School of Family and Nutritional Sciences, for a number of support services critical to the completion of the chapter.

REFERENCES

Adams, B. N. (1979). Mate selection in the United States: A theoretical summarization. In W. Burr, R. Hill, I. Nye, & I. Reiss (Eds.), *Contemporary theories about the family* (Vol. 1, pp. 259-267). New York: Free Press.

Ahrons, C. R. (1979). The binuclear family: Two households, one family. *Alternative Lifestyles, 2,* 499-515.

Ahrons, C. R. (1980a). Divorce: A crisis of family transition and change. *Family Relations, 29,* 533-540.

Ahrons, C. R. (1980b). Redefining the divorced family: A conceptual framework for postdivorce family systems reorganization. *Social Work, 25,* 437-441.

Ahrons, C. R. (1981). The binuclear family: An emerging lifestyle for postdivorce families. In W. Dumon & C. Depaepe (Eds.), *Free papers: The XIXth International CFR Seminar on Divorce and Remarriage* (pp. 1-12). Leuven, Belgium: Committee on Family Research, International Sociological Association.

Baxter, L. A. (1984). Trajectories of relationship disengagement. *Journal of Social and Personal Relationships, 1,* 29-48.

Boss, P. (1980). Normative family stress: Family boundary changes across the life-span. *Family Relations, 29,* 445-450.

Boss, P., McCubbin, H., & Lester, G. (1979). The corporate executive wife's coping patterns in response to routine husband-father absence: Implications for family stress theory. *Family Process, 18,* 79-86.

Boss, P., & Greenberg, J. (1982, October). *The measurement of family boundary ambiguity: A general variable in family stress theory.* Paper presented at the annual meeting of the National Council on Family Relations, Washington, DC.

Burr, W. (1973). *Theory construction and the sociology of the family.* New York: Wiley.

Burr, W. R., Hill, R., Nye, F. I., & Reiss, I. L. (Eds.). (1979) *Contemporary theories about the family* (Vol. 1). New York: The Free Press.

Duck, S. W. (1982). A topography of relationship disengagement and dissolution. In S. W. Duck (Ed.), *Personal relationships 4: Dissolving personal relationships* (pp. 1-30). London: Academic Press.

Duck, S. W. (1984). A perspective on the repair of personal relationships: Repair of what, when? In S. W. Duck (Ed.), *Personal relationships 5: Repairing personal relationships* (pp. 163-184). London: Academic Press.

Duck, S. W., & Sants, S. (1983). On the origin of the specious: Are personal relationships really interpersonal states? *Journal of Social and Clinical Psychology, 1,* 27-41.

Hagestad, G. O. (1981). Problems and promises in the social psychology of intergenerational relations. In R. Fogel, E. Hatfield, S. Kiesler, & J. March (Eds.), *Stability and change in the family* (pp. 11-46). New York: Academic Press.

Hagestad, G. O., & Smyer, M. A. (1982). Dissolving long-term relationships: Patterns of divorcing in middle age. In S. W. Duck (Ed.), *Personal relationships 4: Dissolving personal relationships* (pp. 155-188). London: Academic Press.

Hagestad, G. O., Smyer, M. A., & Stierman, K. (1984). The impact of divorce in middle age. In R. Cohen, B. Cohler, & S. Weissmann (Eds.), *Parenthood: psychodynamic perspectives* (pp. 247-262). New York: Guilford Press.

Hetherington, E. M. (1979). Divorce: A child's perspective. *American Psychologist, 34,* 851-858.

Hetherington, E. M., Cox, H., & Cox, R. (1976). Divorced fathers. *The Family Coordinator, 25,* 417-428.

Hetherington, E. M., Cox, H., & Cox, R. (1978). The aftermath of divorce. In J. H. Stevens, Jr. & M. Matthews (Eds.), *Mother/child, father/child relationships* (pp. 149-176). Washington, DC: NAEYC.

Hetherington, E. M., Cox, H., & Cox, R. (1979). Stress and coping in divorce: Focus on women. In J. Gullahorn (Ed.), *Psychology and women in transition* (pp. 95-128). New York: V. H. Winston and Sons.

Hill, R. (1949). *Families under stress*. New York: Harper.

Kantor, D., & Lehr, W. (1975). *Inside the family*. San Francisco: Jossey-Bass.

Klein, D. M. (1983). Family problem solving and family stress. In H. I. McCubbin, M. B. Sussman, & J. M. Patterson (Eds.), *Social stress and the family: Advances and developments in family stress theory and research* (pp. 85-112). New York: Haworth Press.

Klein, D. M., & Hill, R. (1979). Determinants of family problem-solving effectiveness. In W. R. Burr, R. Hill, I. Nye, & I. Reiss (Eds.), *Contemporary theories about the family* (Vol. 1, pp. 493-598). New York: Free Press.

Lee, L. (1984). Sequences in separation: A framework for investigating endings of the personal (romantic) relationship. *Journal of Social and Personal Relationships. 1,* 49-73.

Lewis, R. A., & Spanier, G. B. (1979). Theorizing about the quality and stability of marriage. In W. Burr, R. Hill, I. Nye, & I. Reiss (Eds.), *Contemporary theories about the family* (Vol. 1, pp. 268-294). New York: Free Press.

McCubbin, H. I., & Patterson, J. M. (1983). The family stress process: The double ABCX model of adjustment and adaptation. In H. I. McCubbin, M. B. Sussman, & J. M. Patterson (Eds.), *Social stress and the family: Advances and developments in family stress theory and research* (pp. 7-37). New York: Haworth Press.

McLanahan, S. S., Wedemeyer, N. V., & Adelberg, T. (1981). Network structure, social support, and psychological well-being in the single-parent family. *Journal of Marriage and the Family, 43,* 601-612.

Reiss, I., & Miller, B. C. (1979) Heterosexual permissiveness: A theoretical analysis. In W. Burr, R. Hill, I. Nye, & I. Reiss (Eds.), *Contemporary theories about the family* (Vol. 1, pp. 57-100). New York: Free Press.

Rodgers, R. H. (1973). *Family interaction and transaction: The developmental approach*. Englewood Cliffs, NJ: Prentice-Hall.

Rodgers, R. H. (1982a). The contributions of the "free papers" to a theory of divorce consequences. In W. Dumon & C. DePaepe (Eds.), *Proceedings: The XIXth International CFR Seminar on Divorce and Remarriage* (pp. 71-104). Leuven, Belgium: Committee on Family Research, International Sociological Association.

Rodgers, R. H. (1982b, October). *Developing a propositional theory of the consequences of divorce/remarriage*. Paper presented at the annual meeting of the National Council on Family Relations, Washington, DC.

Rodgers, R. H. (1984). Developing a propositional theory of the consequences of separation/divorce/remarriage. In I. Koch-Nielson (Ed.), *Parent-child relationship, post-divorce* (pp. 14-53). Copenhagen, Denmark: The Danish National Institute of Social Research.

Wallerstein, J. S., & Kelly, J. B. (1980). *Surviving the breakup: How children and parents cope with divorce*. New York: Basic Books.

10

The Relationship Between Former Spouses

CONSTANCE R. AHRONS
LYNN S. WALLISCH

Although the process of terminating a marital relationship has increasingly received attention among social scientists, the present or current relationship between former spouses remains a neglected area of study. Yet this former spousal relationship has a dynamic history of shared experiences and familial ties that do not necessarily terminate with marital dissolution, particularly in those relationships to which children have been born. This chapter starts by exploring the changes that have taken place in societal views about divorce and then looks at their consequences for child custody and for the ensuing relationship between former spouses.

Divorce: A Historical Overview

A brief look at the historical and sociocultural background surrounding divorce will provide perspective on the "state of the art" of divorce research. Prior to 1975 almost all research was based on the premise that divorce was socially, psychologically, and morally pathological. Psychologists, believing that divorce was caused by psychological determinants, focused their research on identifying adult dysfunction and parental maladjustment as causal factors. This clinical notion of divorce also led to a genre of studies assessing the

AUTHORS' NOTE: This research was funded by the National Institute of Mental Health (Project 34397-01, Postdivorce Relationships: The Binuclear Family).

negative effects of divorce (see Levitan, 1979, for an excellent review of these studies). Since concern was with resulting pathology in children and adults, samples were drawn from clinical caseloads, such as child guidance centers and psychiatric hospitals. Sociologists also perceived divorce as deviant and an indication of the demise of the American family; hence, they focused their concern on the societal ills that either caused divorce or resulted from it.

Underlying both the social clinical pathology notions was the rigidly held belief that divorce was destructive to basic societal values. This notion of divorce as an immoral act set the stage for legal regulation. In order to preserve marriage and family life, getting a divorce was made very difficult, if not impossible. "The judgement that divorce was an immoral act, detrimental to society's stability, necessitated not only control but the employment of repressive sanctions. Thus, although divorce came to be regulated from the bench, the pulpit continued to supply its directives" (Halem, 1980, p. 26). It is only in the past decade, with the sharp increase in divorce rates, that we are beginning to shift away from this "divorce as deviance" perspective. Statutory reform in the form of no-fault legislation was a giant step toward removing both the barriers to divorce and its punitive qualities.

Although the bulk of the literature is still tainted by this early history, research is becoming more concerned with the issues of divorce as viewed from a normative perspective. In so doing, the focus of research is on the specific mediating factors that occur between the event of divorce itself and its subsequent short- and long-range effects on adults, children, and families. Thus the current approach to the study of divorce is changing from that of viewing it as a pathological event to seeing it as a dynamic, complex process of family transitions and change (Ahrons, 1979, 1980a, 1980c). However, much of the research and societal concern still center on the effects of divorce on dependent children. Aside from the exploratory study of midlife divorces conducted by Hagestad and Smyer (1982), the literature is void of work on the effects of divorce on families without dependent children. Although process studies of divorce's effects on childless couples are nonexistent, Hill, Rubin, and Peplau (1976) suggest in their study of 103 break-ups of dating relationships that the processes of uncoupling after divorce and after relationships before marriage have similar dimensions. Because the dissolution of a marital relationship that did not produce children or has no minor children poses no immediate consequence for society, it has not had high research priority. Like most other research, the present chapter looks at divorces of parents of dependent children but examines the nonparental aspect of their relationship as well.

Divorce and Child Custody

Although the study of divorce has become a new and growing area of research, relationships between former spouses did not receive the attention of social scientists until controversy over child custody issues came to the fore. Again, a brief analysis of the character of this movement will shed some light on the choice of research agendas.

Prior to the middle of the 19th century, children were considered the property of the father and custody was arbitrarily awarded to him. Gradually, changes in societal views, reflected in the doctrine of "tender years," shifted the court presumption of custody to the mother. Although the tender years doctrine was meant to apply only to children up to six or seven years of age, the mother has become the generally favored parent, even in custody disputes involving older children. As a result, during the 1960s and 1970s approximately 90% of the custody awards were given to mothers (Halem, 1980). Although there are indications of a trend toward more fathers seeking sole custody, it is not yet clear whether more fathers are actually being granted custody or whether a numerical increase in fathers seeking custody merely reflects the increase in divorce rates.

During the mid-1970s a new arrangement, joint custody, began to emerge. The desire for shared custodial arrangements probably arose from a combination of factors, the most important of these being a trend toward a more egalitarian approach to role-sharing in marriage, the increase of women in the labor force, the women's movement, and a new emphasis on the fathers' role in child development (i.e., more involvement of fathers in the birth and care of infants). The joint custody movement began in California as a grass-roots kind of movement. A small group of fathers, in objection to the prevailing court mandate of mother custody, organized to assert their parental rights. At the same time, there emerged a small group of divorcing spouses who chose joint custody as an agreement outside of the legal decision. Emanating from that development, new legislation in some states was enacted to permit a shared or joint custody arrangement. In virtually every state in the United States, as well as in many European countries, joint custody is now a permissible legal custody arrangement. A recent trend toward joint custody as the preferred arrangement is currently emerging: Several states have enacted legislation that assumes joint custody as a presumption or first choice. In those states, divorcing parents must prove that joint custody is *not* in the best interest of the child—a complete reversal of the issue up until 1980.

As a philosophical concept, joint custody has won the approval of legislators, judges, fathers, some mothers, and many social scientists. However, as a functioning type of custody arrangement we have little empirical evidence on the long-range effects of joint custody on children and the abilities of divorced parents to handle shared childrearing. This is not surprising, given the newness of this type of shared parenting postdivorce and the "divorce as deviance" perspective.

Most of the early studies of joint custody relied on personal accounts, case histories, and samples based on friendship networks and snowball techniques (e.g., Abarbanel, 1979; Steinman, 1981). Other studies have improved on the sampling process by using court records (Ahrons, 1979, 1980c), but all of the currently published research is based on small samples of children and/or adults, lack adequate control groups, and are based almost exclusively on interview data at the early stages of the postdivorce family. In sum, these studies conclude that joint custody is a viable option for those parents who choose it, that childrearing can be shared even though the parents continue to have some conflicts, and that some children can cope with it, at least in the initial stages. Derdeyn and Scott (1984, p. 207) conclude in their critical review of the joint custody literature: "There is a marked disparity between the power of the joint custody movement and the sufficiency of evidence that joint custody can accomplish what we expect of it."

It is because of this movement toward joint custody, however, that the study of the relationship between former spouses gains importance. If, as joint custody presumes, divorced spouses are to continue their role as parents, they must share decision making and childrearing. To do so implies the continuance of some form of relationship with each other. The prevailing assumption, however, is that divorce inevitably severs the relational bonds of the marital pair just as it severs the legal bonds of matrimony. Given the perspective that divorce dissolves the family, there has been little attempt to separate out the relationship dimension from other aspects of the marital union.

Stereotypes About Former Spouse Relationships

What little information we do have on the relationship between former spouses is derived primarily from societal stereotypes and the clinical literature. The clinical literature has long considered a continuing relationship between former spouses to be unhealthy. Contact between divorced spouses is usually perceived as an indication of unresolved marital issues or a "hanging on" to the marriage. It is interesting that while the general public, clergy, and mental health professionals decry the divorce rate and its familial implications, we nevertheless continue to view ex-spousal bonding as pathological or quasi-pathological. In a study that explored the attitudes of lawyers, clergy, and psychotherapists toward divorce, Kressel and his colleagues (1979, p. 259) found:

> With a few exceptions, respondents tended to distrust the ex-spouses' continuing involvement with each other as friends, business partners, or lovers—largely on the grounds that such attachments reflect separation distress rather than realistic caring, and that they drain energies that are more productively spent in forming new relationships.

The general distrust of a continuing relationship after divorce is reflected in the prevailing stereotype that former spouses must, of necessity, be antagonists; otherwise, why would they divorce? This stereotype is again reinforced by a bias in the available clinical material: Clinicians tend to see only the difficult or problematic former spousal relationships, while well-functioning divorced families are less apt to seek professional intervention.

The lack of language to describe the former spousal relationship, except in terms of a past relationship (e.g., "ex" or "former"), is another indication of societal unacceptance of it as a viable form. Margaret Mead's interpretation of the source of our discomfort in acknowledging a continuing relationship between former spouses may indeed still be valid: "Any contact between divorced people somehow smacks of incest; once divorced, they have been declared by law to be sexually inaccessible to each other, and the aura of past sexual relations makes further relationship incriminating" (Mead, 1971, p. 121). Although this taboo may have impeded progress toward developing theoretical formulations of postdivorce relationships, in this chapter we traverse that forbidden territory by providing some empirical data and theoretical beginnings.

The Study

Method

The Binuclear Family Research Project is a longitudinal investigation that takes the family as the unit of analysis and focuses on the consequences of divorce and remarriage for the family system. The term "binuclear family" is a new descriptive concept which assumes that the nuclear family through divorce reorganizes into a binuclear structure with two households defined as one family unit (see Ahrons, 1979, 1980a, 1980b). Gathering data from 98 pairs of former spouses and their current partners at approximately one, three, and five years after divorce, this study has a number of unique characteristics. First, unlike most studies of divorce, the sample was drawn from divorce court records with the intent of identifying a sample that would be representative of a more typical population of divorcing couples. Drawn from the divorce court records of Dane County, Wisconsin, the major restrictions on the sample were related to residency within the county on the part of both spouses, the presence of minor children, and contact between the nonresidential parent and child at least once in the two months prior to the first interview. Second, data were collected from both former spouses as well as from new partners acquired postdivorce. Due to the small number of joint and father custody cases in 1977, divorces finalized in 1978 and the first six months of 1979 were reviewed for the identification of additional non-mother custody cases. Therefore, the sample consists of a random sample of mother custody cases drawn from the 1977 court records and the total populaton of nonmother custody cases in 1977, 1978, and the first six months of 1979.

This sampling procedure yielded a final pool of 379 potentially eligible couples. Letters explaining the study and requesting participation were sent to all eligible individuals (N = 758). The letters were then followed by phone calls which identified those who did not meet the criteria for participation. Of the eligible and locatable sample, 51% agreed to participate. This yielded a final sample of 98 couples: 54 had mother custody, 28 had joint, and 16 father or split custody. At three years postdivorce, 176 of the original 196 divorced parents (90%) were reinterviewed. This resulted in at least one respondent from 96 and both respondents from 80 of the original 98 families. These original 176 study participants identified 124 new partners; of these, 102 met the eligibility required for cohabitation or remarriage, and of these, 91 (89%) were interviewed. (A partner was defined as cohabiting if he or she lived with the respondent 12 or more nights per month.) The data collection of five years postdivorce is still in progress; all respondents are being reinterviewed, and any new partners acquired since the last session will also be interviewed.

Data Collection. In-depth, semi-structured interviews were conducted in the respondents' homes. The interview contained both open-ended and structured questions, two modified Q-sort procedures, and a paper-and-pencil Hopkins Symptom Checklist (HSCL). Multiple indicators were used for most of the major variables under investigation, and the interviews were conducted by graduate social work students with clinical interviewing experience. The interviewers were matched by sex with the subjects, which also ensured that information from one spouse would not be passed on to the other. The interviews focused on a wide range of topics designed to assess the extent and quality of the relationship between former spouses, their relationship with their children, their new partners, if any, their new partner's former spouse, and their own former spouse's new partner. The interviews averaged 1½ hours in the first session and ranged from one to four hours in the second, depending on the binuclear family structure (e.g., whether they were remarried, whether their new partner had children from a prior marriage, etc.; for further details on the methodology of the study, see Ahrons, 1981 and 1983).

Overview of Findings

The findings reported here will be concerned only with the relationship between former spouses. They are based on data from one and three years after divorce and include only those couples in which both partners were interviewed at both times (80 couples). (For additional findings based on specific subsamples of this study at one year postdivorce, see Ahrons, 1981 and 1983, and Bowman & Ahrons, 1985).

Because little research has been done to date on postdivorce relationships, the data presented here will be primarily descriptive in nature. Although the sample is similar to those of other recent longitudinal studies of divorce (e.g., Hetherington, Cox, & Cox, 1976; Wallerstein & Kelly, 1980), the findings should be generalized with caution: They are probably typical of a "normal" (nonclinical) population of divorced people in a mainly white, middle-class, and somewhat liberal community.

Characteristics of the Sample. The respondents were on average in their mid 30s and had been married for around 11 years. Two-thirds of the couples had separated before filing for the divorce, for about one to two years on average. About half of the respondents had completed college, and almost all were engaged in paid employment at the time of both interviews—slightly over half of them in professional, managerial, or administrative positions. Average household income prior to the divorce was approximately $21,000 for both men and women. After the divorce, it had dropped to about $15,000 for women while remaining the same for men.

At the time of the original data collection, the number of children per family ranged from one to six, with an age range of 2 to 18. In all, 70% of the sample had more than one minor child, with an average number per family of two children. At the time of the first interview, 90% of the women and 49% of the men reported at least one child under 18 living in the household. This overlap probably represents not only the cases of split custody, in which each parent has custody of one child, but also the fact that in many cases of joint custody, both parents consider that the same child is part of their household.

By one year after their divorce, approximately 14% of the women and 22% of the men had remarried, and another 13% were planning remarriage in the near future. By the second interview, three years postdivorce, 36% of the women and 59% of the men had remarried. These data are consistent with Bell's (1984) conclusions that men have a greater probability of remarriage after divorce than women. Men traditionally marry younger women, which may explain the gender differences in the remarriage rates, especially in midlife and later parts of the life cycle (in our sample, second wives were on average two years younger than first wives). Another 28% of the women and 19% of the men had cohabitors. Two-fifths of the respondents' new partners had themselves been married before, and most had children from their previous relationships, some of whom were now residing in the respondents' household. About 15% of the married or cohabiting couples had had a new child born of this relationship. These divorced families have changed considerably in structure over the three years since the divorce and, as can be seen in Table 10.1, there is considerable variation and complexity.

TABLE 10.1
Binuclear Family Structures
(three years postdivorce: N = 80 families)

Number of Families	Type of Family Structure
10 (12%)	Neither parent recoupled[a]
7 (9%)	Mother recoupled/Father single
5	Only partner has children[b]
1	Only recoupled pair has children
1	Neither partner nor recoupled pair has children
19 (24%)	Father recoupled/Mother single
13	Only partner has children
1	Only recoupled pair has children
1	Recoupled pair has children and partner has children
4	Neither partner nor recoupled pair has children
44 (55%)	Both parents recoupled
12	Only mother's partner has children
5	Only father's partner has children
5	Both partners only have children
4	Only one recoupled pair has children
6	One recoupled pair and one partner has children
2	One recoupled pair and both partners have children
1	Both recoupled pairs and one partner have children
1	Both recoupled pairs and both partners have children
8	Neither recoupled pair and neither partner has children

a. "Recoupled" includes respondents who are remarried or cohabiting 12 or more nights per month.
b. All respondents had had children in their marriage to each other. This chart only refers to new children since the divorce—either those born to the respondent and his or her new partner or the partner's children from a previous marriage.

Interaction Between Former Spouses

Between a criterion for participation in this study was the presence of children, a certain amount of interaction in areas involving the children might be expected. Interaction in other areas, however, was more voluntary, which is perhaps why it occurred less often among our respondents. In the following sections, we describe the amount and types of both parental and nonparental interaction between former spouses.

Parental Interaction

Respondents were asked a series of ten questions about how often they related to their former spouses in various areas of parenting, such as making major decisions or day-to-day decisions regarding their children's lives; discussing the children's personal, school, or medical problems; planning special events in their children's lives; talking about the problems they were having in raising the children and so on. Their answers could range from "never" (1) to "always" (5) (see Table 10.2). Overall, at one year postdivorce, about 21% of the couples had a relatively high degree of interaction, saying they always or usually shared at least seven of the ten activities. Another 21% reported a very low degree of interaction, saying they rarely or never shared seven or more of the activities. The remaining 59% had a moderate amount of coparental interaction. (We felt that the criterion of seven out of ten activities would best distinguish respondents who had consistently high or low interaction and was more reflective of individual interaction levels than the simple average across all ten activities, as could be calculated from Table 10.2.) The areas of greatest interaction were in making major decisions regarding the children, discussing the children's school and medical problems, and talking about the children's accomplishments and progress; interaction was less frequent in the areas of daily decision making, discussions of how the children were adjusting to the divorce, discussions of problems the respondents may have been having with the coparenting relationship, or discussions of finances in regard to the children.

By three years after the divorce, coparental interaction as a whole had dropped off significantly, with only 9% of respondents reporting a continuing high degree of interaction and 24% a very low amount of interaction, according to the criteria above. The major areas of interaction continued to be making major decisions regarding the children, discussing the children's school and medical problems, and talking about the children's accomplishments and progress, with again little interaction in the areas of daily decision making, discussions of how the children were adjusting to the divorce, discussions of problems the respondents were having with the coparenting relationship, or discussion of child-related finances.

At one year postdivorce, a majority of parents said that they rarely or never argued when discussing parenting issues with each other; however, an equal number felt that there was sometimes tension during such discussions. Although most did not experience overt conflict in their interactions, it is clear that for many these conversations tended to be hostile rather than friendly. About half of the fathers and slightly fewer of the mothers felt that their former spouse understood and was supportive of their needs as a parent. Women more often

TABLE 10.2
Coparental Interaction
(N = 80 couples)

	Percentage of Couples Engaging in Activity					
	First Session			Second Session		
Activity	Never/Rarely[a]	Sometimes	Usually/Always	Never/Rarely	Sometimes	Unusually/Always
1. Share major decisions	29%	17%	54%	37%	11%	52%
2. Share day-to-day decisions	65	23	12	74	20	6
3. Discuss children's personal problems	32	21	47	37	29	34
4. Share children's school, medical problems	22	18	60	27	25	48
5. Plan special events in children's lives	32	18	50	41	23	36
6. Discuss children's progress and accomplishments	26	16	58	26	24	50
7. Discuss childrearing problems	34	19	47	40	32	28
8. Discuss how children are adjusting to divorce	54	13	33	69	16	15
9. Discuss coparenting problems	44	21	35	62	23	15
10. Discuss finances related to children	47	18	35	53	31	16

a. Five-point scale ranging from never (1) to always (5); in the frequency distribution, never and rarely were combined, as were usually and always.

279

than men (62% as compared to 53%) thought that they and their former spouse had basic differences of opinion about childrearing. Women also perceived a higher frequency of arguments, tension, and anger than men.

At three years postdivorce, the reported amount of tension in the relationship had not changed from the amount reported two years before, but while men reported fewer arguments than previously, they also felt that the amount of anger surfacing during coparenting interactions had increased. At this time, unlike at one year postdivorce, they perceived more anger than the women. The feeling that their former spouse was supportive of them as parents remained at the same level for women but declined for men, while the perception of basic disagreements in childrearing rose for men.

The finding that fathers' anger about coparenting issues increases over time is an interesting one that will require further analysis in order to ascertain causes. In research reported elsewhere (Ahrons, 1983), regression analyses conducted on the mother custody subsample revealed that the most important predictor of fathers' involvement with the children at one year postdivorce was the amount of coparental interaction between the parents. Some preliminary data also suggest that noncustodial fathers become less involved with their children over time and more dissatisfied with the custody arrangement. If future analyses show that coparental interaction continues to be a predictor of paternal involvement with children at three and five years postdivorce, then it would follow that the decrease in interaction with and support from their former wives might result in increased anger, especially for noncustodial fathers.

In addition to asking how often the divorced parents interact with each other, we also asked if they actually spent time together with their children. At one year following the divorce, about 45% of the parents reported spending time together with their children. Two years later, only about 30% reported spending time together as a binuclear family. The most frequently mentioned activities participated in together were holidays and celebrations (58%), eating together (42%), and school activities (29%). Only about 10% said that they visited grandparents and other relatives together. Most of the nearly one-third of the parents who reported spending time together did so around family rituals (e.g., child's birthday, school play, or graduation). For these families, the character of the binuclear family is similar to many extended family relationships, when families gather together for ritualistic events even though many of the relationships may be somewhat strained.

Perceptions of the "Ideal" Coparenting Relationship

Given our lack of information about what divorced parents may use as a model for their postdivorce relating, we asked the respondents an open-ended question: What would you say are the characteristics of an ideal divorced parenting relationship? Although the responses were often quite long and detailed, several themes emerged. Open and frequent communication between parents was often mentioned. Cooperation and flexibility—especially in scheduling visitation—were also stressed. Visitation rights should be clearly spelled out, but the children should be allowed to see both parents freely, according to many respondents. Children should not be made pawns in their parents' disagreements, it was emphasized, and should not be made to choose between parents. They need to develop a pattern of closeness with each parent. The parents should be able to separate childrearing issues from marital issues and keep their anger or resentment in the background when dealing with the children. As one respondent put it, "We should show the child that she's safe in our company—that we're both mature people who can handle our own lives."

Many respondents felt that joint custody, implying both joint rights and joint responsibilities, was the ideal coparenting situation, both for the children—allowing them to form close attachments to each parent—and for the parents themselves—freeing them from the burden of single parenthood. Financial tensions seemed to be one common barrier to good continuing relations, and many respondents felt that an ideal relationship needs to take into account both the financial needs and the financial limitations of each parent. "Take only what the child needs," it was admonished, but "make sure the person obligated to pay support really pays."

It is interesting to note that most of the responses would have been the same had we asked married parents what the ideal relationship between parents should be. Indeed, in this era of increased role sharing, or at least the ideal of shared responsibility between parents, the ideals of joint custody parenting are those to which many married parents aspire. However, it is also clear from these findings that there is considerable discrepancy between their ideal relationship and their actual coparental interaction. While most of these parents think they should have frequent interaction around childrearing, the reality is that by three years after the divorce most are not doing so.

Nonparental Interaction Between Former Spouses

For lack of a better term, we have called the relationship between former spouses that does not center on the children the "nonparental" relationship. It is that part of the relationship that has to do with the husband-wife roles, if these could in practice be separated from the mother-father roles.

We asked the respondents a series of 13 questions directed at assessing the frequency of their interaction in a variety of areas, such as talking about old friends and relatives, talking about their past marriage or why they got divorced, helping each other with household tasks, and talking about personal problems or new experiences they were having. For each item, respondents were asked to "think back over the last several months and tell me how often you and your former spouse have related in the following ways." The items were rated on a six-point scale ranging from "never" (1) to "once a week or more" (6) (see Table 10.3).

At one year postdivorce, only about 25% of the respondents continued to interact with each other at least once every few months in half or more of the areas asked about. (Again, we preferred the criterion of seven out of thirteen items to that of taking a simple average across all thirteen categories.) Even among those respondents who had a moderate to high amount of interaction, a large majority said they never talked about their marriage to each other or about why they had divorced, nor did they report continued dating of each other, physical contact, or discussions of reconciling. Only about 5% of all respondents said they were very involved in their former spouse's present life or that their former spouse was involved in theirs, while about 80% reported little or no involvement.

At three years postdivorce, the amount of actual interaction in the variety of areas asked about was even lower than at the first interview, with only 8% interacting at least every few months in half the areas or more. As at the first interview, only about 4% reported that they were involved in the life of their former spouse or that their former spouse was involved in their life.

Perceptions of the "Ideal" Nonparenting Relationship

As in the area of coparental relating, we were also interested in our respondents' perceptions of the ideal nonparenting relationship. Although we did not ask them about it directly, their responses to

TABLE 10.3
Nonparental Interaction
(N = 80 couples)

| | Percentage of Couples Engaging in Activity | | | | | |
| | First Session | | | Second Session | | |
Activity	Twice a month or more[a]	Every few months to once a month	Twice a year or less	Twice a month or more	Every few months to once a month	Twice a year or less
1. Discuss old friends in common	26%	38%	36%	11%	29%	60%
2. Discuss finances not related to children	15	23	62	4	19	76
3. Discuss the past marriage	11	26	63	4	11	86
4. Discuss families, excluding children	26	52	23	9	48	43
5. Discuss new experiences	29	34	37	12	26	63
6. Discuss personal problems	16	26	59	6	13	82
7. Talk about reconciling	3	8	89	1	2	98
8. Talk about why they got divorced	6	12	83	1	6	93
9. Have sexual intercourse	1	3	97	1	0	99
10. Help each other with household task	5	13	82	2	6	92
11. "Date" each other	1	6	93	1	1	98
12. Have physical contact (hug, kiss) without sex	9	6	85	3	4	93
13. Go out to dinner together without the children	1	5	94	1	3	96

a. Six-point scale ranging from once a week or more (6) to never (1); in the frequency distribution, the top two, middle two, and bottom two categories were collapsed.

283

several related questions helped to draw a picture of what that ideal relationship might look like. Respondents were asked first of all: If you didn't have children, do you think you would still want to relate to your former spouse, and why or why not? At one year postdivorce, about 40% said that they would still want to relate to each other now even if they had no children. At three years, the number of people who would still want to continue a relationship with one another had dropped to 32%.

Many of those respondents who said they would continue to relate to each other even if they had no children still considered their former spouse to be a good friend, or even still loved him or her: "Fourteen years of friendship you just don't forget about." "I feel fond of him. He's very much a part of my family. I understand why I married him and I understand why we got divorced." "I love my former spouse, she's a resource." "We care about each other." A few respondents indicated that they felt they sometimes had to defend their continuing relationship against society's idea that not relating to one's former spouse is more "normal."

However, the almost 70% of the respondents who, at three years postdivorce, would not want to continue to relate in the absence of children expressed their reasons this way: "Outside of kids, we don't have anything. Our friendship was long gone. It's like we're on two planets." "We're just so different. We have such opposite natures and personalities. We never should have been married." "I don't like the kind of person he is or the life style he leads." Although most of the respondents cited these feelings of different personalities and a friendship long gone, about one-quarter of the respondents reported actively negative feelings about their former spouse—dislike of them or of their behavior. This latter group most clearly resembles our stereotype of an antagonistic relationship between former spouses; however, the majority appear to be more indifferent than they are angry. In contrast to the prevailing stereotype, however, about one-third continue to have caring feelings and desire a continued relationship.

Respondents were also asked in an open-ended question what they would like to be different about their nonparental relationship. Their responses suggest that dissatisfaction with their current relationship could be due to too much as well as too little interaction. A number of respondents felt that their former spouse was involving them too much in his or her personal life: "My ex-spouse relies on me too much." "I would like him to involve me less in some of his problems which I can't help with." Still others wished their former spouses would not interfere in their private lives: "I wish he wouldn't drop in as frequently; it is especially uncomfortable when I have a date." "I'd like him to be less critical of my social life, to allow me more privacy." "I would like him to stop judging me—quit telling me what to do."

A large proportion of respondents expressed the wish that relations with their ex-spouse would be closer, more friendly, or less antagonistic: "I wish we could greet each other occasionally without hostility." "I wish there were less bitterness between us." "I wish we could be oblivious to what happened to us in the past." A very few respondents expressed the desire to return to predivorce conditions: "I sometimes feel that I love her now more than I did when we lived together." "I would like a time machine to go back 20 years and make it all right." Many respondents mentioned that they would like their ex-spouse to share more and be more understanding: "I wish he talked more about the things that are bothering him." "I would like her to share what's happening in her life." "I would like him to understand how much there is to manage in my life, to have more compassion." A few wanted better acceptance and understanding to extend to their new partners or friends as well: "I would like him to be able to talk to me and my new husband on a social basis—just to relieve some of the tension between the three of us." Some people regretted the dissolution of other relationships due to the divorce: "I really miss hearing about old friends and people he works with. I was really close to many people who were more his friends." "I wish we had more contact with each other's relatives, less hostility between the relatives." "I really liked her family and I wish I could ask her how they're doing."

A number of respondents wished to spend more time together: "I would like us to do some things together." "I would like to talk, to have dinner together." However, one person noted the social pressure this might produce: "If we lived in a larger community, I might take her out some, but here, if we were seen together, suddenly we're getting together again." Some regretted the ambiguity of postdivorce relationships. Finally, several people indicated a sense of continuing responsibility toward their former spouse: "I feel responsibility toward someone I threw out of the house. I want her to be happy." "I'd feel better if she and the guy she's living with would get married." "I would like to see her grow up, diversify her interests." "I wish he were stronger and more in control of his life so I wouldn't have to worry about him."

As in the area of coparental relating, we found that former spouses desire more interaction and a better relationship than they have. The large majority had very little interaction three years following the divorce (four to five years after separation); the interaction they did have usually centered around childrearing, with some still sharing information about extended family and mutual friends. But a third of the respondents wanted to continue the relationship, and an even higher percentage still clung to the ideal of a better relationship. Indeed, these former spouses appeared to have feelings about this relationship similar to those most people have about relationships in general: The real marital or friendship relationship usually falls short of the ideal. It is possible that some will keep striving toward their ideal, and their relationship may improve as the children grow up and custody and child support are no longer an issue. But as the data now appear, it would seem even more likely that they will come to interact less as the need to do so decreases. Even after children leave home, of course, there are still family events (e.g. weddings, grandchildren) that remind divorced parents of their continuing bonds. Our five-year data may provide some additional information and insights about the effect of time on the former spousal relationship.

Variation in Relationships

The preceding sections describe the sample of divorced people overall at one and three years postdivorce. While averages are indicative of the general characteristics and trends of postdivorce relationships, they conceal a certain amount of individual variance in these relationships. In this section we explore how relationships between former spouses vary among couples and what characterizes couples with different levels of interaction. Because it is more "voluntary" and more generally applicable to all divorced couples, we focus here on the nonparental relationship.

In general, by three years postdivorce, nonparental interaction was low for the sample as a whole, with some items used to measure it showing little variance. That is, over 90% of the sample never or rarely talked about reconciling or about why they got divorced, dated, dined together without the children, had physical or sexual contact, or helped each other with housework. The areas in which there was the most variance in the amount of relating were how often they spoke with each other about family, excluding the children, how often they spoke about old friends they had had in common, and how often they spoke about the new experiences they might be having in their present lives.

On the basis of answers to these three questions, which yielded the most varied responses at three years postdivorce, respondents were characterized as having either a "low," "moderate," or "high" amount of nonparental interaction. But couples who interact frequently are not necessarily good friends; their interactions may be fraught with hostility or conflict. Therefore, we decided to combine our interaction measure with a measure of the quality of the relationship so that we could derive our classification on both dimensions. A "quality of relationship" scale was developed measuring the amount of mutual support between former spouses and the relative lack of conflict in their interactions. The scale comprises six questions measuring support (e.g., "Do you feel that your former spouse understands and is supportive of your special needs as a custodian/noncustodial parent?") and four measuring conflict (e.g., "When you and your former spouse discuss parenting issues, how often does an argument result?"). The reliability (Cronbach's alpha) for this scale is .86 (for further details, see Ahrons, 1981). Although the scale was based on support and conflict in parental rather than nonparental interaction, it correlates in the same direction with both forms of interaction. For this analysis, the scale was dichotomized at the median into "high" and "low" quality.

Virtually all the respondents having a low amount of nonparental interaction also had low-quality interaction, while all the respondents with a high amount of interaction had high-quality interaction. However, the moderate group was a mixture of high- and low-quality relationships. About two-fifths of the respondents with moderate interaction levels had a low-quality relationship, and three-fifths a higher-quality relationship. Using both level and quality of interaction, we were thus able to classify respondents according to a four-point typology: 19 couples (24%) had a low amount and low quality of interaction; 21 couples (25%) had a moderate amount but low-quality interaction; 30 couples (38%) moderate, high-quality interaction; and 10 couples (12%) high levels of both amount and quality of interaction. For simplicity in the following discussion, we refer to these groups as low, moderate-low, moderate-high and high. (That the division of couples by level of nonparental interaction reported here is not strictly the same as that which could be calculated from Table 10.3 is due to two reasons: First, for this analysis, we considered respondents who engaged in the activities even once or twice a year to have moderate, rather than low, interaction and those who engaged in them once a month or more to have high, rather than moderate, interaction; second, individual decisions were made in cases of ambiguity (scores falling on the borderline or discrepancies between ex-spouses), which usually resulted in a lower number of couples at the extremes and a larger number in the "moderate" group).

An analysis of variance was undertaken in order to determine whether these four groups were distinguished by differences in other characteristics (see Table 10.4). Although interaction is not always a cause of other characteristics, it has been used as a de facto independent variable in the analysis of variance. However, except in the case of clearly temporally prior factors, such as length of marriage, no direction of causality is hypothesized between interaction and other associated factors, nor is any judgement made a priori about which of the four types of relationship is "best." Because we did not wish to treat the four categories as being strictly linear on a theoretical basis, we chose the method of analysis of variance, which allowed us to examine differences between each category of the independent variable.

We found no significant differences in level of interaction by respondents' age, education, length of marriage, or age of youngest child. Whether or not the wife had remarried was also not associated with former spouse interaction. However, the husband's remarriage was associated with lower levels of interaction. Perhaps one reason for the gender difference is that new wives are more likely than new husbands to discourage continued contacts between the former spouses. Another possible interpretation of this finding could be that men tend to remarry women with children and as such take on new families. Perhaps the dissonance is too great for them to continue to interact with their former family. Nonparental interaction was highest overall among couples in which neither partner had remarried, next highest if both had remarried, and lowest if only the husband had remarried.

Nonparental interaction is also related to custody, with joint custody couples having the highest amount of interaction and mother custody couples the lowest. Since most of the joint custody parents in this study chose that particular custody arrangement, it is not surprising that they continue to relate well after divorce. On the other hand, many of the fathers who were noncustodial felt that they had had no choice and that societal norms and legal structures had dictated the custodial arrangement. On the whole, they were dissatisfied with the custody arrangement and the limited access to their children. These are the "visiting" dads who expressed anger both at the system and at their former wives for making them less of a parent.

Interaction between former spouses is also positively related (if the four groups are considered linearly from low to high) to the amount of contact the noncustodial or nonresidential parent has with the child, net of custody. The largest difference in amount of contact with child was between couples having low and those having moderate-low in-

TABLE 10.4

Means on Selected Variables by Level of Nonparental Interaction at Second Session
(N = 80 couples)

	Low (N = 19)		Moderate-Low (N = 21)		Moderate-High (N = 30)		High (N = 10)		Significant Contrasts[b]
Variable	Women	Men[a]	Women	Men	Women	Men	Women	Men	
REMARRIAGE (1 = no, 2 = yes)									
Neither spouse	1.00		1.24		1.33		1.80		1,2,3,5,6
Both spouses	1.26		1.29		1.23		1.10		—
Wife only	1.21		1.10		1.10		1.10		—
Husband only	1.53		1.38		1.33		1.00		3, 5,6
CUSTODY (1 = no, 2 = yes)									
Joint	1.00		1.29		1.33		1.70		1,2,3,5,6
Mother	1.89		1.52		1.37		1.20		1,2,3
Father/split	1.05		1.10		1.16		1.04		—
Child's contact with noncustodial parent (10-point scale)	4.79	5.56	7.40	8.06	8.00	8.17	8.22	7.90	(W) 1,2,3 (M) 1,2,3
Coparental interaction (5-point scale)	1.54	1.64	2.55	2.86	3.32	3.11	3.39	3.39	(W) 1,2,3,4,5 (M) 1,2,3,5
Spend time together with children (1 = no, 2 = yes)	1.00	1.00	1.19	1.33	1.40	1.37	1.70	1.70	(W) 2,3,5,6, (M) 1,2,3,5,6

(continued)

289

TABLE 10.4 Continued

| | Level of Nonparental Interaction | | | | | | | | |
| | Low (N = 19) | | Moderate-Low (N = 21) | | Moderate-High (N = 30) | | High (N = 10) | | Significant Contrasts[b] |
Variable	Women	Men[a]	Women	Men	Women	Men	Women	Men	
Would relate even without children (1 = no, 2 = yes)	1.21	1.11	1.19	1.14	1.47	1.38	1.60	1.70	(W) 3,4,5 (M) 2,3,4,5,6
Satisfaction with nonparental interaction (5-point scale)	3.74	3.84	3.81	3.71	4.43	4.53	4.00	3.80	(W) 2 (M) 4
Satisfaction with coparental interaction (5-point scale)	3.58	2.84	3.29	3.29	4.33	3.83	4.00	3.80	(W) 2,4 (M) 2,3
Anger (5-point scale)	1.83	1.76	1.61	1.85	1.56	1.26	1.49	1.58	(W) – (M) 2,4,6
Guilt (5-point scale)	1.63	2.11	1.79	1.96	2.19	1.88	2.65	2.52	(W) 2,3,5 (M) 6
Psychological closeness (5-point scale)	1.88	1.87	2.07	2.15	2.34	2.42	2.78	2.80	(W) 2,3,5 (M) 2,3,5
Attachment (5-point scale)	1.37	1.50	1.38	1.62	1.48	1.36	1.90	2.15	(W) 3,5,6 (M) 3,5,6
Positive feelings (5-point scale)	1.83	2.01	2.25	2.17	2.85	2.79	3.38	3.20	(W) 2,3,4,5 (M) 2,3,4,5

a. Remarriage and custody were the same for both spouses, so only a single, "couple" score is given. The other variables differed by gender and are reported separately for women and men.
b. Contrasts are between levels of interaction. They are coded as follows: 1 = between low and moderate-low; 2 = between low and moderate-high; 3 = between low and high; 4 = between moderate-low and moderate-high; 5 = between moderate-low and high; 6 = between moderate-

teraction. Apparently, the lack of any nonparental interaction makes it difficult to maintain contact with the children, while once some interaction exists, differences in its level do not affect differences in the amount of contact with the children. Since we cannot ascertain the cause or effect of these variables, it is of course possible that severance of contact with children "causes" lack of nonparental interaction rather than vice versa (see Bowman and Ahrons, (1985), for a more complete analysis of the relationship between custody, father-child contact, and parental interaction at one year postdivorce).

Nonparental interaction was positively related to coparental interaction, with the largest contrast being again between couples with low and couples with moderate-low interaction. In addition, the higher the amount of nonparental interaction, the more likely couples were to spend time together as parents with their children. As might be expected, there was a positive relationship between the degree of nonparental interaction and the respondents' saying that they would want to continue to relate to one another even if they had no children. Respondents' satisfaction with the present amount of nonparental interaction was the same whether that interaction was of a low, moderate, or high amount. However, when the moderate group was distinguished by high or low quality, it was found that respondents with moderate-high interaction had higher satisfaction than any of the other four groups. This group was also the most satisfied with their coparental relationship. There was no significant difference in satisfaction between women and men. It is interesting to speculate that, while quality appears important in determining satisfaction, perhaps there is a threshold amount of interaction above which satisfaction declines somewhat.

The amount of anger and guilt felt about the divorce have been shown in the clinical literature to affect the quality of the coparental relationship and might be expected to have a bearing on the amount of nonparental interaction between former spouses. The amount of anger felt was measured by an index of eight items, such as "I feel angry for the hurt I have gone through" and "I want to get back at my former spouse." Guilt was measured as a four-item index composed of questions such as "I feel guilty about the divorce" and "I wish I could make up for the hurt I have caused my former spouse." (The reliability for the anger scale is .82 for women and .78 for men, and for the guilt scale, .82 for women and .74 for men).

For women, the higher the amount and quality of interaction, the higher the level of guilt, but interaction was not significantly related to anger. For men, the relationship was not linear. Both anger and guilt were lowest for men with moderate levels but high-quality interaction. However, as for women, guilt was highest among men with high interaction. From these data it appears that guilt over the divorce may work to keep some former spouses involved with each other as a way of assuaging their guilt. We usually attribute negative characteristics to guilt and certainly would not see it as a constructive basis for continuing a relationship, but it may be that some level of guilt may have a positive effect on relationships as well. In the case of some of these former spouse relationships, a little guilt may be a good thing. For others, however, it may keep them involved in a relationship that has ceased to meet their needs in other ways.

We looked at some additional variables that might provide more information about the relationship. Indices of psychological closeness, measured by such items as "I feel neutral about my former spouse," attachment ("I feel I will never get over the divorce"), and positive feelings ("I have warm feelings for my former spouse") were all positively associated with the amount of nonparental interaction for both men and women, although for men the amount of attachment dipped for those with moderate-high interaction.

In summary, we can say that couples with higher levels and quality of nonparental interaction were less often remarried; most often had joint custody and least often mother custody; had the most amount of contact between the noncustodial parent and the child; had better coparental interaction; spent more time together as parents with their children; would most often like to continue their nonparental relationship even if they had no children; had the highest levels of psychological closeness, attachment, and positive feelings; and had the least amount of anger but the most amount of guilt. These more interactive pairs of former spouses who cooperate well in childrearing after divorce and maintain their friendship make up only about 10% of this sample. However, the approximately 40% who had a high-quality but moderate level of interaction seemed to be the most satisfied with the amount of parental and nonparental interaction.

Conclusions

A major conclusion that can be drawn from the findings presented here is that the former spouse relationship is a complex one involving perhaps as many variations as we find with married couples. We have found that at least half of the sample do have relationships similar to ones depicted in the prevailing stereotypes. Although some of them do continue to have rare interactions, these are concerned with children. In general, what interaction they do have is negative and their feelings toward each other are usually hostile. Some may be indifferent, but many still harbor the anger arising from the marriage and divorce. Not only is the marital union dissolved, but so are their relationships.

On the other hand, we have found that a large minority of the sample have what Duck (1982) has described as a "declined" relationship. These former spouses have at least a moderate amount of interaction that includes shared information about issues that are child-related and issues that also have a component of friendship. Within this group there are also variations: a small proportion whom we could certainly label friends, and perhaps some who are even intimates, and the larger group who have an amicable relationship but not a close friendship. Although the measures and sample of Bell's study (1984) and ours are quite different, the frequencies of relationship patterns are similar. We have found a somewhat higher percentage of angry or hostile relationships, but our findings concur on the low frequency of "friendly" ex-spouse relationships. Our data suggest, however, that it is perhaps this small group of friendly ex-spouses who are most satisfied with the nature of their relationship.

As is consistent with the purpose of exploratory research, more questions are raised than answered. One major question is whether a declined relationship is more functional than a dissolved one. To assign a value, however, to which type of relationship is better would require answering several questions: Better for whom? At what points in the postdivorce period? And on what specific dimensions or aspects of the relationships? If it is dependent children we are concerned about, then we can say with some certainty that they will withstand the divorce better if their parents remain friendly. Recent longitudinal studies examining the effects of divorce on children (e.g., Hetherington et al., 1976; Wallerstein & Kelly, 1980) have concluded that it is in the best interests of children that their divorced parents be cooperative and congenial. The children who suffered the most psychological distress were those who experienced the continual conflict of their parents and whose fathers had minimal or no contact with them after the divorce.

Given that our findings suggest that perhaps half of the divorced spouses have dissolved relationships, with continuing conflict and anger that is negatively correlated with the continued involvement of the noncustodial parent, we can assume that those relationships are not in the best interests of children. Although there are few data available on the effects on adult children, it seems reasonable to hypothesize that their distress about their parents' divorce might be lessened if their parents had a declined rather than a dissolved relationship.

For the divorced spouses themselves, assigning a value to which type of relationship is better is more difficult. Although the clinical literature has moved away from its earlier stance on the dysfunctional aspects of continuing relations between former spouses, it only addresses that relationship now in terms of its importance for children. Given that for most of the sample the ideal relationship would be more amicable, we can only assume that they would be happier if it were so. Certainly for former spouses who have to continue to see each other because they live in the same community or have familial obligations that require some contact, it would be much more comfortable to be at least on "speaking terms."

The findings here are quite positive, given the numbers of divorced spouses who do have declined as opposed to dissolved relationships. It should be noted, however, that we probably found a somewhat higher percentage of declined relationships than might be found in the general population, based on the criteria used for inclusion in the study. Nevertheless, it is clearly possible for former spouses to continue to relate in constructive ways. This in itself is surprising, since they do so without the support of the community and without adequate role models. One can only wonder whether, if divorce was not viewed from a pathological framework but instead was interpreted as a normative development process in many family careers (see Rodgers, this volume), with the expectation that relationships change but do not dissolve after divorce, more ex-spouses would not have an amicable relationship of sorts. The respondents themselves noted that they were very unsure of "appropriate" ways to relate, often asking the interviewer how they were "supposed" to relate.

Since data collection and additional data analyses are still in progress and include information from current partners as well as from the former spouses themselves, we will be able to explore how these variations in former spousal relationships affect their new partnerships, step relationships, and extended family relationships. For example, we will want to explore whether dissolved relationships are related to better marital adjustment in the second marriage. Do new partners feel that the continuing relationship between their spouse and his or her ex-spouse intrudes on the new relationship? Do those former spouses with declined but not dissolved relationships have more difficulty, such as role conflict, in relation to their new stepfamily? Since remarriage is less likely to occur in the group with the highest amount and quality of former spousal interaction, does this type of relationship present a barrier to remarriage? And is this group more likely to reconcile?

Our data set does not include many variables on marital history. As we explored these data, we of course found many questions that we wish we had asked. Some of these are related to the marital history of the ex-spouses and their individual personality characteristics. Identifying the fact that there are many variants of former spouse relationships should now pave the way for research that will examine specific groups in more depth, perhaps with the intent of specifying the relationships between marital interaction styles and divorced interaction styles. As we have done in some of the marital research, we need to look at personality types in relation to divorcing relationship patterns.

Our findings suggest that, as is true for married spouses, divorced spouses relate in a variety of ways. As we move from a deviant or pathological model of divorce to a normative one, we will have to begin thinking about functional and dysfunctional relationship styles for divorced spouses. This change in our approach to studying divorce as a transition of family change will necessitate a change in our basic research questions. The surge in the divorce and remarriage rates over the past decade has resulted in family relationships about which we know very little. We now need to focus our research efforts on investigating the patterns of postdivorce family relationships over time and determine the positive and negative components of family reorganization.

REFERENCES

Abarbanel, A. (1979). Shared parenting after separation and divorce: A study of joint custody. *American Journal of Orthopsychiatry, 49,* 320-329.

Ahrons, C. R. (1979). The binuclear family: Two households, one family. *Alternative Lifestyles, 2,* 499-515.

Ahrons, C. R. (1980a). Divorce: A crisis of family transition and change. *Family Relations, 29,* 533-540.

Ahrons, C. R. (1980b). Joint custody arrangements in the postdivorce family. *Journal of Divorce, 3,* 189-205.

Ahrons, C. R. (1980c). Redefining the divorced family: A conceptual framework for postdivorce family system reorganization. *Social Work, 25,* 437-441.

Ahrons, C. R. (1981). The continuing coparental relationship between divorced spouses. *American Journal of Orthopsychiatry, 51,* 315-328.

Ahrons, C. R. (1983). Predictors of paternal involvement postdivorce: Mothers' and fathers' perceptions. *Journal of Divorce, 6,* 55-59.

Bell, R. R. (1984). *Friendship and divorce.* Unpublished manuscript, Temple University, Philadelphia.

Bowman, M. E., & Ahrons, C. R. (1985). Impact of legal custody status on fathers' parenting postdivorce. *Journal of Marriage and the Family, 47*, 481-488.

Derdeyn, A., & Scott, E. (1984). Joint custody: A critical analysis and appraisal, *American Journal of Orthopsychiatry, 54*, 199-209.

Duck, S. (1982). A topography of relationship disengagement and dissolution. In S. Duck (Ed.), *Personal relationships* (Vol. 4, pp. 1-30). London: Academic Press.

Hagestad, G. O., & Smyer, M. A. (1982). Dissolving long-term relationships: Patterns of divorcing in middle age. In S. Duck (Ed.) *Personal relationships* (Vol. 4, pp. 155-188). London: Academic Press.

Halem, L. (1980). *Divorce reform*. New York: Macmillan.

Hetherington, E., Cox, M., & Cox, R. (1976). Divorced fathers. *Family Coordinator, 25*, 417-428.

Hill, C., Rubin, Z., & Peplau, L. (1976). Breakups before marriage: The end of 103 affairs. *Journal of Social Issues, 32*(1), 147-168.

Kressel, K., Lopez-Morillas, M., Weinglass, J., & Deutsch, M. (1979). Professional intervention in divorce: The views of lawyers, psychotherapists, and clergy. In G. Levinger & O. Moles (Eds.), *Divorce and separation* (pp. 246-272). New York: Basic Books.

Levitan, T. (1979). Children of divorce: An introduction. *Journal of Social Issues, 34*(4), 1-25.

Mead, M. (1971). Anomalies in American postdivorce relationships. In P. Bohannan (Ed.), *Divorce and after* (pp. 107-125). New York: Anchor Books.

Steinman, S. (1981). The experience of children in a joint custody arrangement: A report of a study. *American Journal of Orthopsychiatry, 51*, 403-414.

Wallerstein, J., & Kelly, J. (1980). *Surviving the breakup*. New York: Basic Books.

11

Intimacy as the Proverbial Elephant

LINDA K. ACITELLI
STEVE DUCK

Final chapters, prefaces, and editors' summaries rarely do full justice to the richness and complexity of authors' contributions to a volume such as this. However, in making a general assessment of the volume and its contribution—as well as identifying lines for future work—it is necessary to summarize, encapsulate, and characterize both the individual and the collective issues raised in the volume. Given this, we see the chapters in the first section as indicating that the development of intimacy is guided by partners' feelings, by social and cultural rules for expressing those feelings, and by behavioral constraints on the form of a relationship. The second and third sections likewise indicate that, in the context of problematic relationships and declining intimacy, feelings, social rules, and behavioral constraints are major influences on the postintimate aftermath of relating. Other recent work indicating that friendship between former spouses is a conceivable outcome, in addition to the traditional view that divorce means estrangement (see Ahrons & Wallisch, Chapter 10, this volume), also suggests that these are the main elements of intimacy in its broadest sense (Masheter & Harris, 1986).

To extract from this the "central" issues for future work is a grand intention and one that we do not have. However, we do see some key issues emerging from the foregoing chapters and from the general trends in the field noted in the editors' chapter in *Understanding Personal Relationships* (Duck & Perlman, 1985). We therefore have some thoughts to add to those already in this volume. The issues that seem most important to us are these:

AUTHORS' NOTE: We are grateful to Rosalie Burnett for her careful reading of this chapter and for her helpful comments.

(1) Does intimacy reside in persons or between persons—or doesn't the question even make sense?
(2) Is intimacy a state or a process—or could it be both?
(3) How do perspectives on intimacy differ in intimate couples, and what does the existence of such differences mean for our work?

The Locus of Intimacy

As indicated by Perlman and Fehr in the introductory chapter here, both theories and measures of intimacy differ in their implicit or explicit views about the locus of intimacy, and we take the view that methods embody unstated "theories" about the phenomena (Acitelli, 1984; Duck, 1977; Duck & Sants, 1983). The question is whether intimacy is a quality of persons or of interactions. Rather than decide between them, we opt for an amalgamation of the two—with an additional observation—since we do not see these two possibilities as either exhaustive or exclusive. Intimacy can be a property of persons and of interactions once we clarify the meaning of the term.

Sullivan's (1953), Erikson's (1959, 1963), or McAdams' (1985) conceptualizations most explicitly approach intimacy as an individual capacity, while the social exchange, equilibrium, and systems approaches are most explicitly interactional (see Perlman & Fehr, Chapter 1, this volume, or Acitelli, 1984). Each theory recognizes individual capacities and behavioral interactions that are necessary for intimacy to occur, but they differ with respect to their relative emphases.

The opposing assumptions underlying this issue are: (1) An individual with certain capacities for relating to others will behave in ways consistent with those capacities, and he or she relates to everyone in a consistent fashion over time; and (2) the interaction between two people is determined by the reinforcing influence that each partner's behavior has upon the other, and each relationship is uniquely shaped by the behavioral interactions of the partners.

A conceptualization of intimacy must acknowledge both perspectives, just as many researchers acknowledge that individual behavior is determined by the interaction between person and situation. However, more emphasis should be placed by relationship researchers on locating intimacy between partners rather than within each individual, just as the origins of relationships are to be found in the interactions of partners, not in their "entry characteristics" or properties that pre-existed their relating (Duck & Sants, 1983; Duck & Perlman, 1985).

That the intimacy we are interested in is something relational becomes obvious when evaluating the statements: "I am intimate" versus "We are intimate." The former really indicates a tendency to act in a particular way and makes better sense when qualified by stating "I am intimate *with* someone." The latter makes sense only if it is understood as an interactional or relational description. Thus individual capacities should be identified not as ends in themselves but, to the extent that they influence intimate behavior between partners, so that intimacy is seen as a particular blend of individual and social influences. Since partners, ex hypothesi, must always retain their capacity for intimacy but may not achieve it in full in a particular interaction or relationship, it is obvious that measures of intimacy are inadequate for our research (but may not be for other purposes) if they assess only static characteristics of persons rather than dynamic features of interactions.

Although we do not have space here to give a full review of all measures of intimacy (but see Perlman & Fehr, Chapter 1, this volume, or Acitelli, 1984), we have some points to make about some of them. Most measures of intimacy (with the exception of the Intimacy Status Interview; Orlofsky, Marcia, & Lesser, 1973; Orlofsky, 1974; in press) claim to have operationalized a construct that occurs between two people, yet, surprisingly, most are self-report inventories that assess the attitudes and perceptions that an individual has about his or her closest relationship. Whilst, as Baucom (Chapter 7, this volume) shows, these are legitimate foci for researchers who will eventually pool their knowledge about particular parts of the topic, they do not tap such variables as the nonverbal communication (NVC) occurring in specific intimate interactions, as Noller has indicated in Chapter 5, nor the structural reorganization of routine that is important as relationships develop (Surra & Huston, Chapter 4, this volume) or decline (Rodgers, Chapter 9, and Ahrons & Wallisch, Chapter 10, this volume).

The PAIR inventory (Schaefer & Olson, 1981) is the only self-report instrument that was constructed with the intention of measuring the perceptions of both partners. No other instrument taps individual and conjoint perspectives simultaneously. No instrument by itself relates individual and conjoint perspectives to actual behavior nor taps into both individual and interactional aspects of intimacy. What seems to us to be necessary now is an approach that combines such methods and styles whilst maintaining the primary emphasis on the relationship.

We note that Snyder and Simpson (Chapter 2) consider feelings of intimacy rather than capacities for intimacy, whilst Kelley and Rolker-Dolinsky (Chapter 3) indicate that intimacy has to be initiated by someone and that cultural rules or expectations therefore affect our interpretation of that action. We therefore conclude that there are two aspects of intimacy locatable in persons (i.e., their capacity for it in general terms and their feelings toward a particular partner) as well as two locatable elsewhere (i.e., cultural norms about expression of intimacy and particular types of intimate behavior in a given interaction). We also note that the general level of intimacy in a relationship (as distinct from that in a given interaction) is another feature of intimacy, equally locatable in these two domains. Researchers could therefore measure an individual's capacity for it in general or in specific interactions with specific partners, as well as assessing the person's feelings toward a given partner in general and also the average level of intimacy expressed (e.g., in words or nonverbally) in given interactions or in a relationship, composed of series of interactions, measured across time.

State or Process?

The preceding discussion raises several overlapping issues that are significant for the future progress of the field. One of them involves deciding whether intimacy is a state or a process. A process can be distinguished from a state by its emphasis on movement through time, much like a verb can be distinguished from a noun. ("State" as it is used here is not to be confused with the temporary or fleeting emotion that is usually contrasted with "trait.") In its extreme form, intimacy as a state is seen as a relatively static end product or goal: Once achieved, it is constantly present and is measurable objectively or in terms of the congruence of the two partners' perspectives on it. Likewise, intimacy as a process is seen to develop, fluctuate, and change over time; it may be measurable by behavioral means, perhaps taken together with behavioral self-report. There is no necessary implication of consistency in such reports or behavior across time, and the very notion of process implies that there will be changes in subjects' reports about their feelings and behavior over time. A relationship may be intimate overall, but interactions can be intimate at one moment and not intimate the next (see Surra & Huston, Chapter 4, this volume). Again, intimacy can incorporate facets of both perspectives. Intimacy could be regarded as a process, a characteristic way of relating that develops over time, subject to change but nevertheless acquiring relatively stable defining features. Without some stable defining features, intimate relationships could not easily be distinguished from nonintimate ones, except that subjects, at a specific point in time, may report them to be such (i.e., may report a state as a "readout" from a process; Buck, 1985).

Erikson and the object relations theorists implicitly approach intimacy as a state occurring in a relationship between two people who possess the requisite capacities. How these two people interact in time to attain this goal is not clearly articulated. Sullivan identifies, in general terms, how intimacy develops. However, this process ultimately results in intimacy as a state. Social exchange and social learning perspectives do emphasize behavioral interactions that occur over time but, like systems theorists, seem to focus on prescribed patterns of interaction to maintain intimacy at a relatively fixed level. This is not to say that these approaches are static, but rather that they "sum up" discrete behaviors, assuming that intimacy is defined by "the quantity or distribution of certain activities" (Duck & Sants, 1983, p. 31)

Humanistic and social psychological perspectives (Kelley et al., 1983) attempt to conceptualize intimacy in terms of a continuous, flexible process. Kelley et al. focus more on discrete elements than the humanists do but appear less rigid than other theorists in prescribing just what intimacy should be. Humanists, on the other hand, conceptualize relationships to be "in the process of becoming" (Rogers, 1972). While humanists prescribe certain requisite conditions for intimacy, there is no end product but rather a fluid process that emerges from the necessary conditions. With these theorists, however, intimacy becomes a rather foggy concept.

From the present volume, by contrast, it is clear that some elements of intimacy are both dynamic and static, both personal and situational: The mediating factor is the perspective on it that is taken by the participants, particularly their judgments about the level of intimacy appropriate for a given situation or occasion. Thus Noller's work (Chapter 5) sustains the point that intimate behavior and failure to act intimately (both dynamic or processual perspectives) convey to partners a view of the state of intimacy existing between them. In other words, from (non)intimate behavior, partners infer (non)intimacy of feelings in their partner and hence infer (non)intimacy in the relationship as a whole. Similarly, both Baucom (Chapter 7) and Buunk and Bringle (Chapter 6) illustrate the point that a dynamic style of intimate action or interpretation leads to partners' deductions about the state of (non)intimacy that, for them, characterizes their relationship. We note also, in passing, that our analysis shows that researchers act in like manner but that some measure dynamics and infer state, whilst some measure state and infer dynamics (compare Surra & Huston, Chapter 4, and Rodgers, Chapter 9, this volume).

What is important is that we recognize that self-report inventories tap into partners' views of their relationships at one point in time. True, the views may result from an accumulation of events over time, but the measures indicate only the individuals' perspectives as they are in the present. We should therefore be circumspect about their claims to view the processual aspects of relationships, since they often create a picture of a relationship that consists of "a description of the characteristics of its constituent interactions, or (worse) of one of its interactions, rather than as a phenomenon that emerges from this series of interactions over time—just as one might describe a movie as a series of still shots and omit the importance of showing them in rapid succession" (Duck & Sants, 1983, p. 39). Duck and Sants (1983) recommend that future research be directed not only toward charting "the geographic course of a relationship" but also toward describing "the characteristic tides, fluctuations, and behavior of the relationship within and beyond those bounds" (p. 39). Likewise, intimacy, as an important dimension of relationships, should be conceptualized and assessed from just such a perspective.

Intimacy from Whose Perspective?

Whether researchers choose to study intimacy from insiders' or outsiders' perspectives reflects not only a methodological preference but also a philosophical and theoretical orientation (Olson, 1977). Phenomenologists value the subjective (insiders') frame of reference, while the behaviorists prefer the objective (outsiders') frame of reference. Thus we have theories of intimacy that lie at the extremes of the continuum—humanists and behaviorists—and theories that fall somewhere in between. On the surface, measures of intimacy seem to adopt perspectives that are clear-cut—either insiders' or outsiders'. A closer look, however, reveals that it is practically impossible to categorize the work so neatly and suggest that a concept of relationship awareness should be introduced into the discussion (Acitelli, 1984; Burnett, 1984).

The Intimacy Status Interview, for example, with its semi-structured, open-ended format appears to tap into a subjective frame of reference more than any other measure. However, the topics explored in the interview are chosen by outsiders, and the resulting intimacy status is thus ascertained somewhat externally (objectively). This instrument thus results in an intimacy status derived from an outsider's perspective on one insider's frame of reference. Similarly, self-report inventories that measure insiders' attitudes and perceptions, which are chosen by outsiders to assess, result in scores that are evaluated against some external (objective) frame of reference. Among these, only the PAIR inventory was constructed with the intention of measuring the subjective viewpoint of each partner.

Subjective and objective measures of intimacy have been shown to produce discrepant results (Klos & Loomis, 1979; Olson, 1977). Yet these discrepancies should not be interpreted to mean that one perspective is more valid than the other. Given the different orientations of researchers constructing these methods, "it should be not only expected but assumed that there will generally be discrepancies between data from self-report and from behavior methods" (Olson, 1977, p. 127). Olson further hypothesizes that these methods are "tapping two different domains, the subjective and the objective realities."

Duck and Sants (1983, pp. 34-35) concur in this judgment but believe that "insider-outsider perspectives are not all that there is to think about here ... There is not only *one* outsider perspective nor only *one* insider perspective. Insiders may disagree with each other and hence provide another sort of discrepant data; furthermore, outsiders may disagree not only with the insiders but also among themselves. Furthermore, insiders and outsiders may themselves be aware of the existence of different perspectives." Instead of viewing the discrepancies as sources of error, these authors believe that the many different perspectives provide useful information about the nature of the relationship. For example, a relationship that is agreed to be intimate by outsiders and by both insiders may be a different relationship from one that appears intimate only to the insiders (or just to one insider). Therefore, the significant issue is not that there are discrepancies but "how such discrepant data can be used to develop theoretical formulations" (Olson, 1977, p. 128).

This issue is especially relevant to those chapters in the third section of this volume that concern partners' responses to the breakdown of intimacy. Discrepancies between views of the "state of the relationship" are known to be a major source of upheaval in relationships (Baxter & Wilmot, 1985), and discrepant views of potential intimacy in relationships are a major source of discussion about breakdown

(Duck, 1982). As Rusbult (Chapter 8), Baucom (Chapter 7), and Buunk and Bringle (Chapter 6) clearly show, whilst one person's own view of a relationship is sometimes a motivator for changing the level of intimacy in a relationship, far more often the motive is provided by an awareness of discrepancies between one's own view and that of the partner. Thus discrepancies in views are a relevant concern for future researchers rather than a dismissible source of "error" or "biased data."

What seems to us to be presently lacking in models and measures of intimacy is a key concept that can provide the necessary distinctions between intimacy and love, intimacy and marital satisfaction, and intimacy and marital adjustment. Evidence provides high correlations between intimacy and marital happiness but also indicates that happy couples are not always intimate, and intimate couples are not always happy (Glazer-Malbin, 1975; Raush, Barry, Hertel, & Swain, 1974). This difference, we feel, is only partly explained by the points that we have made about the location of intimacy and state-process differences. An additional concept is necessary to help out here.

We offer the concept of relationship awareness proposed by Acitelli (1984, 1985). It is more than self-awareness and more than knowledge of the other person. It suggests that couples have a "metaperspective" of their relationship, just as researchers do—yet few have sought to explore relationship awareness as a variable in its own right (Acitelli, 1984; Burnett, 1984, 1985). Nonetheless, many marital therapies implicitly seek to enhance a couple's relationship awareness but explicitly strive for smoother conflict resolution, more effective communication skills, reciprocal self-disclosure, and so on (Duck, 1984). Relationship awareness is more than an individual capacity. It can be said to exist from the perspective of each individual partner, but it cannot develop on its own. Couples must not only be self-aware, self-disclosing, and understanding (White, 1985); they must mutually explore what they have discovered about themselves and each other and how it affects their particular relationship. Relationship awareness can be considered a conscious process, developing over time and requiring effort to maintain.

Relationship awareness is a conceptualization similar to but distinct from "interpersonal attribution," a category proposed by Newman (1981, pp. 60-61) as an addition to the dispositional and situational attribution categories. Interpersonal attributions are causal explanations that focus on the relationship, attributing the cause of an actor's behavior to "something about the actor in relation to the observer," as opposed to either the situation or the actor's disposition. This concept (interpersonal attribution) is similar to relationship awareness in its emphasis on the dyadic unit.

Relationship awareness can be distinguished from interpersonal attribution in two ways. First, relationship awareness includes but encompasses more than causal explanations of an actor's behavior. It involves an acknowledgment of behavioral, cognitive, and affective interaction patterns that describe a relationship. This distinction parallels the difference between two of Aristotle's "four causes" (1952, cited in Rychlak, 1984). The efficient cause, that which an interpersonal attribution seems to seek, is the "impetus that assembles things or brings events about instrumentally" (Rychlak, 1984, pp. 364-365). The formal cause—that which is acknowledged through relationship awareness—is a "pattern in events as well as various shapes that things assume" (p. 365). Thus an interpersonal attribution may be a part of the relationship of which a person is aware, making up just a subset of the entire interaction pattern. Second, an interpersonal attribution is not always conscious (acknowledged), yet relationship awareness is. Such awareness may not always be verbalized or communicated; however, it involves at least thinking about the relationship. Relationship awareness has also been called relationship construal or relationship "mindfulness" (Burnett, 1984). Burnett focuses on whether or not partners attend to, think about, and communicate about their relationship, implying a conscious and deliberate analysis or acknowledgment of relationship processes.

The concept of relationship awareness may resolve the dilemma that researchers have faced when trying to distinguish intimacy from marital satisfaction (Waring, 1984). Relationship awareness may not guarantee satisfaction, and indeed may make couples more cognizant of their problems. However, in the long run it can be a major determinant of marital satisfaction. Relationship awareness plus positive affect, combined with a commitment to the relationship, might be the better predictor of marital satisfaction and stability than any of these variables alone. This and other hypotheses regarding relationship awareness and its interaction with other components of intimacy seem to us to merit further study (Acitelli, 1985).

Towards . . .

Conceptualizing, hypothesizing about, and measuring with regard to a global aspect of a relationship are much more complex than summing the concepts, hypotheses, and measurements regarding two individuals in a relationship. What is needed is both an interactional model of marital intimacy as a construct and an interactional model of the measurement and assessment of such a construct (Margolin, 1983). The central focus of an interactional model would be the relationship. What goes on between couples behaviorally, cognitively and affectively? How are their cognitions and affects expressed? What patterning of interactions and communications over time, distinguishes the intimate relationship from the nonintimate one, and what patterning of interactions and communications across networks and individuals (see Milardo, Johnson & Huston, 1983) indicates the change of overall levels of intimacy in a relationship?

An interactional model of intimacy should encompass both the objective and the subjective frames of reference and account for differences between them (both inside and outside the relationship). Also, conceptualizations of intimacy that focus on individual characteristics should be evaluated by testing whether or not these variables are actually reflected in behavioral interactions (e.g., are two "intimate" individuals guaranteed to have intimate interactions, and how do intimate interactions sum up into an intimate relationship?).

Historical variables also deserve attention. Information about each spouse's family of origin serves as a "context for understanding the spouses' current expectations and appraisals of their relationship" (Margolin, 1983, p. 118). In addition, the developmental history of the relationship would need to be conceptualized. How do ultimately intimate relationships typically begin, develop in intimacy, and change in character over time? Does the level of intimacy continuously increase, or does it fluctuate depending on the couple's situation? Or do we observe a shift from partners' discrepancies about the level of intimacy to agreement with each other and with outsiders? As intimate relationships develop, so will the "rules" for expressing the intimacy and for the behavioral constraints affecting relationships become more easily assessed and more publicly available as influences, because they are clearer for the well-established sorts of relationship, like marriage (Argyle & Henderson, 1984).

These, then, are our major concerns and hopes for the future development of research into this topic. We feel that the work in the present volume shows that the various parts of the elephant are already being felt quite vigorously by various researchers. Although the proverb has it that blind men feeling an elephant reach different conclusions about the shape of the beast, our conclusion is optimistic: It is a necessary and valuable part of the research enterprise that some researchers *must* feel some parts of the creature whilst others probe other areas. We will, however, remain blind only if we fail to relate the different reports to one another or if we see them as exclusive or competitive rather than compatible and complementary. We hope that the advantages of the present volume are precisely that it shows that the relating of different contributions to the Big Picture is possible and, indeed, that the volume has itself begun that process.

REFERENCES

Acitelli, L. (1984). *Marital intimacy: Theories, values and measures.* Unpublished manuscript, University of Michigan, Ann Arbor.

Acitelli, L. (1985). *The influence of relationship awareness on perceived marital satisfaction and stability.* Unpublished manuscript, University of Michigan, Ann Arbor.

Argyle, M., & Henderson, M. (1984). The rules of friendship. *Journal of Social and Personal Relationships, 1,* 211-237.

Baxter, L. A., & Wilmot, W. (1985). Taboo topics in close relationships. *Journal of Social and Personal Relationships, 2,* 253-269.

Buck, R. (1985). Prime theory: An integral view of motivation and emotion. *Psychological Review, 92,* 389-413.

Burnett, R. (1984, July). *Thinking and communicating about personal relationships: Some sex differences.* Paper presented at the Second International Conference on Personal Relationships, Madison, WI.

Burnett, R. (1985). *Content and incidence of conceptualisation of personal relationships.* Unpublished doctoral dissertation, Oxford University.

Duck, S. W. (1977). *The study of acquaintance.* Farnborough: Gower Press.

Duck, S. W. (1982). A topography of relationship disengagement and dissolution. In S. W. Duck (Ed.), *Personal relationships 4: Dissolving personal relationships* (pp. 1-30). Orlando, FL: Academic Press.

Duck, S. W. (1984). A perspective on the repair of relationships: Repair of what, when? In S. W. Duck (Ed.), *Personal relationships 5: Repairing personal relationships* (pp. 163-184). New York: Academic Press.

Duck, S. W., & Perlman, D. (1985). The thousand islands of personal relationships: A prescriptive analysis for future explorations. In S. W. Duck & D. Perlman (Eds.), *Understanding personal relationships: An interdisciplinary approach* (pp. 1-15). London: Sage.

Duck, S. W., & Sants, H.K.A. (1983). On the origins of the specious: Are personal relationships really interpersonal states? *Journal of Clinical and Social Psychology, 1,* 27-41.

Erikson, E. (1959). *Childhood and society.* New York: Norton.

Erikson, E. (1963). *Identity, youth and crisis.* New York: Norton.

Glazer-Malbin, N. (1975). Man and woman: Interpersonal relationships in the marital pair. In N. Glazer-Malbin (Ed.), *Old family/new family.* New York: Van Nostrand.

Kelley, H. H., Berscheid, E., Christensen, A., Harvey, J. H., Huston, T. L., Levinger, G., McClintock, E., Peplau, L. A., & Peterson, D. R. (1983). *Close relationships.* New York: W. H. Freeman.

Klos, D. S., & Loomis, D. F. (1979). A rating scale of intimate disclosure between late adolescents and their friends. *Psychological Reports, 42,* 815-820.

Margolin, G. (1983). An interactional model for the behavioral assessment of marital relationships. *Behavioral Assessment, 5,* 103-127.

Masheter, C., & Harris, L. (1986). From divorce to friendship: A study of dialectical relationship development. *Journal of Social and Personal Relationships, 3,* 177-189.

McAdams, D. (1985). Motivation and friendship. In S. W. Duck & D. Perlman (Eds.), *Understanding personal relationships: An interdisciplinary approach* (pp. 85-105). London: Sage.

Milardo, R. M., Johnson, M. P., & Huston, T. L. (1983). Developing close relationships: Changing patterns of interaction between pair members and social networks. *Journal of Personality and Social Psychology, 44,* 964-976.

Newman, H. (1981). Communication within ongoing intimate relationships: An attributional perspective. *Personality and Social Psychology Bulletin, 7,* 59-70.

Olson, D. H. (1977). Insiders' and outsiders' views of relationships: Research studies. In G. Levinger and H. L. Raush (Eds.), *Close relationships: Perspectives on the meaning of intimacy* (pp. 115-135). Amherst: University of Massachusetts Press.

Orlofsky, J. L. (1974). *Intimacy status, partner perception and resolution of previous developmental crises.* Unpublished doctoral dissertation, SUNY, Buffalo.

Orlofsky, J. L. (in press). Intimacy status: Theory and research. In J. E. Marcia (Ed.), *Ego identity.* Hillsdale, NJ: Erlbaum.

Orlofsky, J. L., Marcia, J. E., & Lesser, I. (1973). Ego identity status and the intimacy vs. isolation crisis of young adulthood. *Journal of Personality and Social Psychology, 27,* 211-219.

Raush, H. L., Barry, W. A., Hertel, R. K., & Swain, M. A. (1974). *Communication, conflict and marriage.* San Francisco: Jossey-Bass.

Rogers, C. (1972). *Becoming partners: Marriage and its alternatives.* New York: Dell.

Rychlak, J. E. (1984). Relationship theory: An historical development in psychology leading to a teleological image of humanity. *Journal of Social and Personal Relationships, 1,* 363-386.

Schaefer, M. T., & Olson, D. H. (1981). Assessing intimacy: The PAIR inventory. *Journal of Marital and Family Therapy, 7,* 47-60.

Sullivan, H. S. (1953). *The interpersonal theory of psychiatry.* New York: Norton.

Waring, E. M. (1984). The measurement of marital intimacy. *Journal of Marital and Family Therapy, 10,* 185-192.

White, J. M. (1985). Perceived similarity and understanding in married couples. *Journal of Social and Personal Relationships, 2,* 45-57.

INDEX

Wills, T., 152
Wilmot, W., 303
Wilson, C., 218
Winter, D. G., 74
Wishnoff, R., 80
Wong, P.T.P., 178, 179, 181
Woodworth, W. 47
Wright, J. L., 210, 220

Yablon, G., 223

Yoppi, B., 150, 202, 210
Young, J. E., 36

Zaidel, S. F., 163, 167
Zajonc, R. B., 125
Zanna, M. P., 47
Zembrodt, I. M., 212, 220, 224, 225, 226
Zillmann, D., 81
Zuckerman, M., 191

About the Contributors

LINDA K. ACITELLI, a former instructor of psychology at Hillsdale College and Concordia College, received a Ph.D. from the Department of Psychology at the University of Michigan, Ann Arbor, for her dissertation, "The Influence of Relationship Awareness on Perceived Marital Satisfaction and Stability." She is currently a Research Associate, Department of Psychology, University of Connecticut, Storrs.

CONSTANCE R. AHRONS is an Associate Professor of Sociology at the University of Southern California, Los Angeles. Prior to this she was on the faculty at the University of Wisconsin, Madison, for 13 years. She is principal investigator of a major five-year longitudinal study on postdivorce family relationships funded by NIMH. In addition to her teaching, research, and writing, she is a practicing family therapist. She is a Fellow and Approved Supervisor in the American Association of Marriage and Family Therapists, a Fellow in the American Orthopsychiatric Association, and a member of a number of other professional and scholarly organizations, including the National Council on Family Relations, the Committee on Family Research of the International Sociological Association, and the American Psychological Association. She has contributed to a number of international meetings and publications and is currently preparing a co-authored book, *Beyond the Nuclear Family: The Divorce/Remarriage Transition,* to be published by W. W. Norton.

DONALD H. BAUCOM is Associate Professor of Clinical Psychology at the University of North Carolina at Chapel Hill. He obtained his B.A. and Ph.D. from UNC. His primary research area involves evaluating the effectiveness of different treatments for maritally distressed couples, working from a behavioral and skills-oriented approach. He has conducted some of the major controlled outcome studies of behavioral marital therapy and recently has focused on developing and evaluating cognitive restructuring procedures as an adjunct to behavioral marital therapy.

316

ROBERT G. BRINGLE took his doctoral training in social psychology at the University of Massachusetts. He is now an Associate Professor of psychology at Purdue University, Indianapolis. His interests include interpersonal processes, the evaluation of social and health problems, cognitive development, and the psychology of aging. For the past several years he has been programmatically investigating jealousy.

BRAM BUUNK is a leading Dutch social psychologist, teaching at the University of Nijmegen. His research centers on jealousy, extramarital relations, and friendships. His contribution for this volume was prepared while he was a Fulbright Visiting Professor at UCLA.

STEVE DUCK has been one of the key people in establishing personal relationships as an identifiable field. He edited what many consider the handbook of the area, the five-volume Academic Press PR series. He founded both the International Conferences on Personal Relations and the *Journal of Social and Personal Relationships*. Educated at Oxford and Sheffield, he has spent the last few years on the faculty in psychology at the University of Lancaster. Besides his numerous contributions to the PR area, Steve has done research on television and extended personal construct theory. A Fellow of the British Psychological Society, he has represented his country as a British Council Visiting Scholar in Canada, the Soviet Union, and the United States. In 1986 he became the Daniel and Amy Starch Research Professor in the Communications Department at the University of Iowa.

BEVERLEY FEHR is a doctoral candidate in social psychology at the University of British Columbia. Her current research is on a prototype approach to love and commitment. This grows out of her important 1984 *Journal of Experimental Psychology* article on a prototype approach to emotion. She has also recently contributed a chapter to L. L'Abate's *Handbook of Family Psychology and Therapy*. She holds a Social Sciences and Humanities Research Council of Canada Fellowship.

TED L. HUSTON moved to the University of Texas at Austin in 1984 as the Amy Johnson McLaughlin Centennial Professor. Trained as a social psychologist, he has been a leading figure in the personal relations area for the past decade. He has authored a number of publications, including such noteworthy contributions as his classic 1978 *Annual Review of Psychology* chapter on interpersonal attraction and his from UCLA and her M.A. at California State University, Sacramento. Her major interests lie in the areas of sex roles, sex differences, and health psychology.

CARYL E. RUSBULT is an Associate Professor of Psychology at the University of North Carolina at Chapel Hill. Her research interests include the study of commitment, problem-solving behavior, and responses to dissatisfaction in both close relationships and work settings. Having received her Ph.D. from the University of North Carolina at Chapel Hill in 1978, she has published widely in such major psychological journals as the *Journal of Personality and Social Psychology* and the *Journal of Applied Psychology*. For her excellence in teaching, Caryl received the 1983 Kentucky Psi-Chi Award. In 1986 she will be on sabbatical at UCLA, her undergraduate alma mater, where she was invited to teach a graduate course on relationships.

JEFFRY A. SIMPSON received his B.A. summa cum laude from the University of Illinois in 1981. En route, he spent a term at Oxford. Currently he is a doctoral student in social psychology at the University of Minnesota. He has begun his publishing career with two articles on self-monitoring and relationships in the *Journal of Personality and Social Psychology*. He has numerous broad interests: as an undergraduate, he had a double major (psychology plus political sciences), and he has worked on research projects in departments of zoology, marketing, family practice, and community health.

MARK SNYDER is a Professor of Psychology at the University of Minnesota. A Canadian by birth, he took his undergraduate training at McGill University. His 1972 Ph.D. thesis at Stanford received the Dissertation Award from the Society for Experimental Social Psychology. He developed the self-monitoring concept and has creatively explored its ramifications during the past dozen years. Among his other persisting interests are the self-fulfilling nature of social perception and the relationship between personality and situations. In 1980-81 he was a Fellow at the Center for Advanced Study in the Behavioral Sciences. He is currently Associate Editor of *Contemporary Psychology* and has recently written the chapter on personality and social behavior for the new *Handbook of Social Psychology*. His career has been most distinguished and as a recent analysis of citation patterns documented, his work is having a great impact on the field of personality and social psychology.

more recent volume, *Close Relationships,* with Kelley's UCLA group. Currently he is bringing to fruition his exciting PAIR project, a longitudinal study of the transition to marriage.

KATHRYN KELLEY teaches personality, human sexuality, and health psychology at SUNY Albany. She completed her Ph.D. in social and personality psychology at Purdue Univesity in West Lafayette, Indiana. She has recently developed the Chronic Self-Destructiveness Scale, and with her husband, Donn Byrne, she has done research on responses to erotica.

PATRICIA NOLLER is a lecturer in the Psychology Department at the University of Queensland in Australia. She is the author of *Nonverbal Communication and Marital Interaction,* published by Pergamon Press in 1984, as well as several articles in developmental and social psychology journals.

DANIEL PERLMAN is a Professor of Family Science and a Lecturer in Psychology at the University of British Columbia. A Fellow of both the American and the Canadian Psychological Associations, he is best known for his work with L. Anne Peplau on loneliness. He has edited *Canadian Psychology* as well as a social psychology textbook sponsored by the Society for the Psychological Study of Social Issues. At the time of submitting the present manuscript, he has just completed writing two papers: "Theories of Interpersonal Attraction," for a volume by Derlega and Winstead, and "The Wisdom of Solomon: Avoiding Bias in the Editorial Review Process," for Sage's forthcoming volume on *Scientific Excellence: Origins and Assessment.*

ROY H. RODGERS, who took his Ph.D. in Family Sociology at the University of Minnesota, has achieved distinction as both an administrator and a scholar. Formerly the chair of the Sociology Department at the University of Oregon, he is now the director of the School of Family and Nutritional Sciences at the University of British Columbia. Most noted for his theoretical writing, he has been a leading champion of the developmental approach to family interaction. For several years, he served as an editorial board member for the *Journal of Marriage and the Family.* With Connie Ahrons, he is currently writing a book on postmarital family reorganization.

BEVERLY ROLKER-DOLINSKY is currently working toward her Ph.D. in social psychology at SUNY Albany. She received her B.A.

CATHERINE A. SURRA received her Ph.D. in the Human Development and Family Program at Pennsylvania State University and is currently on the faculty at the University of Illinois. The 1979 recipient of the National Council on Family Relations Outstanding Graduate Student Award, her recent research has focused on courtship. Based on how quickly their relationships progress, she has developed a typology of different courtship styles. She has also investigated the effects of courtship on people's social networks.

LYNN S. WALLISCH served as the research analyst for the Binuclear Family Research Project at the University of Wisconsin at Madison. She is a graduate of Mount Holyoke College, holds an M.A. in both French literature and sociology, and is presently a doctoral candidate in sociology/demography at the University of Michigan. She has done research in social development and demography at the Organization for Economic Cooperation and Development in Paris and at the Alan Guttmacher Institute in New York. Her publications have been in the areas of women's role in development, gender roles and fertility, and the availability of abortion to poor women in the United States.